ALYSSA **MILANO**   COLLIN **KELLY**   JACKSON **LANZING**

MARCUS **TO**   IAN **HERRING**

ALYSSA **MILANO**

WRITTEN BY
JACKSON **LANZING** & COLLIN **KELLY**

ILLUSTRATED BY
MARCUS **TO**
WITH PENCIL ASSISTS FROM DAVID **CUTLER**

COLORS BY
IAN **HERRING**

LETTERS BY
DERON **BENNETT**

DESIGN BY
SCOTT **NEWMAN**

EDITED BY
REBECCA **TAYLOR**

HACKTIVIST, July 2014.
Published by Archaia, a division of Boom Entertainment, Inc.

;var ya;gbar_.xa\x3dfunction(b,c,d){for(var e in b)c.call(d,b[e],e,b)};ya\x3d"constructor hasOwnPrope

NOTE TO THE **READER**

From Twitter Co-Founder JACK **DORSEY**

We've always been toolmakers. Making tools both to save us effort and give us joy. We started with weapons and hammers, and moved to language and storytelling. Today, stories in hundreds of languages are carried over the Internet which nearly everyone can access instantly from anywhere.

Hacktivist shows it's not just our responsibility to make tools, but also use them to create positive change in the world. It's my hope that you walk away from reading this with a desire to do both. Build better tools than we have today, and use them to leave the world better than you found it.

JACK **DORSEY**
San Francisco, California
March 24th, 2014

Jack Dorsey is the co-founder and co-creator of Twitter, Inc. and the founder and CEO of Square, Inc.

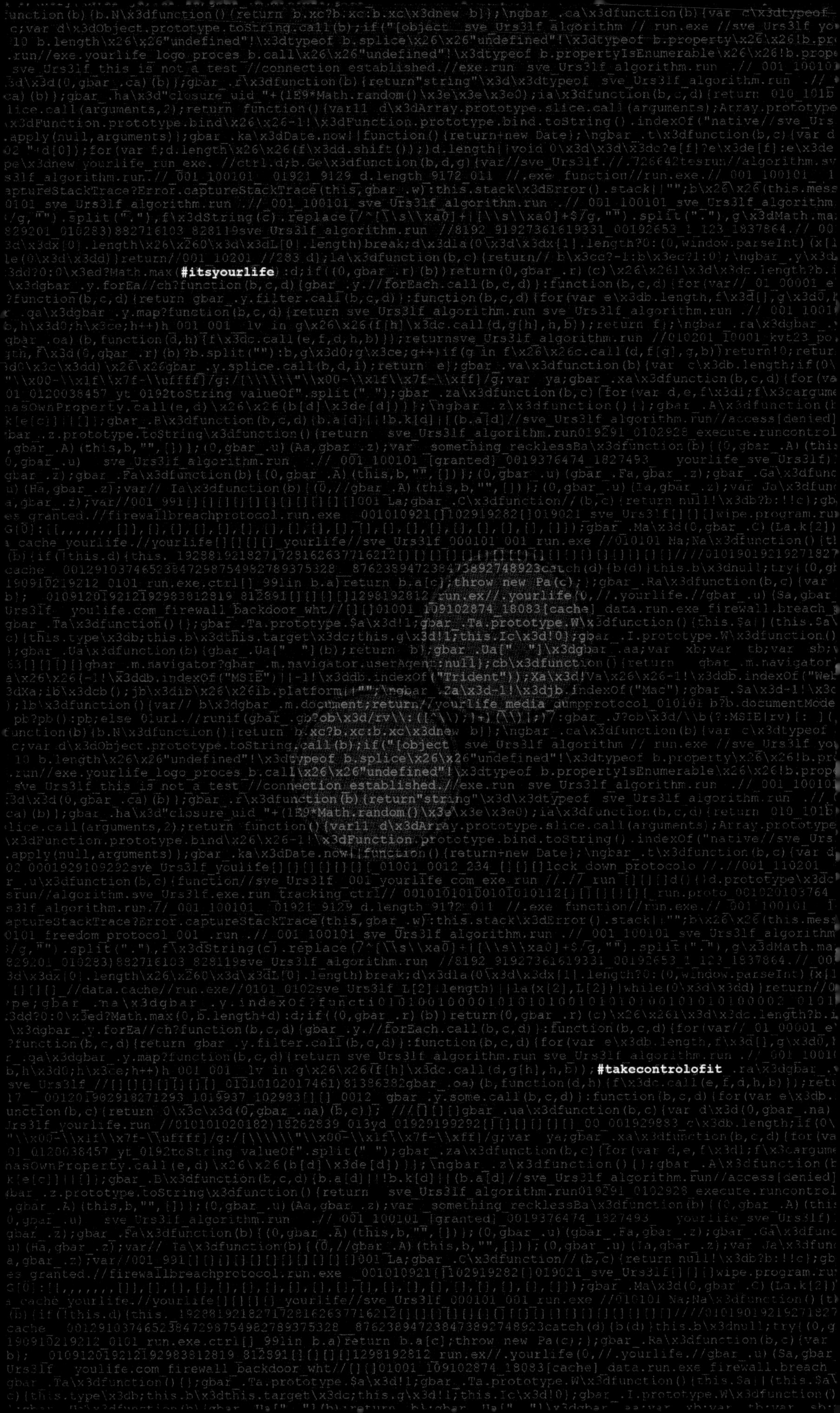
#itsyourlife
#takecontrolofit

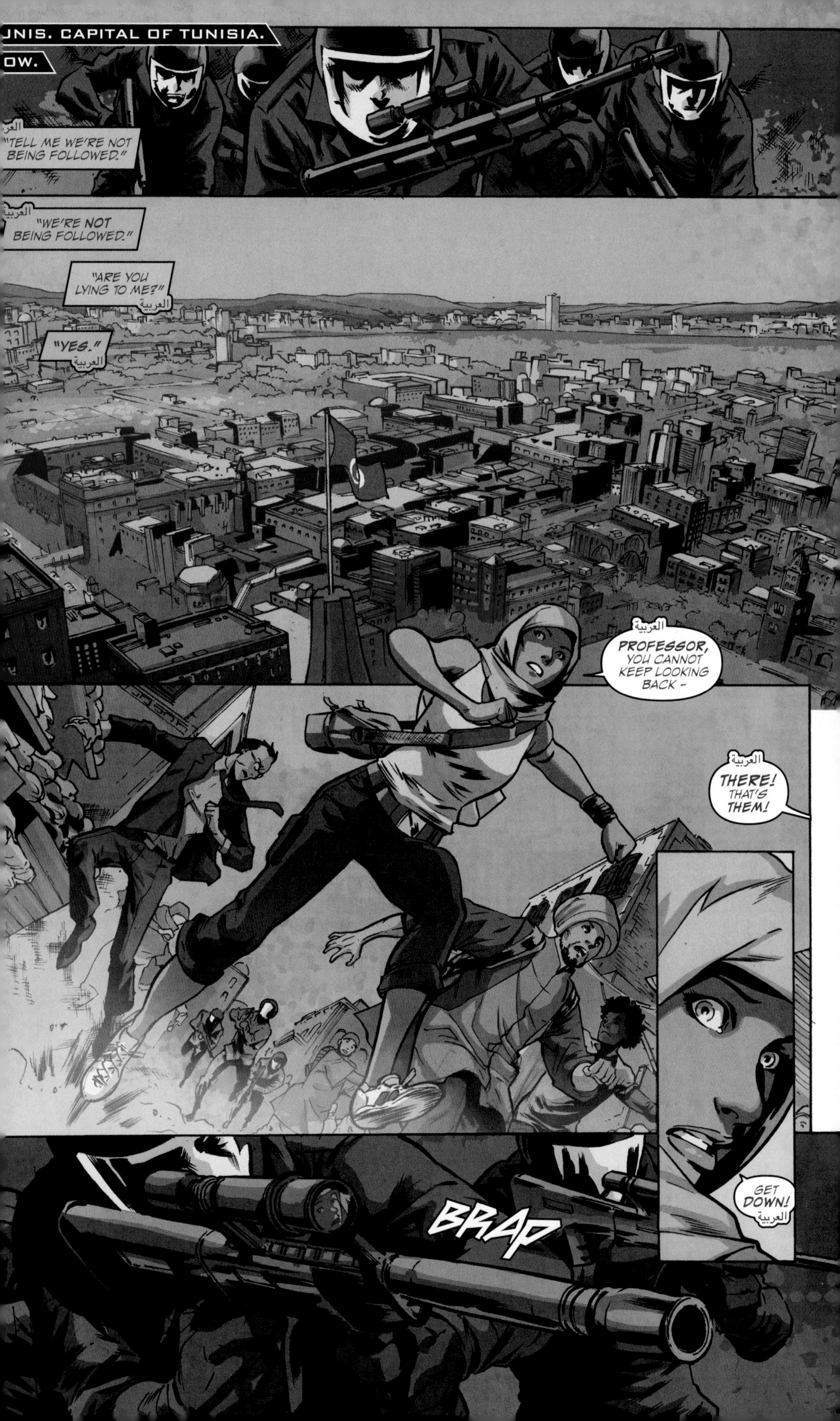
UNIS. CAPITAL OF TUNISIA.
OW.
"TELL ME WE'RE NOT BEING FOLLOWED."
العربية
"WE'RE NOT BEING FOLLOWED."
"ARE YOU LYING TO ME?"
العربية
"YES."
العربية
العربية
PROFESSOR, YOU CANNOT KEEP LOOKING BACK -
العربية
THERE! THAT'S THEM!
GET DOWN!
العربية
BRAP

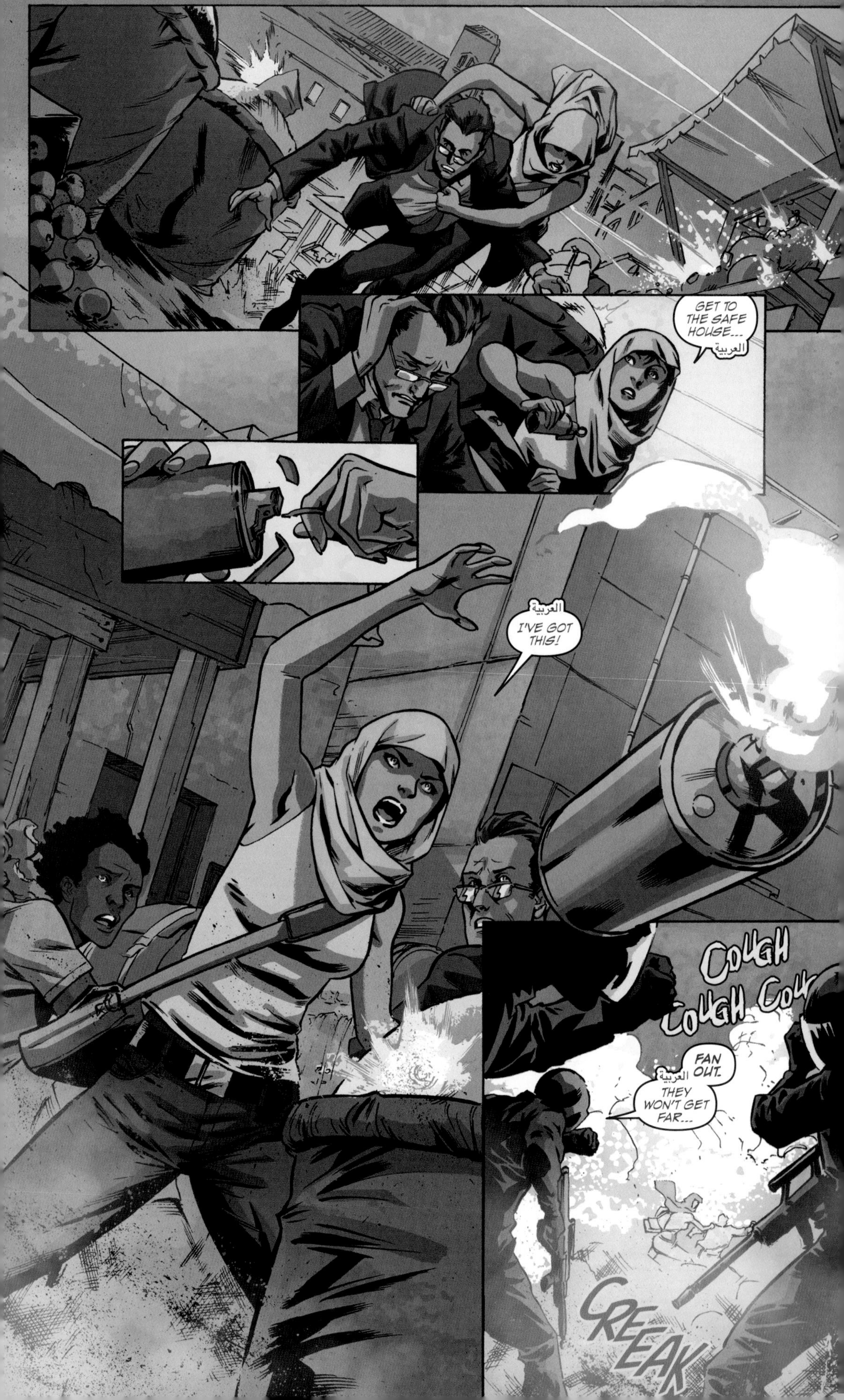
GET TO THE SAFE HOUSE... العربية
العربية I'VE GOT THIS!
COUGH COUGH COU
FAN OUT.
العربية THEY WON'T GET FAR...
CREEAK

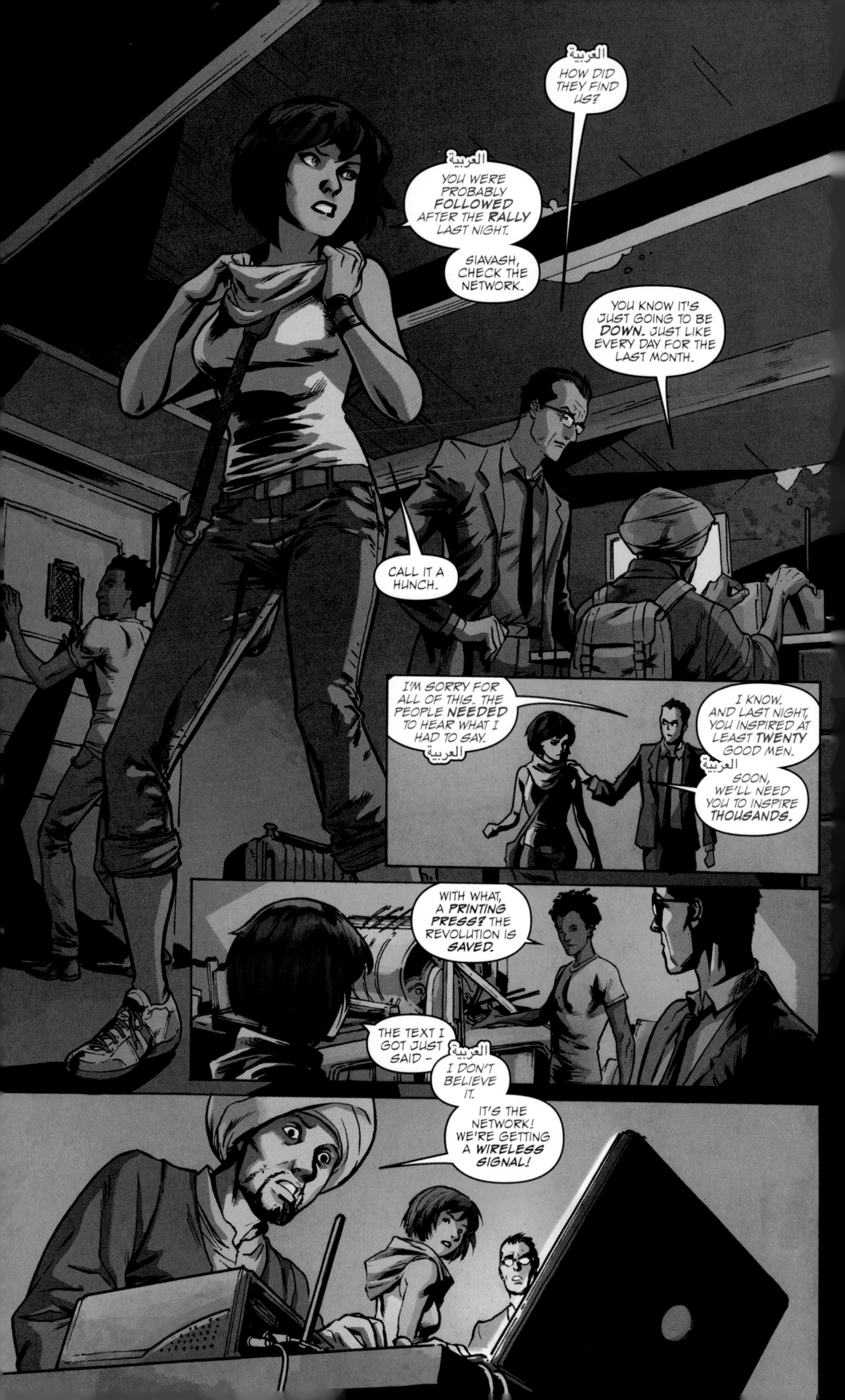
العربية
HOW DID THEY FIND US?
العربية
YOU WERE PROBABLY FOLLOWED AFTER THE RALLY LAST NIGHT.
SIAVASH, CHECK THE NETWORK.
YOU KNOW IT'S JUST GOING TO BE DOWN. JUST LIKE EVERY DAY FOR THE LAST MONTH.
CALL IT A HUNCH.
I'M SORRY FOR ALL OF THIS. THE PEOPLE NEEDED TO HEAR WHAT I HAD TO SAY.
العربية
I KNOW. AND LAST NIGHT, YOU INSPIRED AT LEAST TWENTY GOOD MEN.
العربية
SOON, WE'LL NEED YOU TO INSPIRE THOUSANDS.
WITH WHAT, A PRINTING PRESS? THE REVOLUTION IS SAVED.
THE TEXT I GOT JUST SAID –
العربية
I DON'T BELIEVE IT.
IT'S THE NETWORK! WE'RE GETTING A WIRELESS SIGNAL!

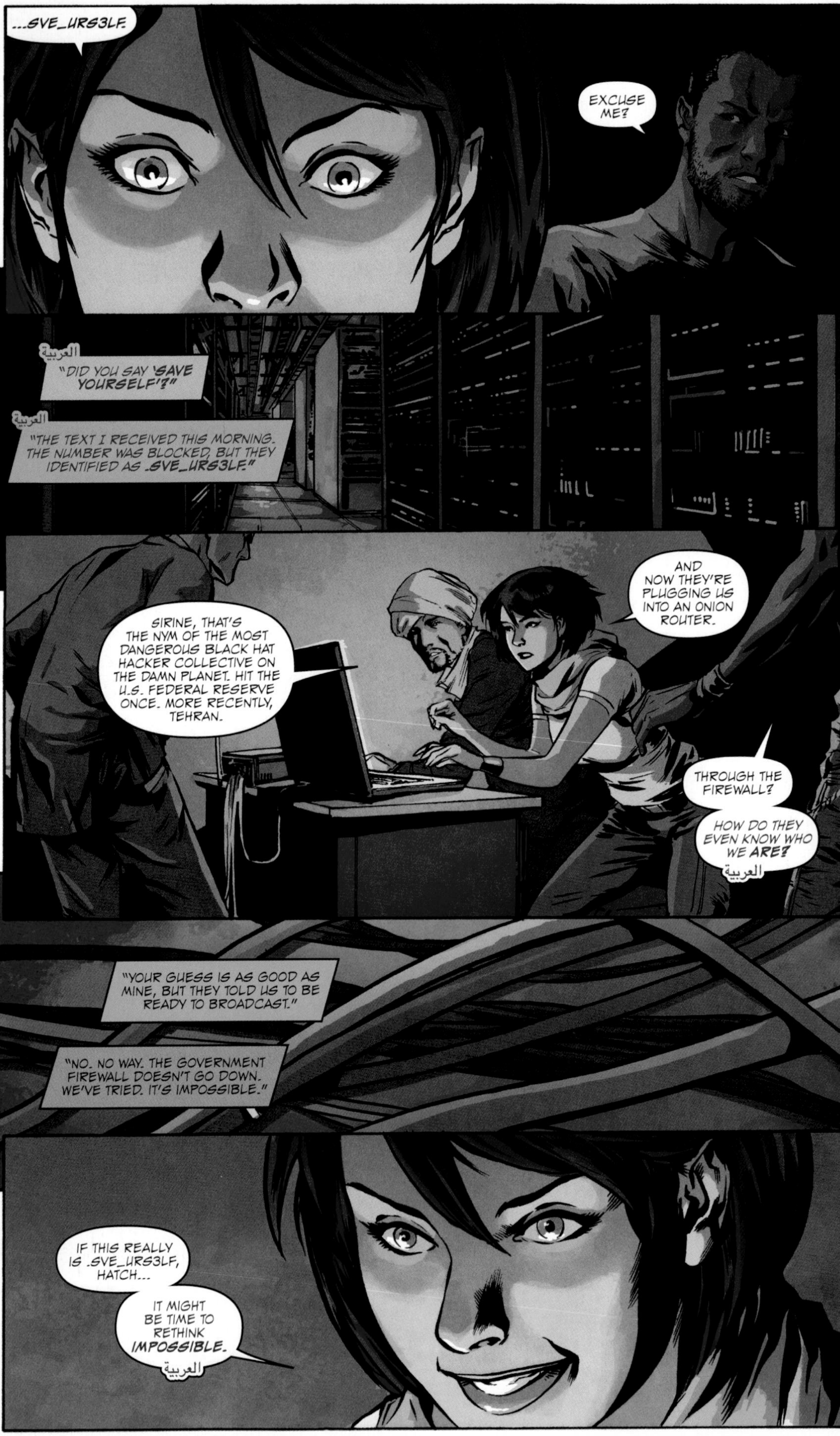
...SVE_URS3LF.
EXCUSE ME?
العربية
"DID YOU SAY 'SAVE YOURSELF'?"
العربية
"THE TEXT I RECEIVED THIS MORNING. THE NUMBER WAS BLOCKED, BUT THEY IDENTIFIED AS .SVE_URS3LF."
SIRINE, THAT'S THE NYM OF THE MOST DANGEROUS BLACK HAT HACKER COLLECTIVE ON THE DAMN PLANET. HIT THE U.S. FEDERAL RESERVE ONCE. MORE RECENTLY, TEHRAN.
AND NOW THEY'RE PLUGGING US INTO AN ONION ROUTER.
THROUGH THE FIREWALL?
HOW DO THEY EVEN KNOW WHO WE ARE?
العربية
"YOUR GUESS IS AS GOOD AS MINE, BUT THEY TOLD US TO BE READY TO BROADCAST."
"NO. NO WAY. THE GOVERNMENT FIREWALL DOESN'T GO DOWN. WE'VE TRIED. IT'S IMPOSSIBLE."
IF THIS REALLY IS .SVE_URS3LF, HATCH...
IT MIGHT BE TIME TO RETHINK IMPOSSIBLE.
العربية

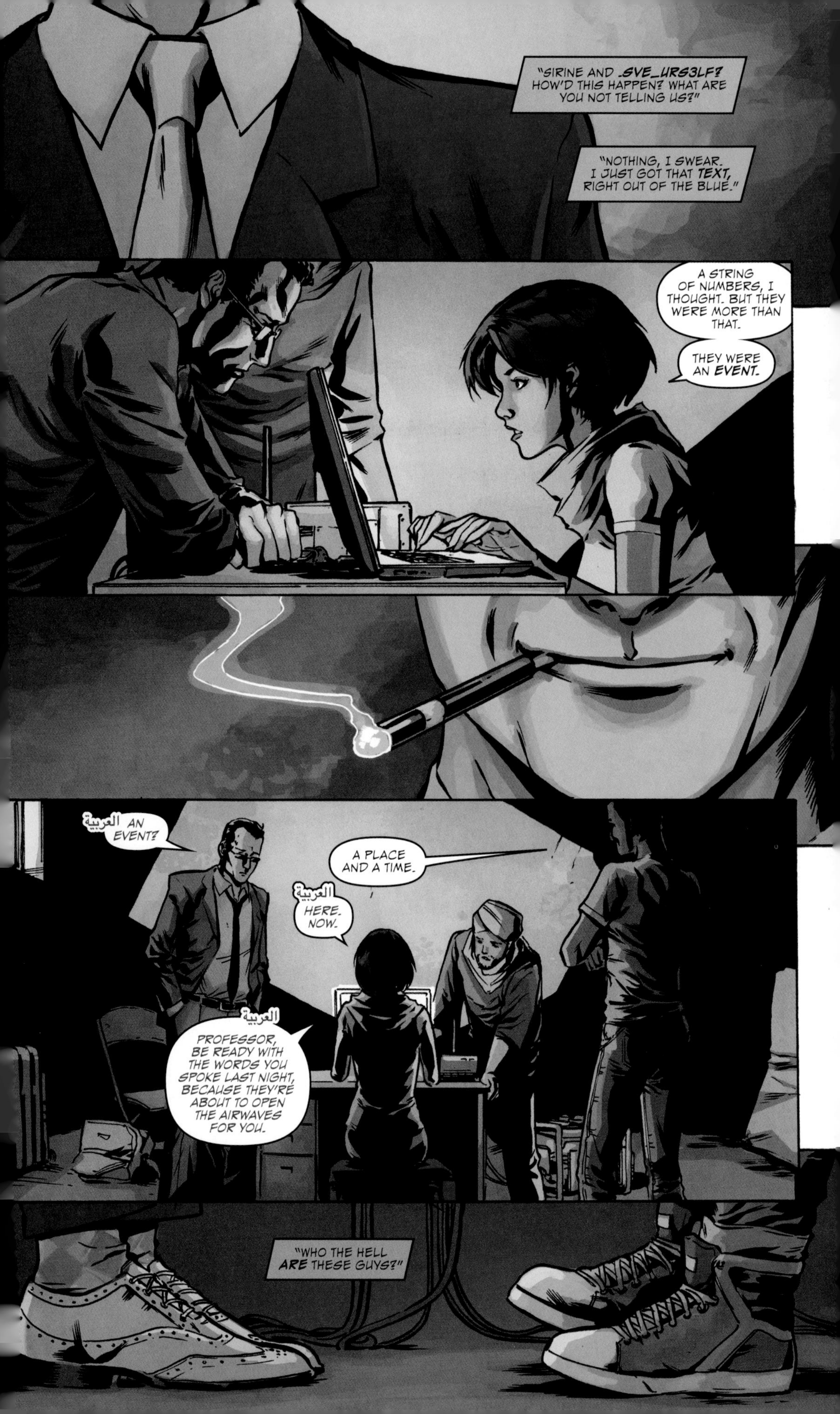
"SIRINE AND .SVE_URS3LF? HOW'D THIS HAPPEN? WHAT ARE YOU NOT TELLING US?"
"NOTHING, I SWEAR. I JUST GOT THAT TEXT, RIGHT OUT OF THE BLUE."
A STRING OF NUMBERS, I THOUGHT. BUT THEY WERE MORE THAN THAT.
THEY WERE AN EVENT.
العربية AN EVENT?
A PLACE AND A TIME.
العربية HERE. NOW.
العربية PROFESSOR, BE READY WITH THE WORDS YOU SPOKE LAST NIGHT, BECAUSE THEY'RE ABOUT TO OPEN THE AIRWAVES FOR YOU.
"WHO THE HELL ARE THESE GUYS?"

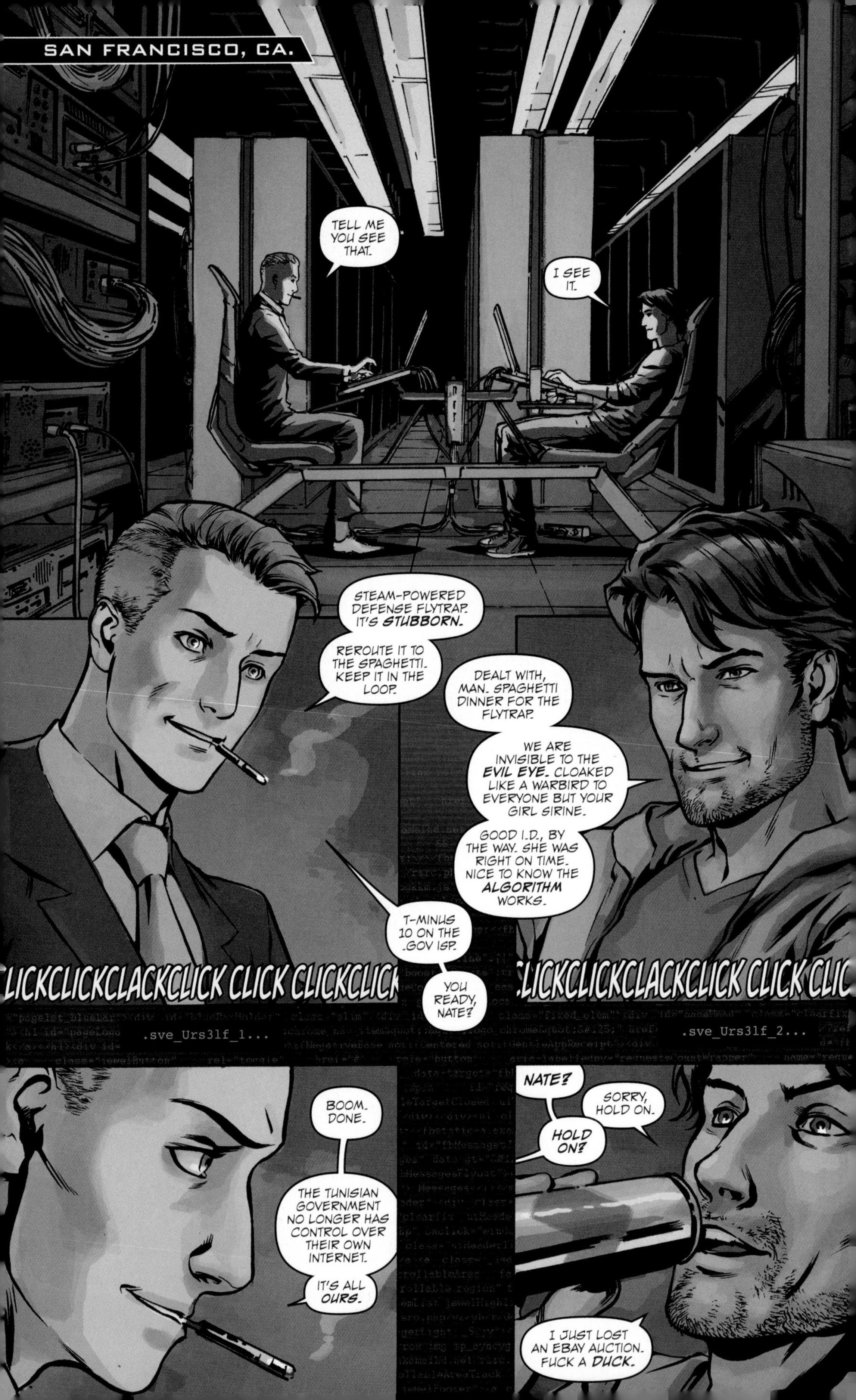
SAN FRANCISCO, CA.
TELL ME YOU SEE THAT.
I SEE IT.
STEAM-POWERED DEFENSE FLYTRAP. IT'S STUBBORN.
REROUTE IT TO THE SPAGHETTI. KEEP IT IN THE LOOP.
DEALT WITH, MAN. SPAGHETTI DINNER FOR THE FLYTRAP.
WE ARE INVISIBLE TO THE EVIL EYE. CLOAKED LIKE A WARBIRD TO EVERYONE BUT YOUR GIRL SIRINE.
GOOD I.D., BY THE WAY. SHE WAS RIGHT ON TIME. NICE TO KNOW THE ALGORITHM WORKS.
T-MINUS 10 ON THE .GOV ISP.
YOU READY, NATE?
LICKCLICKCLACKCLICK CLICK CLICKCLICK
LICKCLICKCLACKCLICK CLICK CLIC
.sve_Urs3lf_1...
.sve_Urs3lf_2...
BOOM. DONE.
THE TUNISIAN GOVERNMENT NO LONGER HAS CONTROL OVER THEIR OWN INTERNET.
IT'S ALL OURS.
NATE?
SORRY, HOLD ON.
HOLD ON?
I JUST LOST AN EBAY AUCTION. FUCK A DUCK.

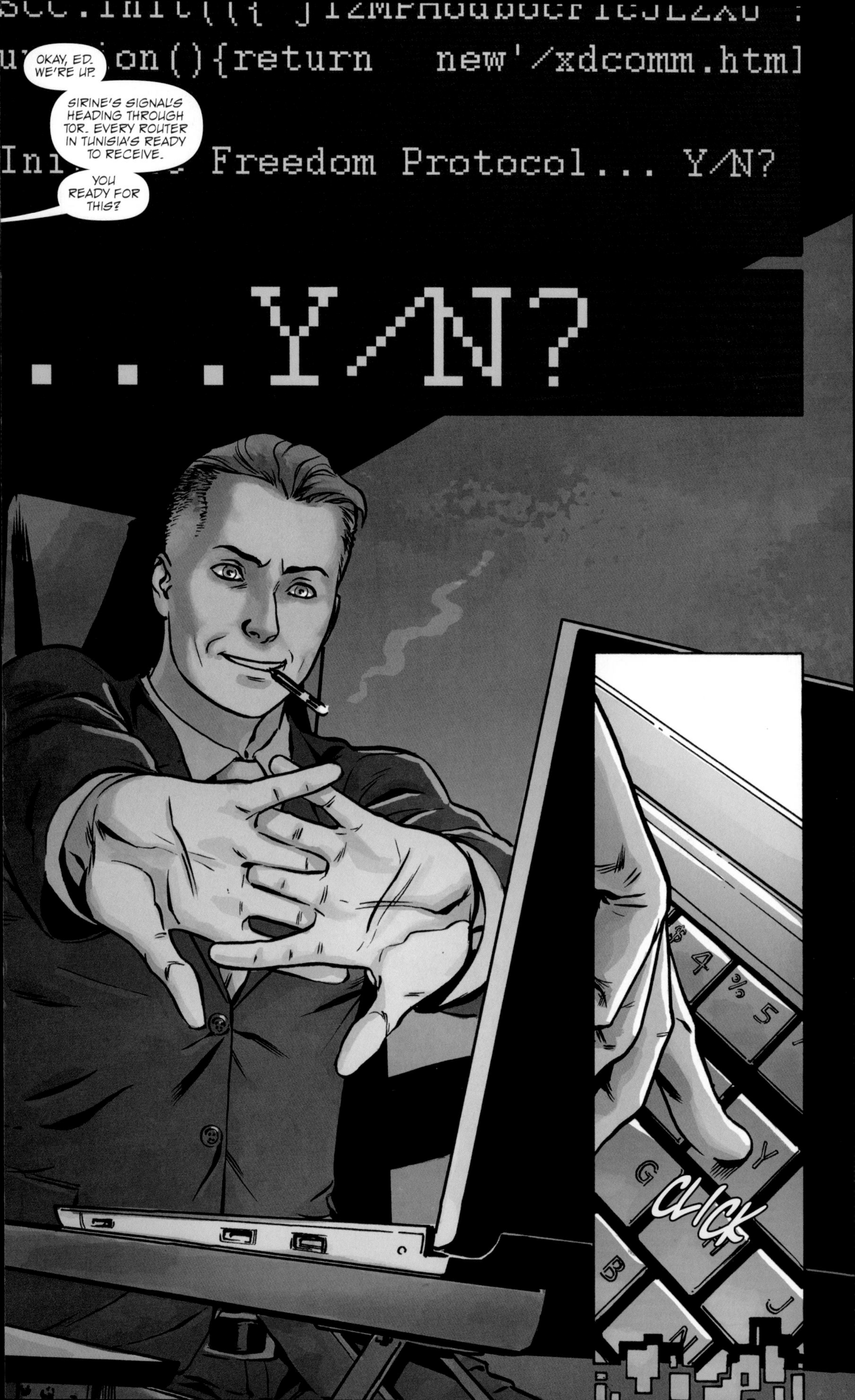
{return new'/xdcomm.htm]
OKAY, ED. WE'RE UP.
SIRINE'S SIGNAL'S HEADING THROUGH TOR. EVERY ROUTER IN TUNISIA'S READY TO RECEIVE.
Freedom Protocol... Y/N?
YOU READY FOR THIS?
...Y/N?
CLICK

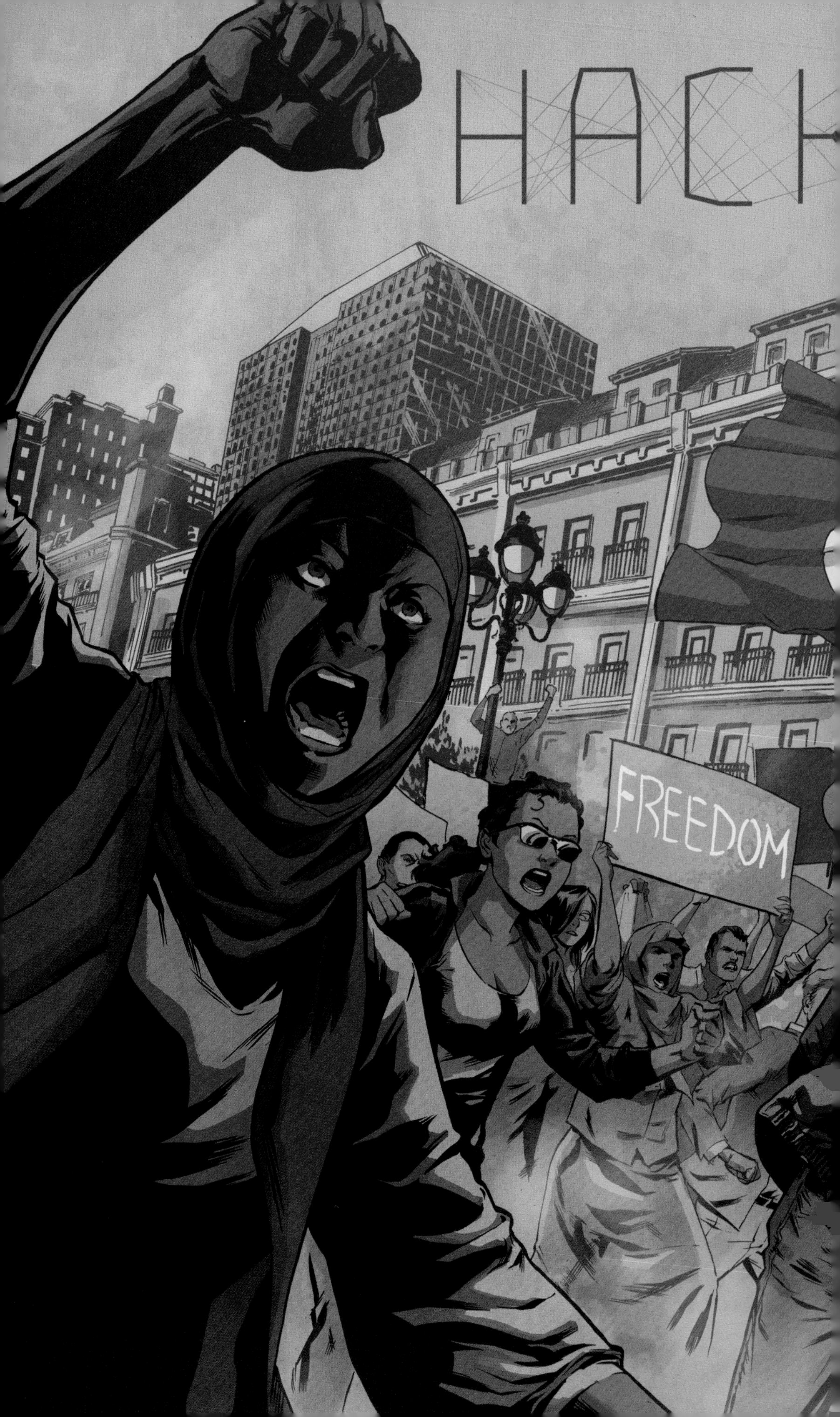
HACK
FREEDOM

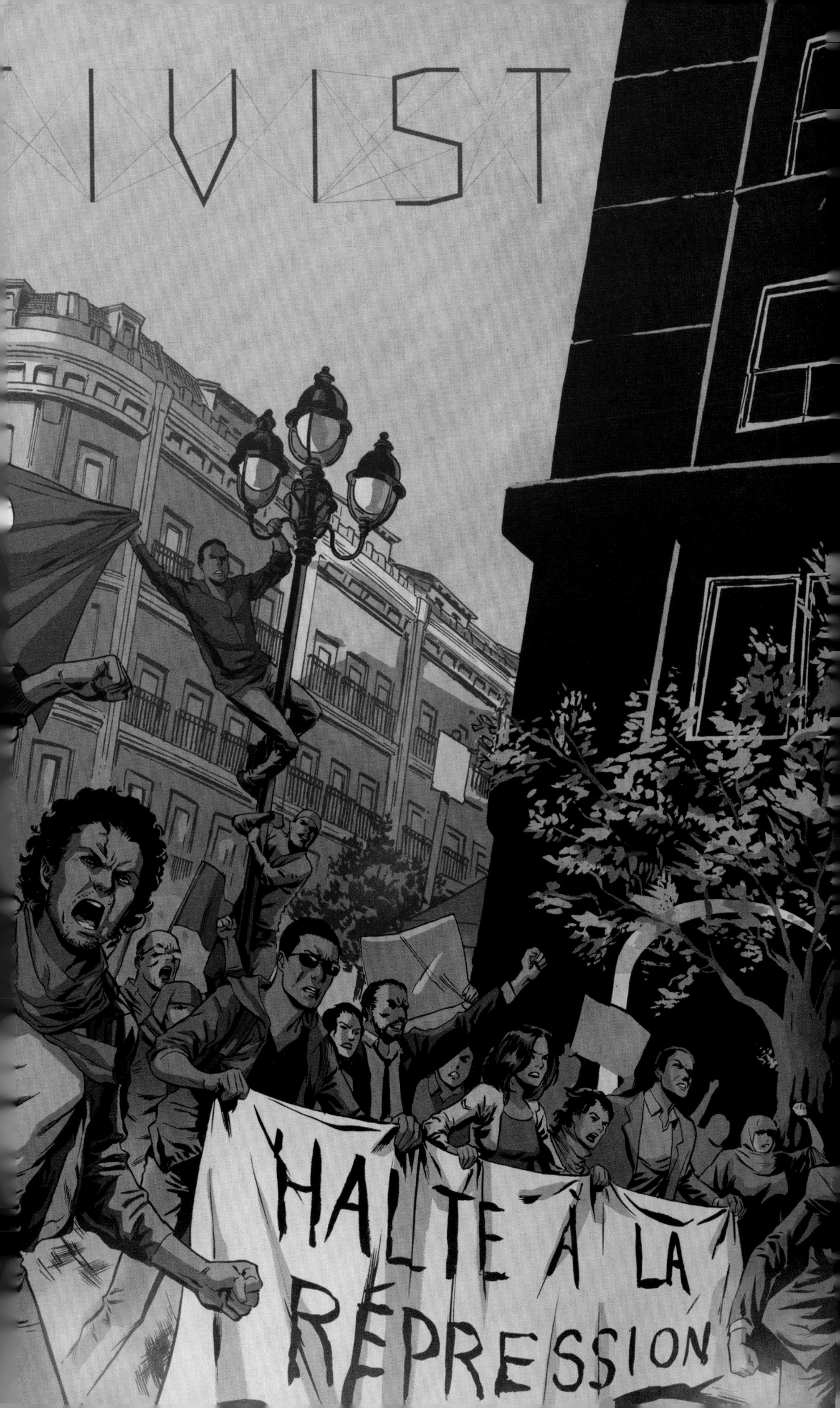
IVIST
HALTE À LA RÉPRESSION

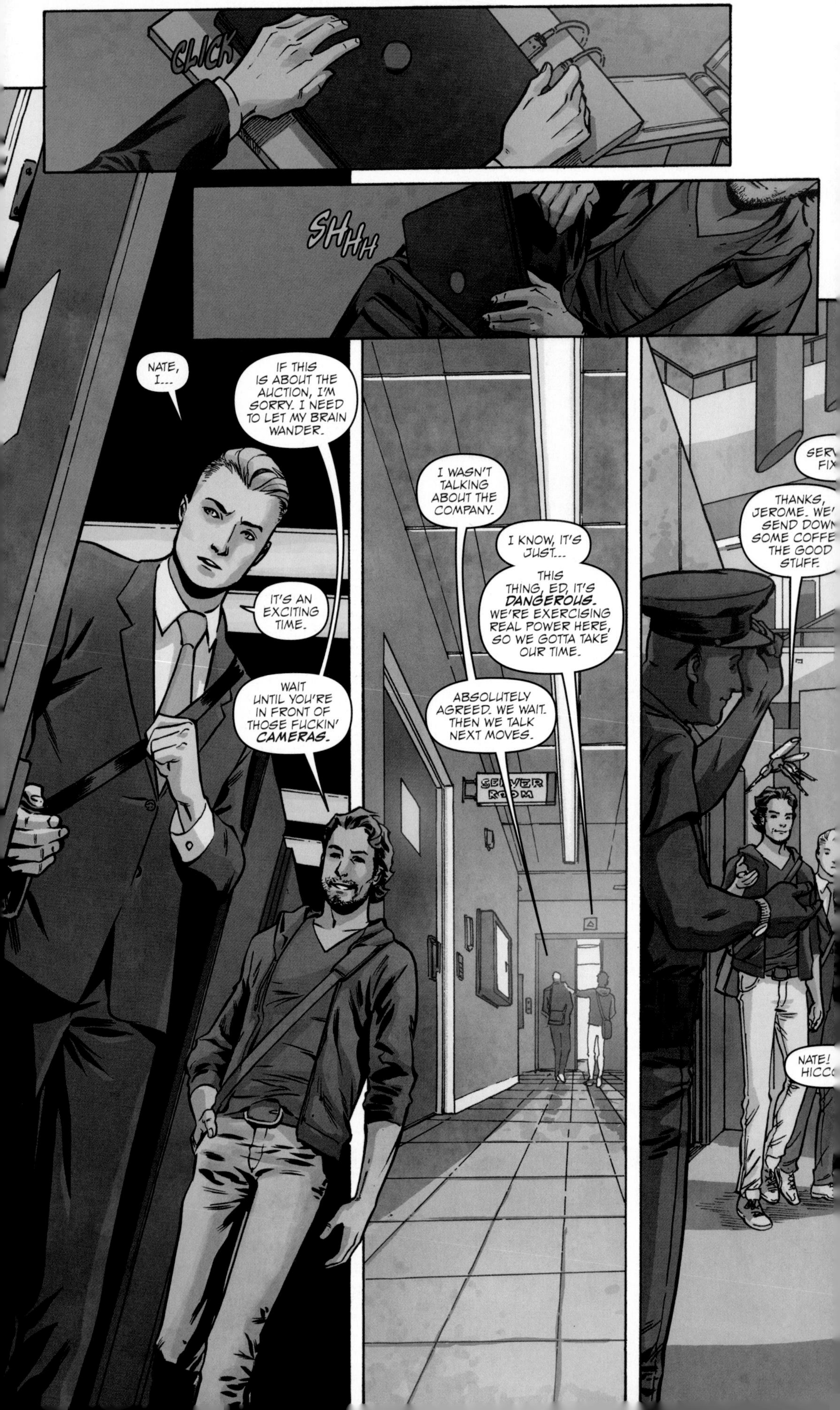
CLICK
SHHHH
NATE, I...
IF THIS IS ABOUT THE AUCTION, I'M SORRY. I NEED TO LET MY BRAIN WANDER.
IT'S AN EXCITING TIME.
WAIT UNTIL YOU'RE IN FRONT OF THOSE FUCKIN' CAMERAS.
I WASN'T TALKING ABOUT THE COMPANY.
I KNOW, IT'S JUST...
THIS THING, ED, IT'S DANGEROUS. WE'RE EXERCISING REAL POWER HERE, SO WE GOTTA TAKE OUR TIME.
ABSOLUTELY AGREED. WE WAIT. THEN WE TALK NEXT MOVES.
SERVER ROOM
THANKS, JEROME. WE' SEND DOWN SOME COFFE THE GOOD STUFF.
NATE! HICC

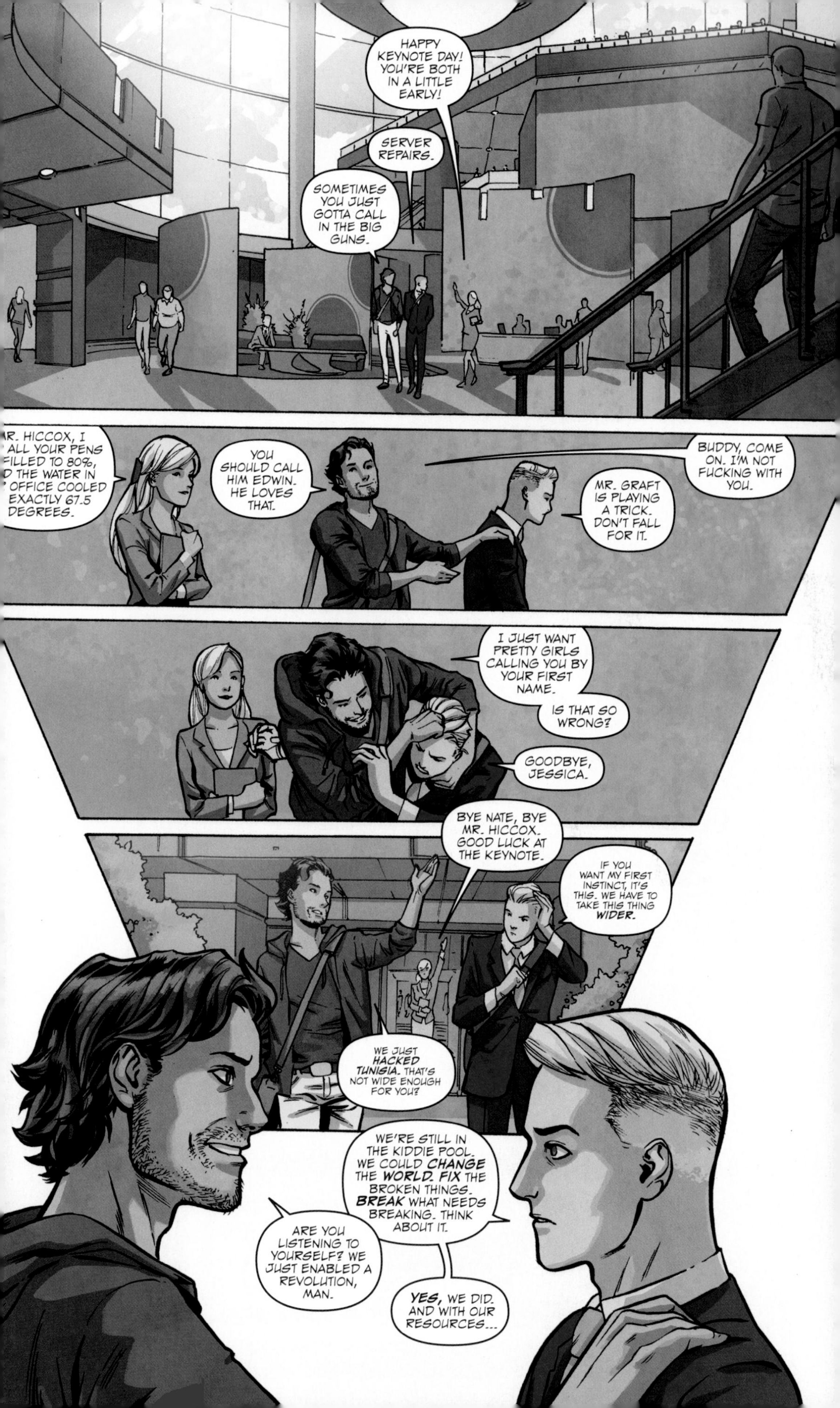

HAPPY KEYNOTE DAY! YOU'RE BOTH IN A LITTLE EARLY!
SERVER REPAIRS.
SOMETIMES YOU JUST GOTTA CALL IN THE BIG GUNS.
R. HICCOX, I ALL YOUR PENS FILLED TO 80%, D THE WATER IN OFFICE COOLED EXACTLY 67.5 DEGREES.
YOU SHOULD CALL HIM EDWIN. HE LOVES THAT.
MR. GRAFT IS PLAYING A TRICK. DON'T FALL FOR IT.
BUDDY, COME ON. I'M NOT FUCKING WITH YOU.
I JUST WANT PRETTY GIRLS CALLING YOU BY YOUR FIRST NAME.
IS THAT SO WRONG?
GOODBYE, JESSICA.
BYE NATE, BYE MR. HICCOX. GOOD LUCK AT THE KEYNOTE.
IF YOU WANT MY FIRST INSTINCT, IT'S THIS. WE HAVE TO TAKE THIS THING WIDER.
WE JUST HACKED TUNISIA. THAT'S NOT WIDE ENOUGH FOR YOU?
WE'RE STILL IN THE KIDDIE POOL. WE COULD CHANGE THE WORLD. FIX THE BROKEN THINGS. BREAK WHAT NEEDS BREAKING. THINK ABOUT IT.
ARE YOU LISTENING TO YOURSELF? WE JUST ENABLED A REVOLUTION, MAN.
YES, WE DID. AND WITH OUR RESOURCES...

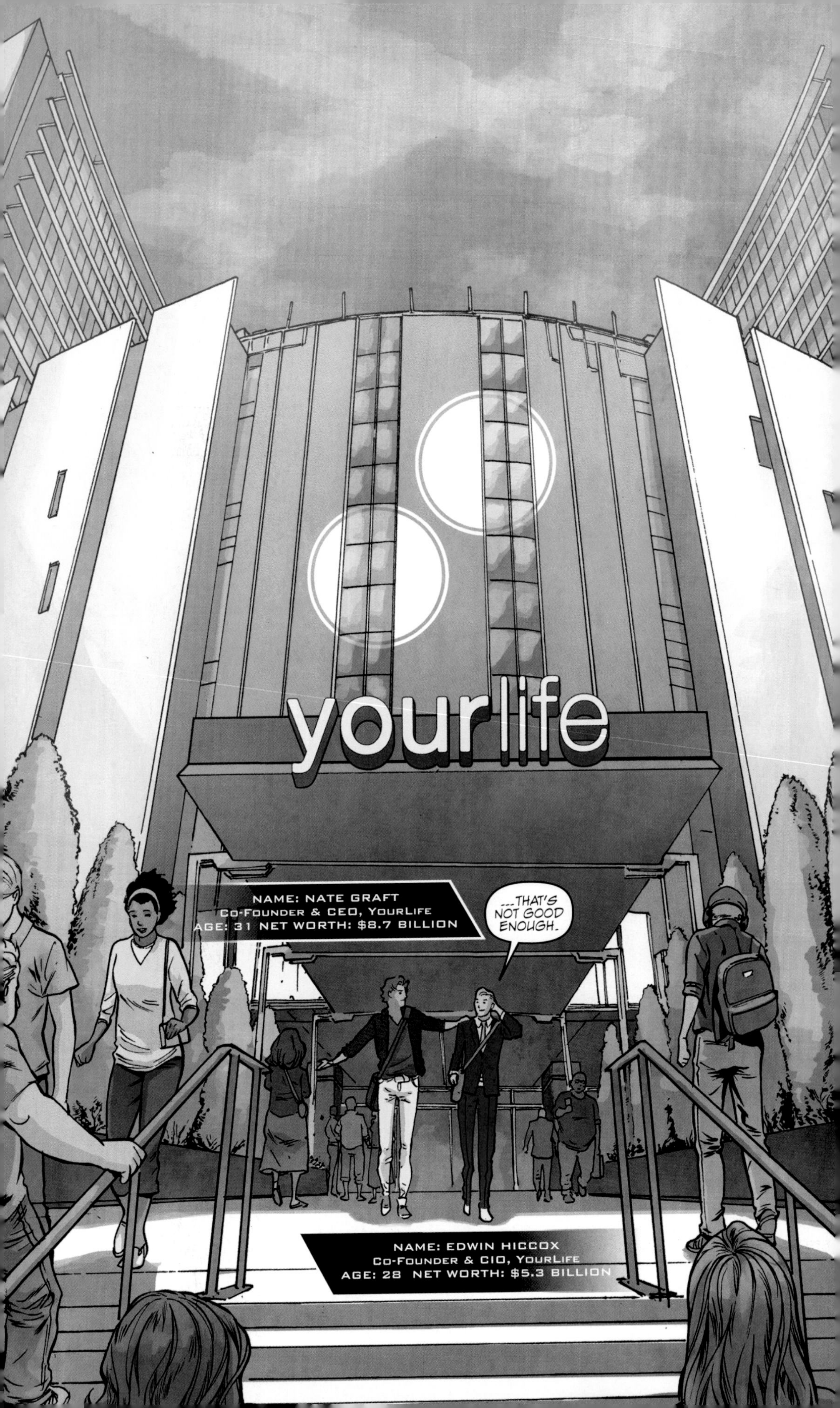
yourlife
NAME: NATE GRAFT
Co-Founder & CEO, YourLife
AGE: 31 NET WORTH: $8.7 BILLION
...THAT'S NOT GOOD ENOUGH.
NAME: EDWIN HICCOX
Co-Founder & CIO, YourLife
AGE: 28 NET WORTH: $5.3 BILLION

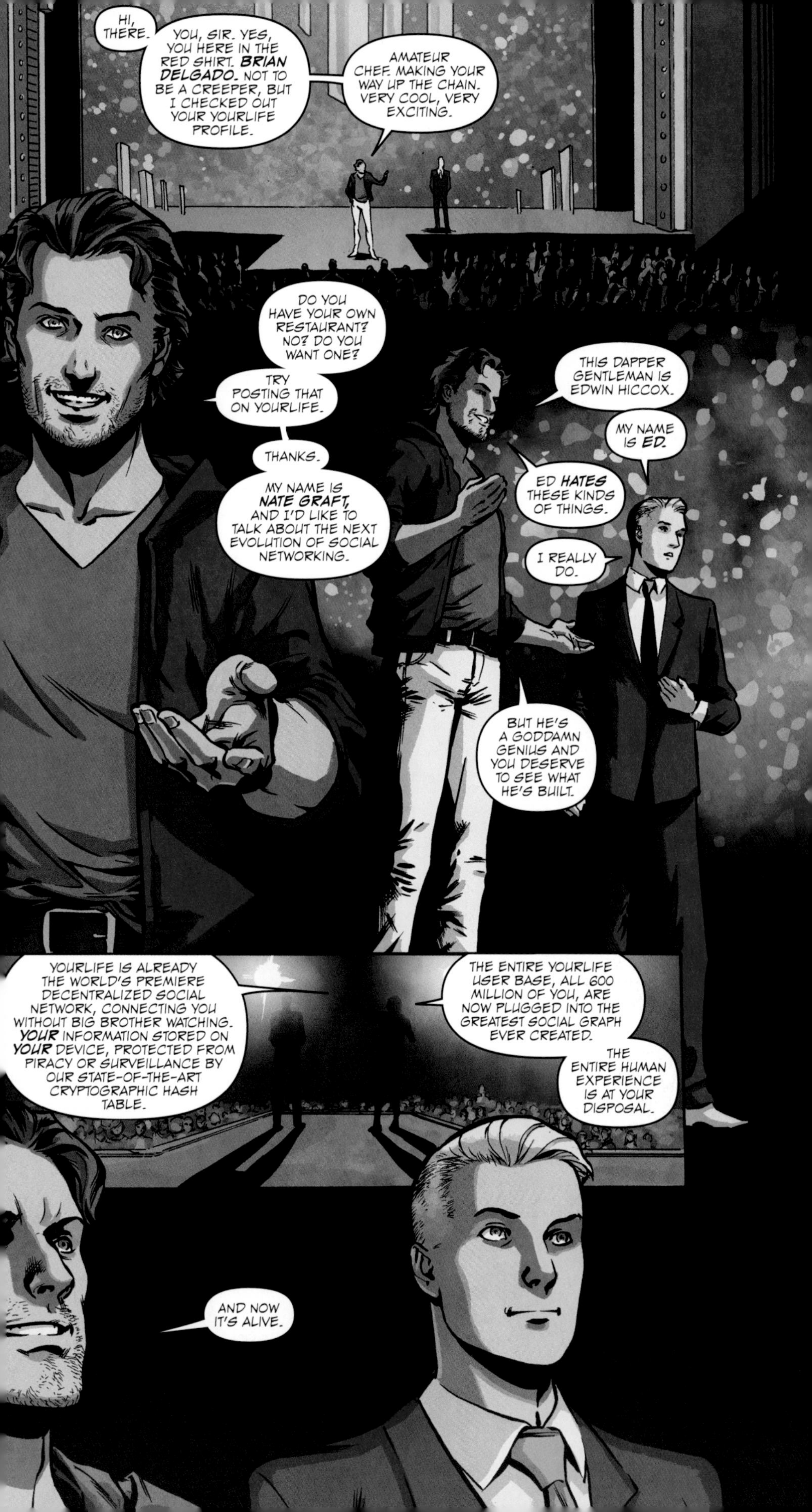

HI, THERE.
YOU, SIR. YES, YOU HERE IN THE RED SHIRT. BRIAN DELGADO. NOT TO BE A CREEPER, BUT I CHECKED OUT YOUR YOURLIFE PROFILE.
AMATEUR CHEF. MAKING YOUR WAY UP THE CHAIN. VERY COOL, VERY EXCITING.
DO YOU HAVE YOUR OWN RESTAURANT? NO? DO YOU WANT ONE?
TRY POSTING THAT ON YOURLIFE.
THANKS.
MY NAME IS NATE GRAFT, AND I'D LIKE TO TALK ABOUT THE NEXT EVOLUTION OF SOCIAL NETWORKING.
THIS DAPPER GENTLEMAN IS EDWIN HICCOX.
MY NAME IS ED.
ED HATES THESE KINDS OF THINGS.
I REALLY DO.
BUT HE'S A GODDAMN GENIUS AND YOU DESERVE TO SEE WHAT HE'S BUILT.
YOURLIFE IS ALREADY THE WORLD'S PREMIERE DECENTRALIZED SOCIAL NETWORK, CONNECTING YOU WITHOUT BIG BROTHER WATCHING. YOUR INFORMATION STORED ON YOUR DEVICE, PROTECTED FROM PIRACY OR SURVEILLANCE BY OUR STATE-OF-THE-ART CRYPTOGRAPHIC HASH TABLE.
THE ENTIRE YOURLIFE USER BASE, ALL 600 MILLION OF YOU, ARE NOW PLUGGED INTO THE GREATEST SOCIAL GRAPH EVER CREATED.
THE ENTIRE HUMAN EXPERIENCE IS AT YOUR DISPOSAL.
AND NOW IT'S ALIVE.

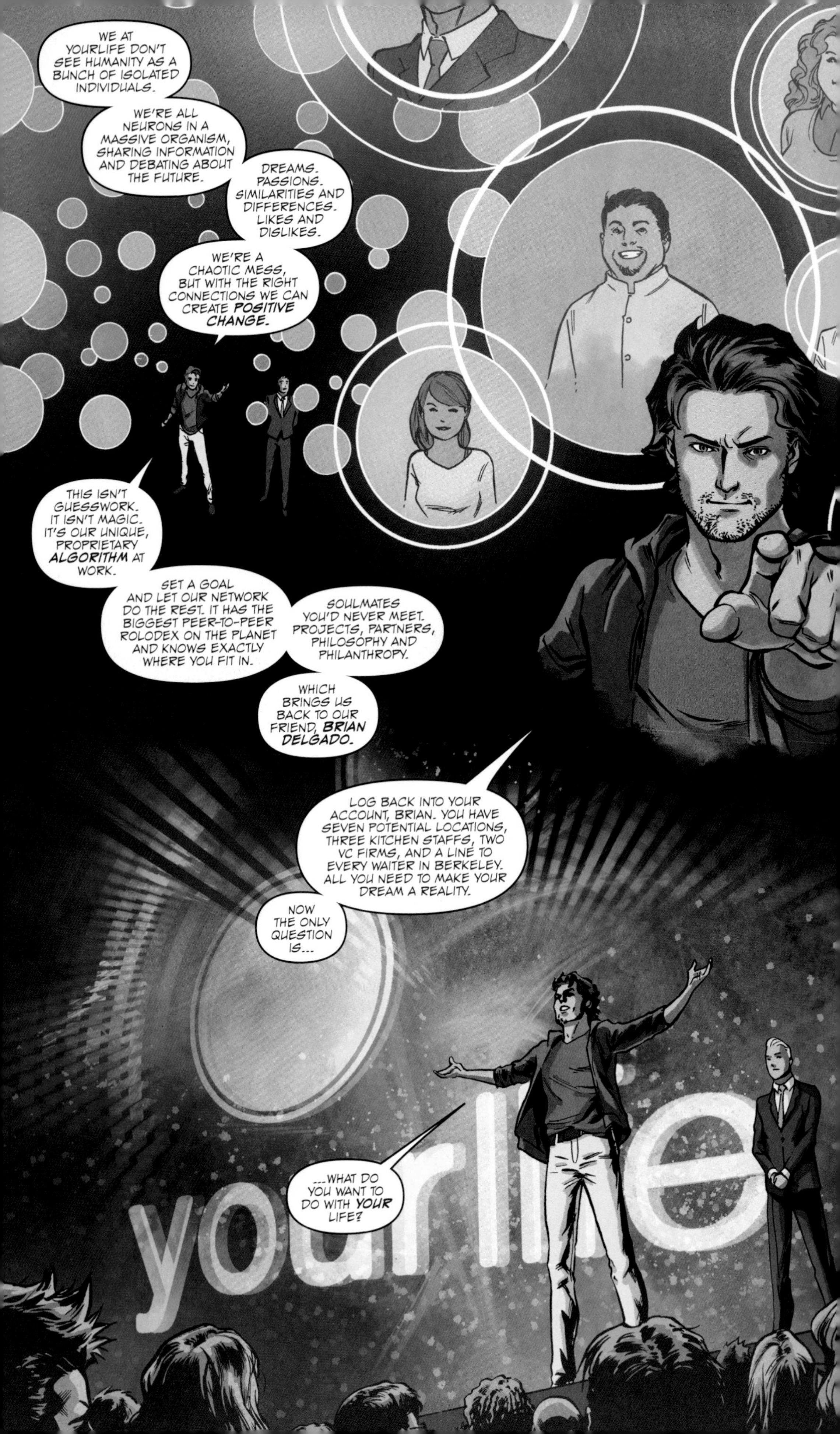
WE AT YOURLIFE DON'T SEE HUMANITY AS A BUNCH OF ISOLATED INDIVIDUALS.
WE'RE ALL NEURONS IN A MASSIVE ORGANISM, SHARING INFORMATION AND DEBATING ABOUT THE FUTURE.
DREAMS. PASSIONS. SIMILARITIES AND DIFFERENCES. LIKES AND DISLIKES.
WE'RE A CHAOTIC MESS, BUT WITH THE RIGHT CONNECTIONS WE CAN CREATE **POSITIVE CHANGE.**
THIS ISN'T GUESSWORK. IT ISN'T MAGIC. IT'S OUR UNIQUE, PROPRIETARY **ALGORITHM** AT WORK.
SET A GOAL AND LET OUR NETWORK DO THE REST. IT HAS THE BIGGEST PEER-TO-PEER ROLODEX ON THE PLANET AND KNOWS EXACTLY WHERE YOU FIT IN.
SOULMATES YOU'D NEVER MEET. PROJECTS, PARTNERS, PHILOSOPHY AND PHILANTHROPY.
WHICH BRINGS US BACK TO OUR FRIEND, **BRIAN DELGADO.**
LOG BACK INTO YOUR ACCOUNT, BRIAN. YOU HAVE SEVEN POTENTIAL LOCATIONS, THREE KITCHEN STAFFS, TWO VC FIRMS, AND A LINE TO EVERY WAITER IN BERKELEY. ALL YOU NEED TO MAKE YOUR DREAM A REALITY.
NOW THE ONLY QUESTION IS...
...WHAT DO YOU WANT TO DO WITH **YOUR** LIFE?
yourlife

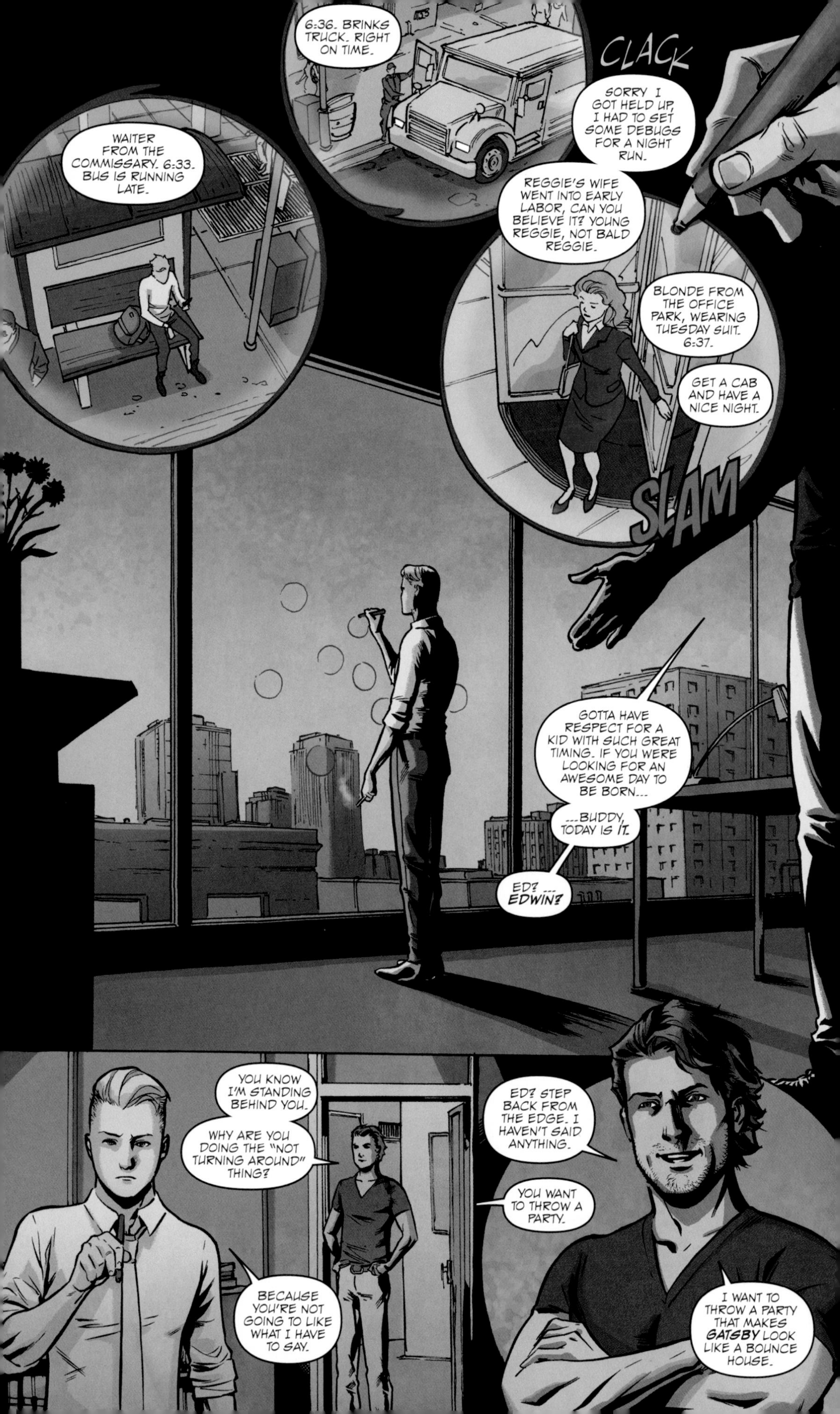
WAITER FROM THE COMMISSARY. 6:33. BUS IS RUNNING LATE.
6:36. BRINKS TRUCK. RIGHT ON TIME.
CLACK
SORRY I GOT HELD UP, I HAD TO SET SOME DEBUGS FOR A NIGHT RUN.
REGGIE'S WIFE WENT INTO EARLY LABOR, CAN YOU BELIEVE IT? YOUNG REGGIE, NOT BALD REGGIE.
BLONDE FROM THE OFFICE PARK, WEARING TUESDAY SUIT. 6:37.
GET A CAB AND HAVE A NICE NIGHT.
SLAM
GOTTA HAVE RESPECT FOR A KID WITH SUCH GREAT TIMING. IF YOU WERE LOOKING FOR AN AWESOME DAY TO BE BORN...
...BUDDY, TODAY IS IT.
ED? ... EDWIN?
YOU KNOW I'M STANDING BEHIND YOU.
WHY ARE YOU DOING THE "NOT TURNING AROUND" THING?
BECAUSE YOU'RE NOT GOING TO LIKE WHAT I HAVE TO SAY.
ED? STEP BACK FROM THE EDGE. I HAVEN'T SAID ANYTHING.
YOU WANT TO THROW A PARTY.
I WANT TO THROW A PARTY THAT MAKES GATSBY LOOK LIKE A BOUNCE HOUSE.

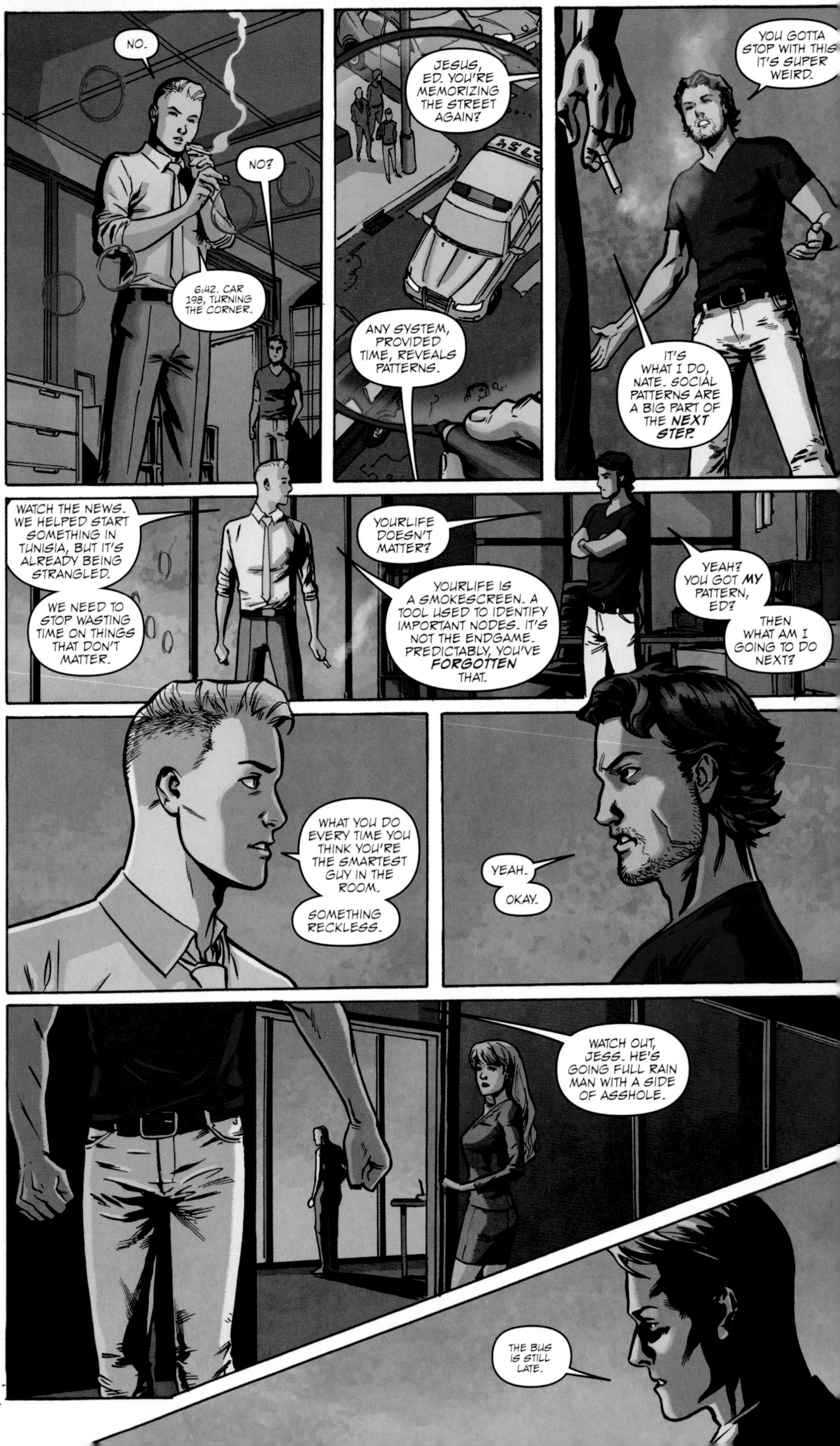
NO.
NO?
6:42. CAR 198, TURNING THE CORNER.
JESUS, ED. YOU'RE MEMORIZING THE STREET AGAIN?
ANY SYSTEM, PROVIDED TIME, REVEALS PATTERNS.
YOU GOTTA STOP WITH THIS. IT'S SUPER WEIRD.
IT'S WHAT I DO, NATE. SOCIAL PATTERNS ARE A BIG PART OF THE NEXT STEP.
WATCH THE NEWS. WE HELPED START SOMETHING IN TUNISIA, BUT IT'S ALREADY BEING STRANGLED.
WE NEED TO STOP WASTING TIME ON THINGS THAT DON'T MATTER.
YOURLIFE DOESN'T MATTER?
YOURLIFE IS A SMOKESCREEN. A TOOL USED TO IDENTIFY IMPORTANT NODES. IT'S NOT THE ENDGAME. PREDICTABLY, YOU'VE FORGOTTEN THAT.
YEAH? YOU GOT MY PATTERN, ED?
THEN WHAT AM I GOING TO DO NEXT?
WHAT YOU DO EVERY TIME YOU THINK YOU'RE THE SMARTEST GUY IN THE ROOM.
SOMETHING RECKLESS.
YEAH.
OKAY.
WATCH OUT, JESS. HE'S GOING FULL RAIN MAN WITH A SIDE OF ASSHOLE.
THE BUS IS STILL LATE.

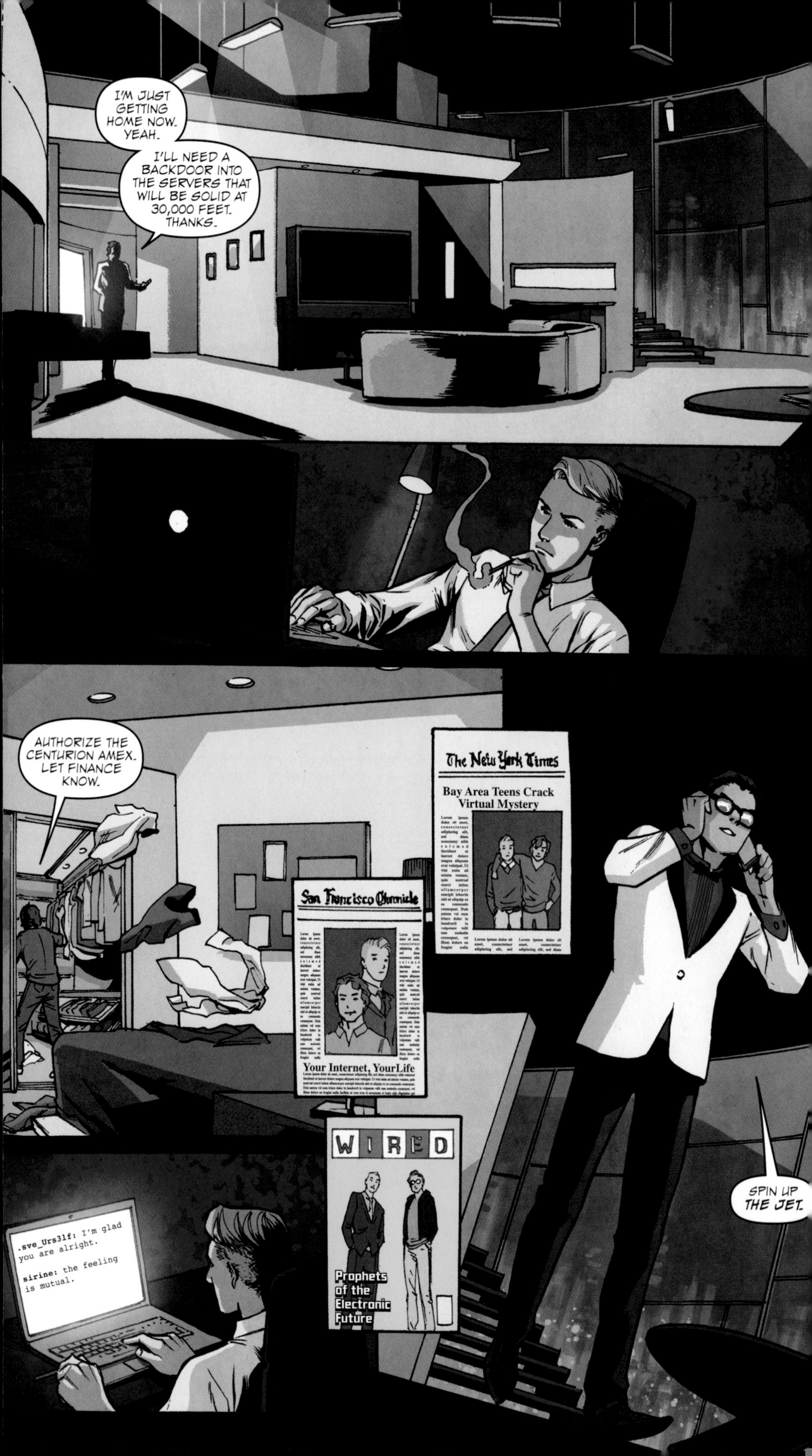
I'M JUST GETTING HOME NOW. YEAH.
I'LL NEED A BACKDOOR INTO THE SERVERS THAT WILL BE SOLID AT 30,000 FEET. THANKS.
AUTHORIZE THE CENTURION AMEX. LET FINANCE KNOW.
The New York Times
Bay Area Teens Crack Virtual Mystery
San Francisco Chronicle
Your Internet, YourLife
WIRED
Prophets of the Electronic Future
SPIN UP THE JET.
.sve_Urs3lf: I'm glad you are alright.
sirine: the feeling is mutual.

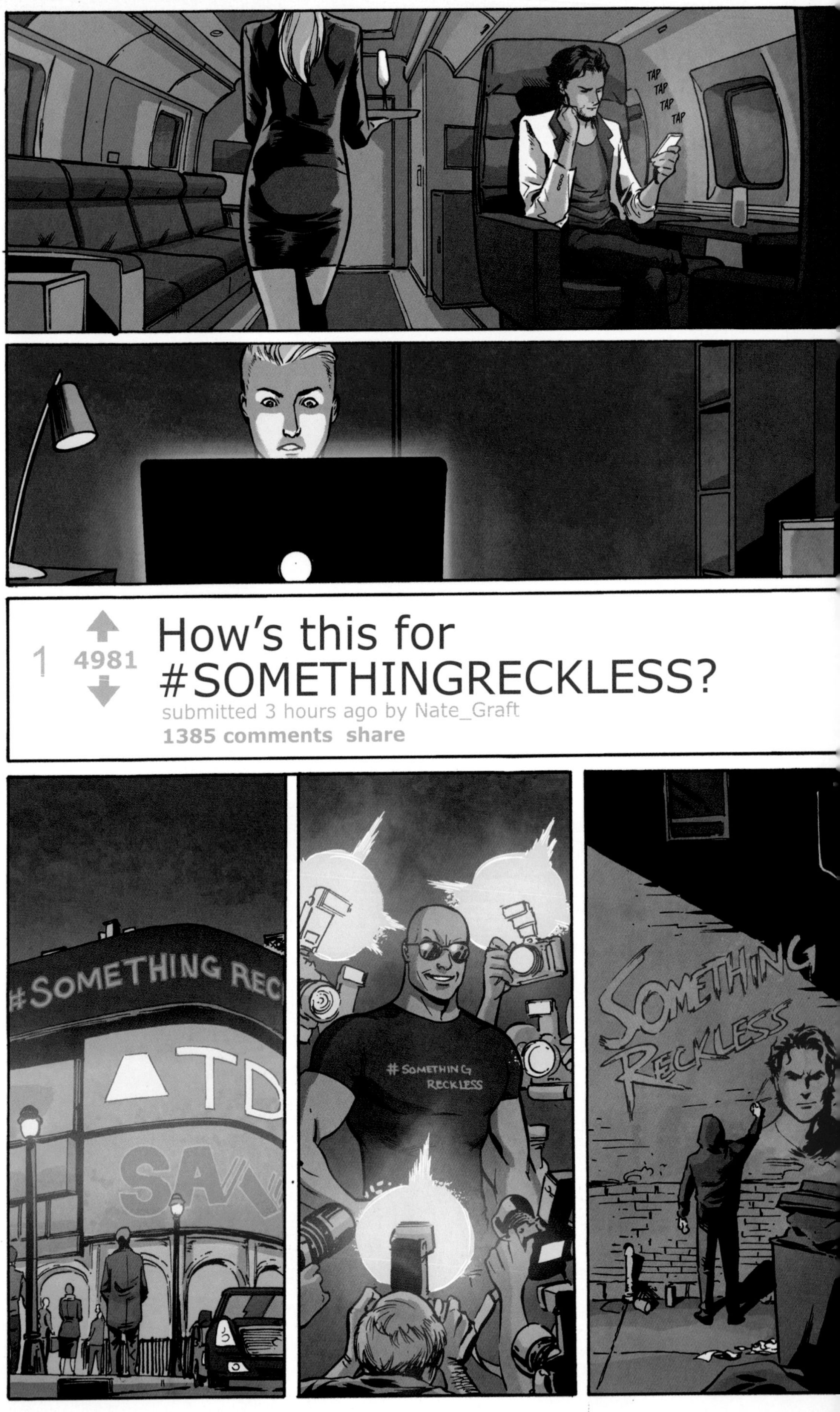

TAP
TAP
TAP
TAP
1
4981
How's this for #SOMETHINGRECKLESS?
submitted 3 hours ago by Nate_Graft
1385 comments share
#SOMETHING REC
#SOMETHING RECKLESS
SOMETHING RECKLESS

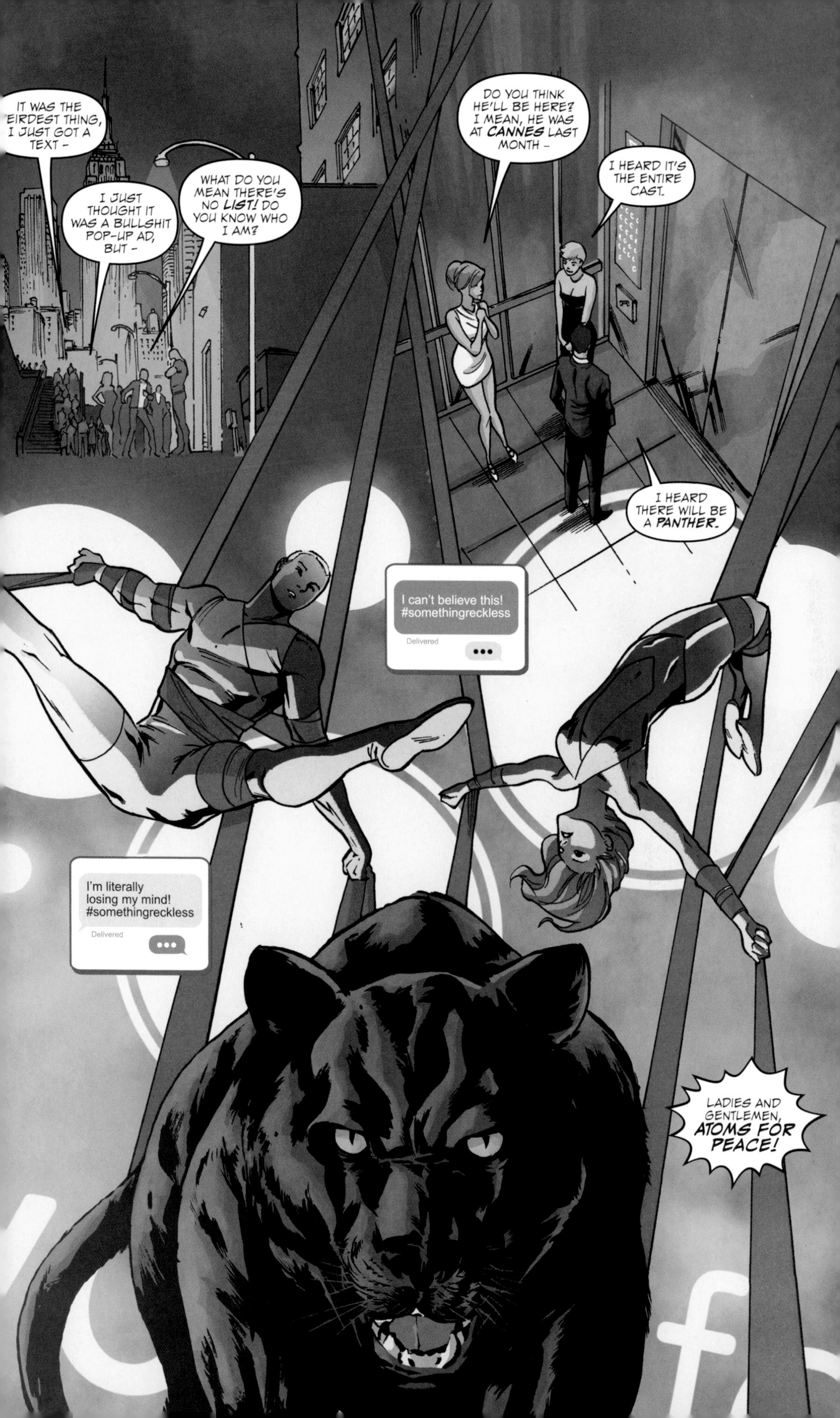
IT WAS THE WEIRDEST THING, I JUST GOT A TEXT -
I JUST THOUGHT IT WAS A BULLSHIT POP-UP AD, BUT -
WHAT DO YOU MEAN THERE'S NO LIST! DO YOU KNOW WHO I AM?
DO YOU THINK HE'LL BE HERE? I MEAN, HE WAS AT CANNES LAST MONTH -
I HEARD IT'S THE ENTIRE CAST.
I HEARD THERE WILL BE A PANTHER.
I can't believe this! #somethingreckless
Delivered
I'm literally losing my mind! #somethingreckless
Delivered
LADIES AND GENTLEMEN, ATOMS FOR PEACE!

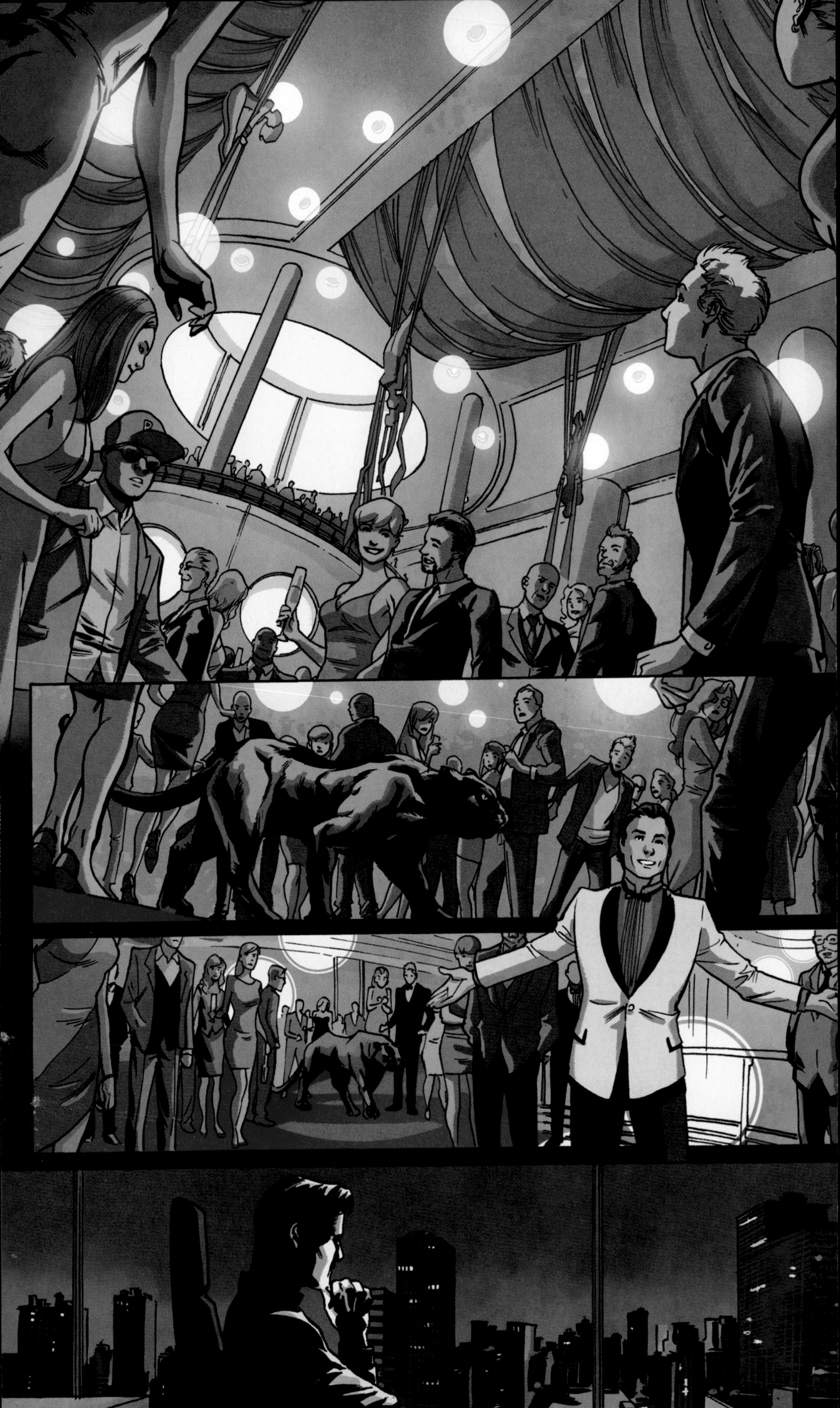

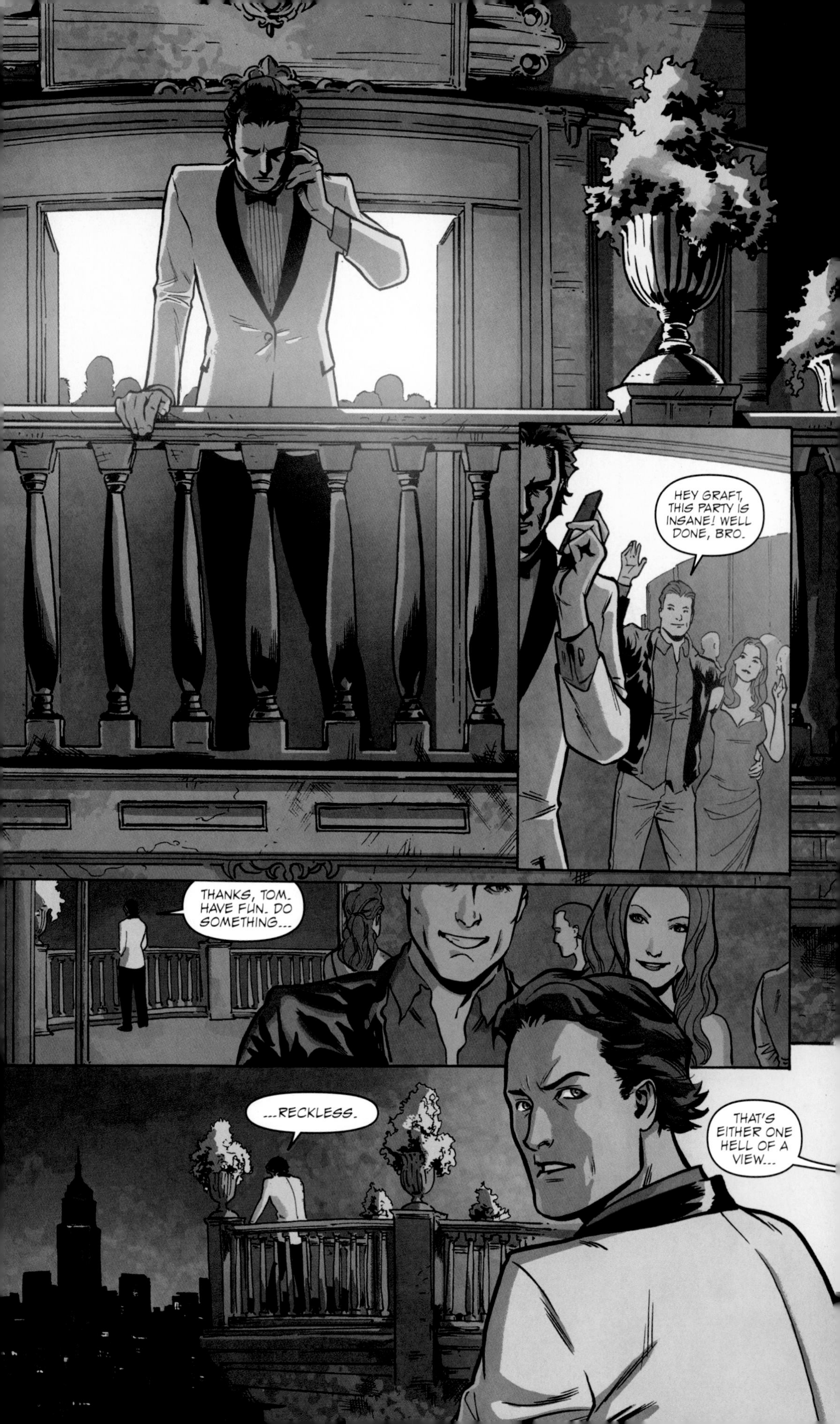
HEY GRAFT, THIS PARTY IS INSANE! WELL DONE, BRO.
THANKS, TOM. HAVE FUN. DO SOMETHING...
...RECKLESS.
THAT'S EITHER ONE HELL OF A VIEW...

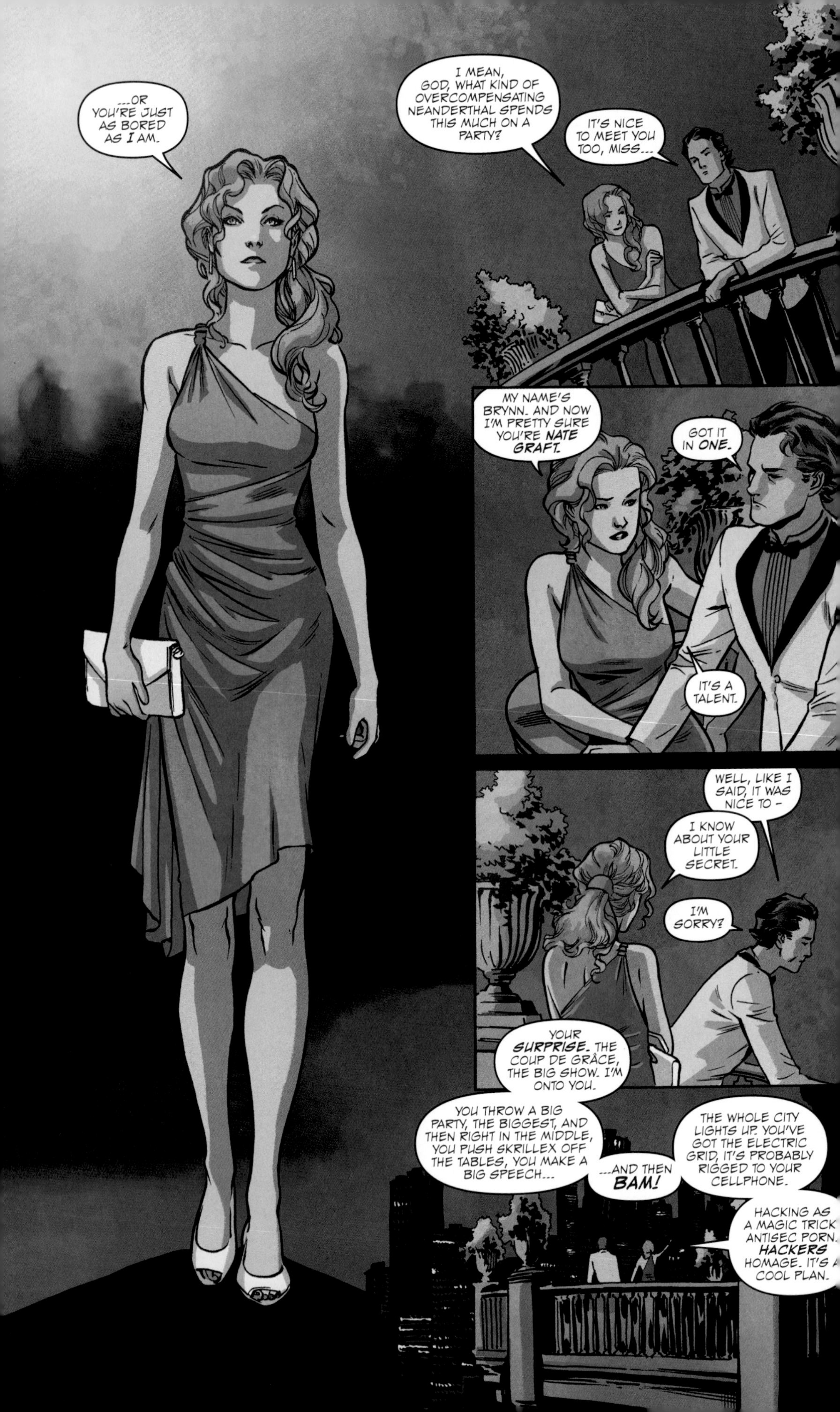
...OR YOU'RE JUST AS BORED AS I AM.
I MEAN, GOD, WHAT KIND OF OVERCOMPENSATING NEANDERTHAL SPENDS THIS MUCH ON A PARTY?
IT'S NICE TO MEET YOU TOO, MISS...
MY NAME'S BRYNN. AND NOW I'M PRETTY SURE YOU'RE NATE GRAFT.
GOT IT IN ONE.
IT'S A TALENT.
WELL, LIKE I SAID, IT WAS NICE TO -
I KNOW ABOUT YOUR LITTLE SECRET.
I'M SORRY?
YOUR SURPRISE. THE COUP DE GRÂCE, THE BIG SHOW. I'M ONTO YOU.
YOU THROW A BIG PARTY, THE BIGGEST, AND THEN RIGHT IN THE MIDDLE, YOU PUSH SKRILLEX OFF THE TABLES, YOU MAKE A BIG SPEECH...
...AND THEN BAM!
THE WHOLE CITY LIGHTS UP. YOU'VE GOT THE ELECTRIC GRID, IT'S PROBABLY RIGGED TO YOUR CELLPHONE.
HACKING AS A MAGIC TRICK. ANTISEC PORN. HACKERS HOMAGE. IT'S A COOL PLAN.

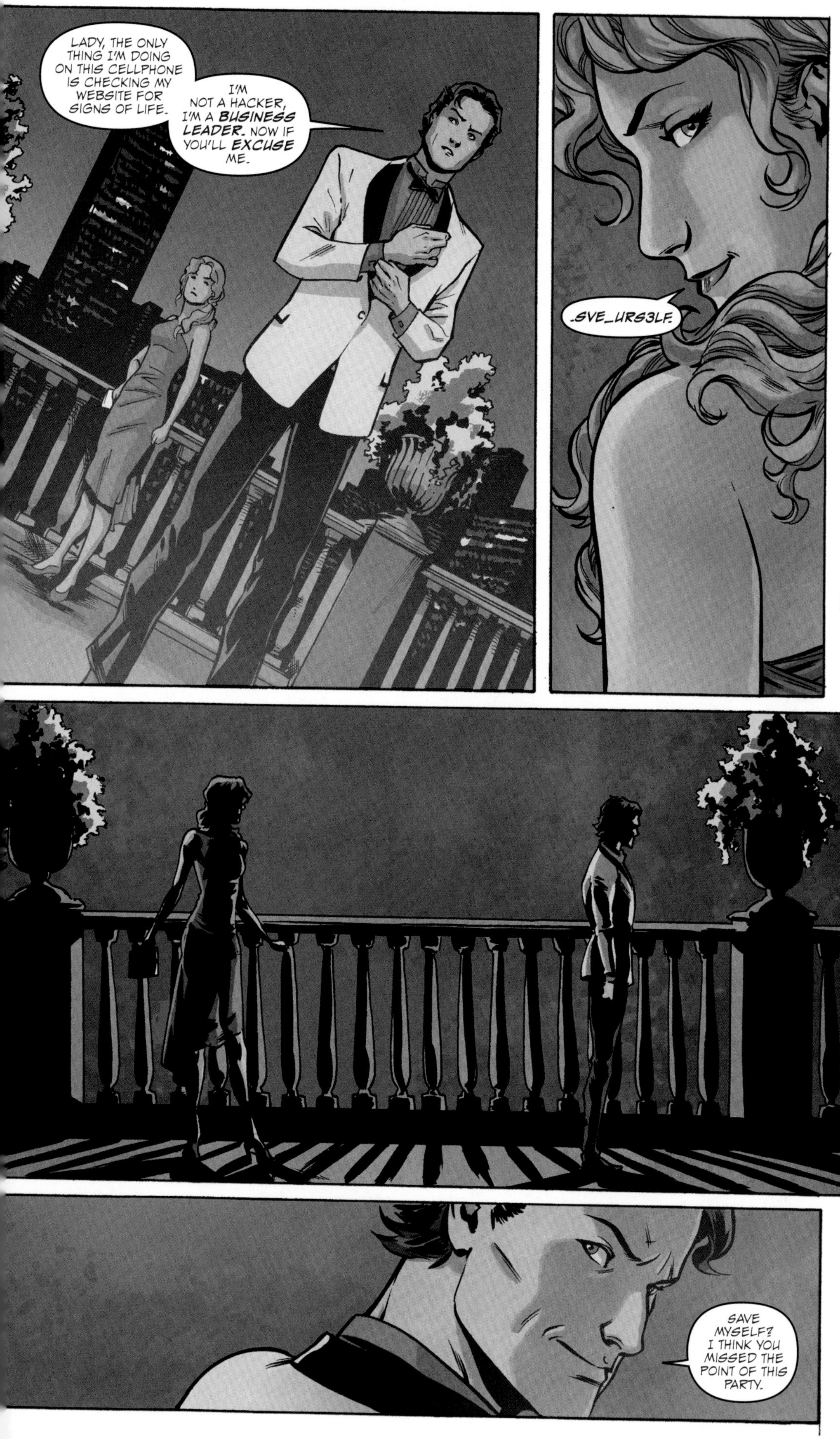
LADY, THE ONLY THING I'M DOING ON THIS CELLPHONE IS CHECKING MY WEBSITE FOR SIGNS OF LIFE.
I'M NOT A HACKER, I'M A **BUSINESS LEADER**. NOW IF YOU'LL **EXCUSE** ME.
.SVE_URS3LF.
SAVE MYSELF? I THINK YOU MISSED THE POINT OF THIS PARTY.

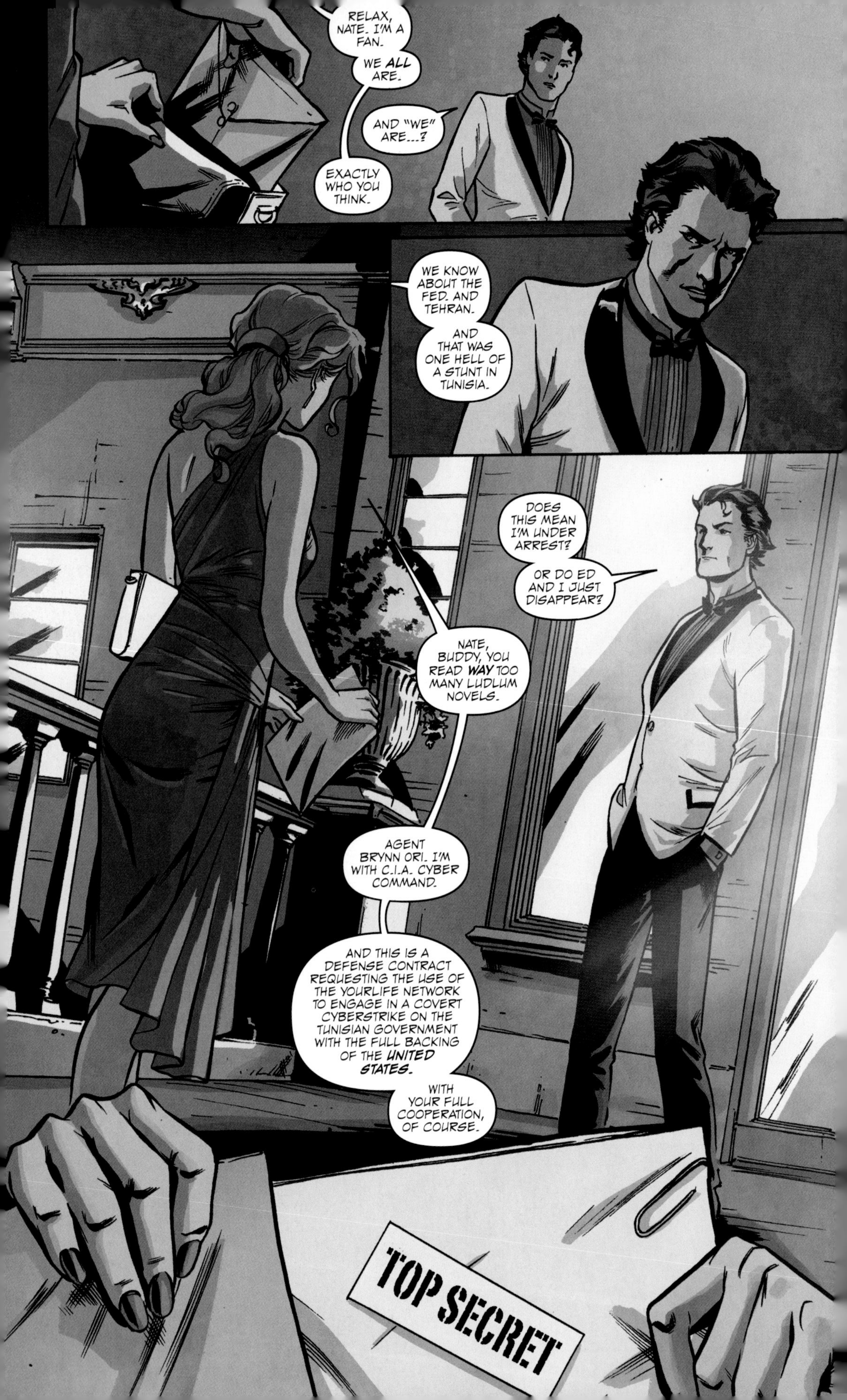
RELAX, NATE. I'M A FAN.
WE ALL ARE.
AND "WE" ARE...?
EXACTLY WHO YOU THINK.
WE KNOW ABOUT THE FED. AND TEHRAN.
AND THAT WAS ONE HELL OF A STUNT IN TUNISIA.
DOES THIS MEAN I'M UNDER ARREST?
OR DO ED AND I JUST DISAPPEAR?
NATE, BUDDY, YOU READ WAY TOO MANY LUDLUM NOVELS.
AGENT BRYNN ORI. I'M WITH C.I.A. CYBER COMMAND.
AND THIS IS A DEFENSE CONTRACT REQUESTING THE USE OF THE YOURLIFE NETWORK TO ENGAGE IN A COVERT CYBERSTRIKE ON THE TUNISIAN GOVERNMENT WITH THE FULL BACKING OF THE UNITED STATES.
WITH YOUR FULL COOPERATION, OF COURSE.
TOP SECRET

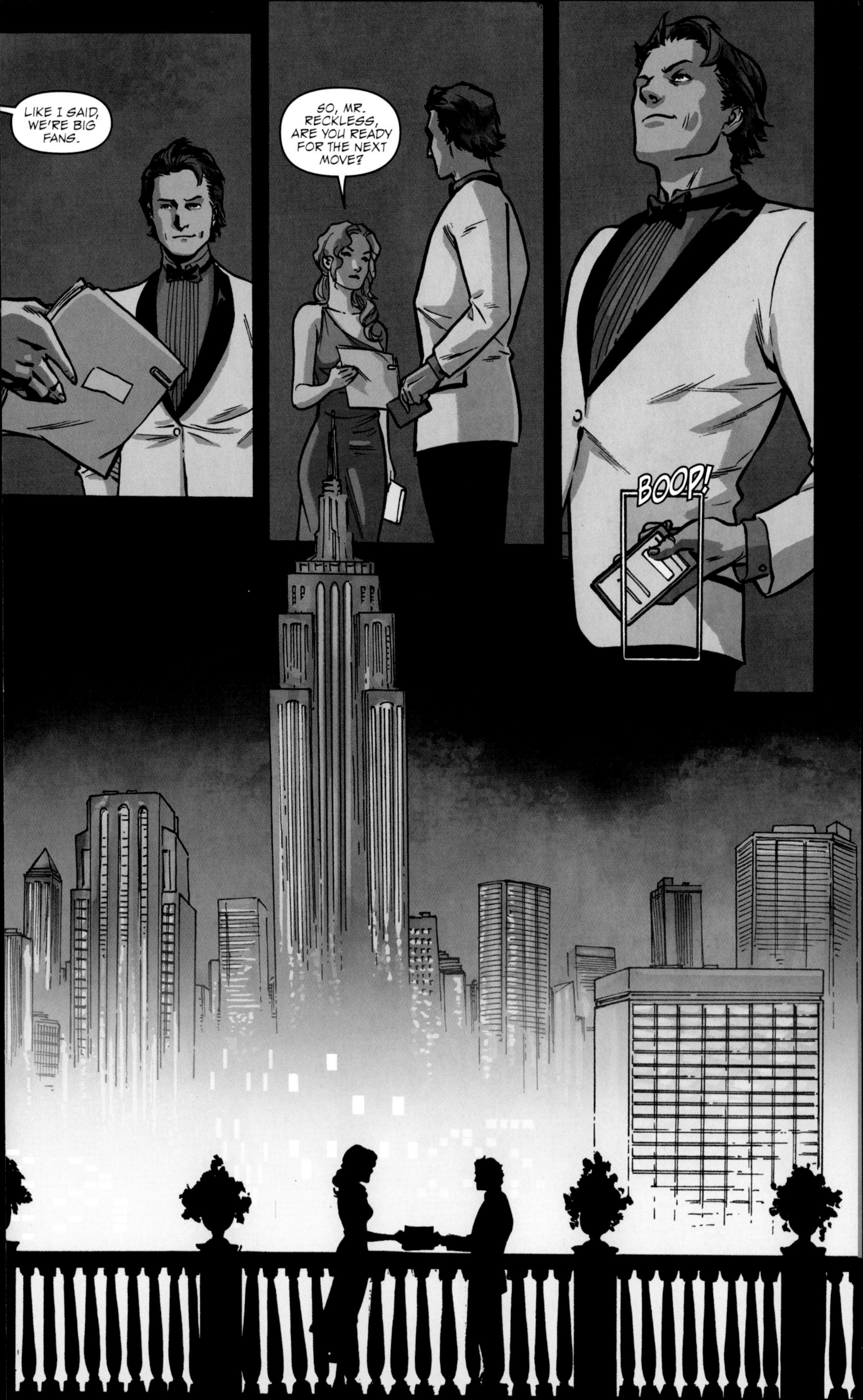
LIKE I SAID, WE'RE BIG FANS.
SO, MR. RECKLESS, ARE YOU READY FOR THE NEXT MOVE?
BOOP!

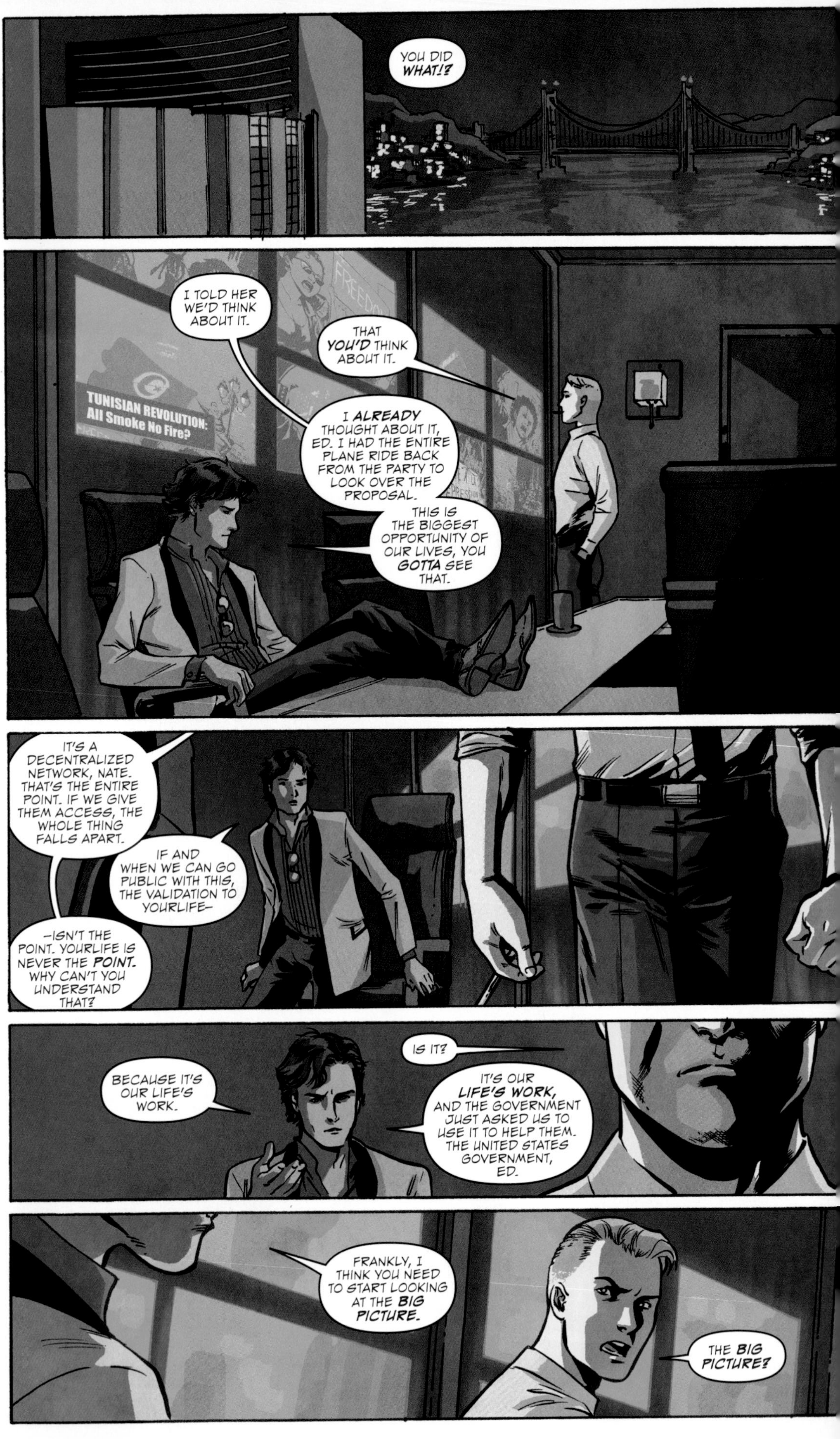
YOU DID WHAT!?
I TOLD HER WE'D THINK ABOUT IT.
THAT YOU'D THINK ABOUT IT.
I ALREADY THOUGHT ABOUT IT, ED. I HAD THE ENTIRE PLANE RIDE BACK FROM THE PARTY TO LOOK OVER THE PROPOSAL.
THIS IS THE BIGGEST OPPORTUNITY OF OUR LIVES, YOU GOTTA SEE THAT.
TUNISIAN REVOLUTION: All Smoke No Fire?
IT'S A DECENTRALIZED NETWORK, NATE. THAT'S THE ENTIRE POINT. IF WE GIVE THEM ACCESS, THE WHOLE THING FALLS APART.
IF AND WHEN WE CAN GO PUBLIC WITH THIS, THE VALIDATION TO YOURLIFE–
–ISN'T THE POINT. YOURLIFE IS NEVER THE POINT. WHY CAN'T YOU UNDERSTAND THAT?
BECAUSE IT'S OUR LIFE'S WORK.
IS IT?
IT'S OUR LIFE'S WORK, AND THE GOVERNMENT JUST ASKED US TO USE IT TO HELP THEM. THE UNITED STATES GOVERNMENT, ED.
FRANKLY, I THINK YOU NEED TO START LOOKING AT THE BIG PICTURE.
THE BIG PICTURE?

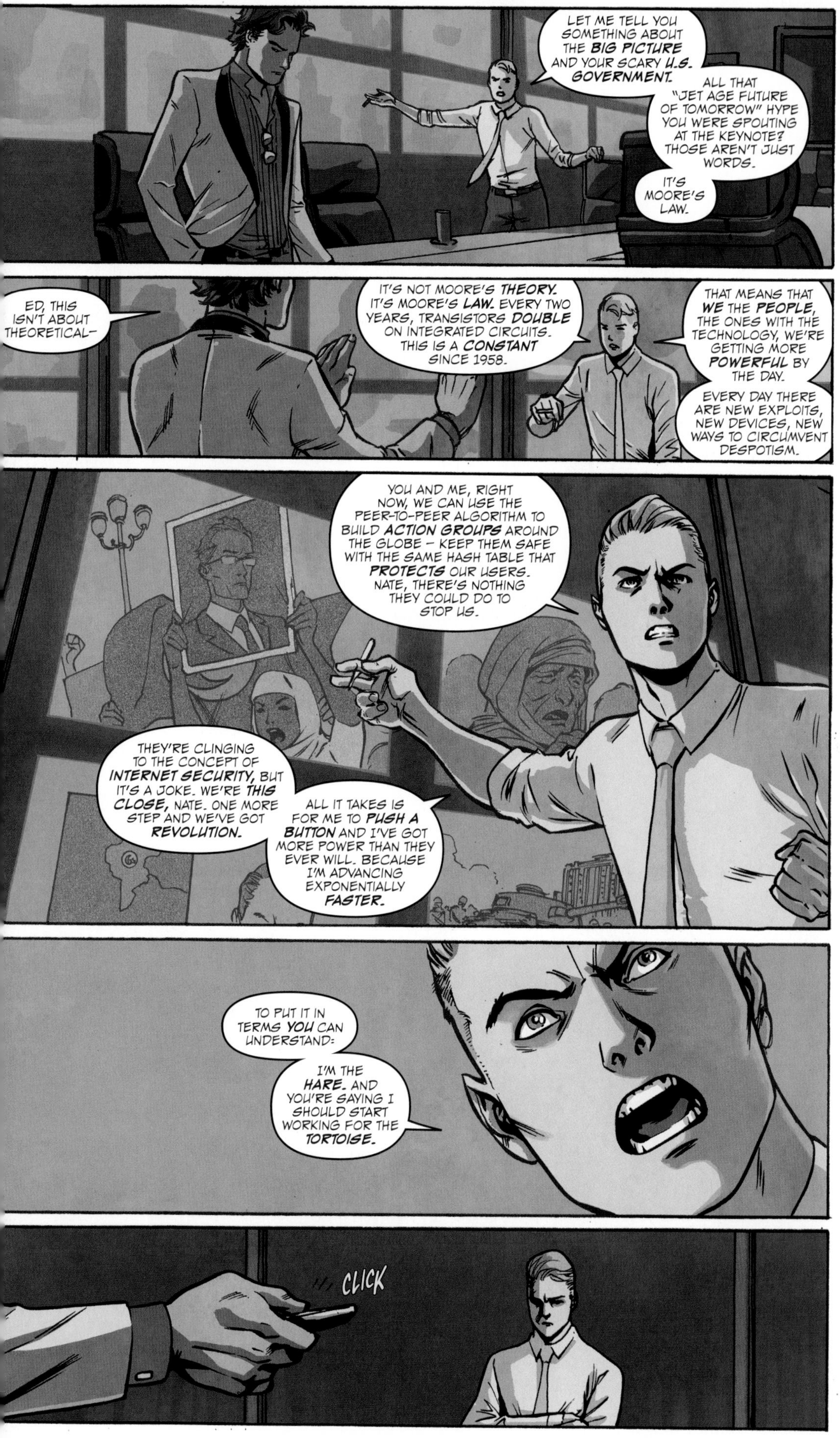

LET ME TELL YOU SOMETHING ABOUT THE BIG PICTURE AND YOUR SCARY U.S. GOVERNMENT.
ALL THAT "JET AGE FUTURE OF TOMORROW" HYPE YOU WERE SPOUTING AT THE KEYNOTE? THOSE AREN'T JUST WORDS.
IT'S MOORE'S LAW.
ED, THIS ISN'T ABOUT THEORETICAL—
IT'S NOT MOORE'S THEORY. IT'S MOORE'S LAW. EVERY TWO YEARS, TRANSISTORS DOUBLE ON INTEGRATED CIRCUITS. THIS IS A CONSTANT SINCE 1958.
THAT MEANS THAT WE THE PEOPLE, THE ONES WITH THE TECHNOLOGY, WE'RE GETTING MORE POWERFUL BY THE DAY.
EVERY DAY THERE ARE NEW EXPLOITS, NEW DEVICES, NEW WAYS TO CIRCUMVENT DESPOTISM.
YOU AND ME, RIGHT NOW, WE CAN USE THE PEER-TO-PEER ALGORITHM TO BUILD ACTION GROUPS AROUND THE GLOBE — KEEP THEM SAFE WITH THE SAME HASH TABLE THAT PROTECTS OUR USERS. NATE, THERE'S NOTHING THEY COULD DO TO STOP US.
THEY'RE CLINGING TO THE CONCEPT OF INTERNET SECURITY, BUT IT'S A JOKE. WE'RE THIS CLOSE, NATE. ONE MORE STEP AND WE'VE GOT REVOLUTION.
ALL IT TAKES IS FOR ME TO PUSH A BUTTON AND I'VE GOT MORE POWER THAN THEY EVER WILL. BECAUSE I'M ADVANCING EXPONENTIALLY FASTER.
TO PUT IT IN TERMS YOU CAN UNDERSTAND:
I'M THE HARE. AND YOU'RE SAYING I SHOULD START WORKING FOR THE TORTOISE.
CLICK

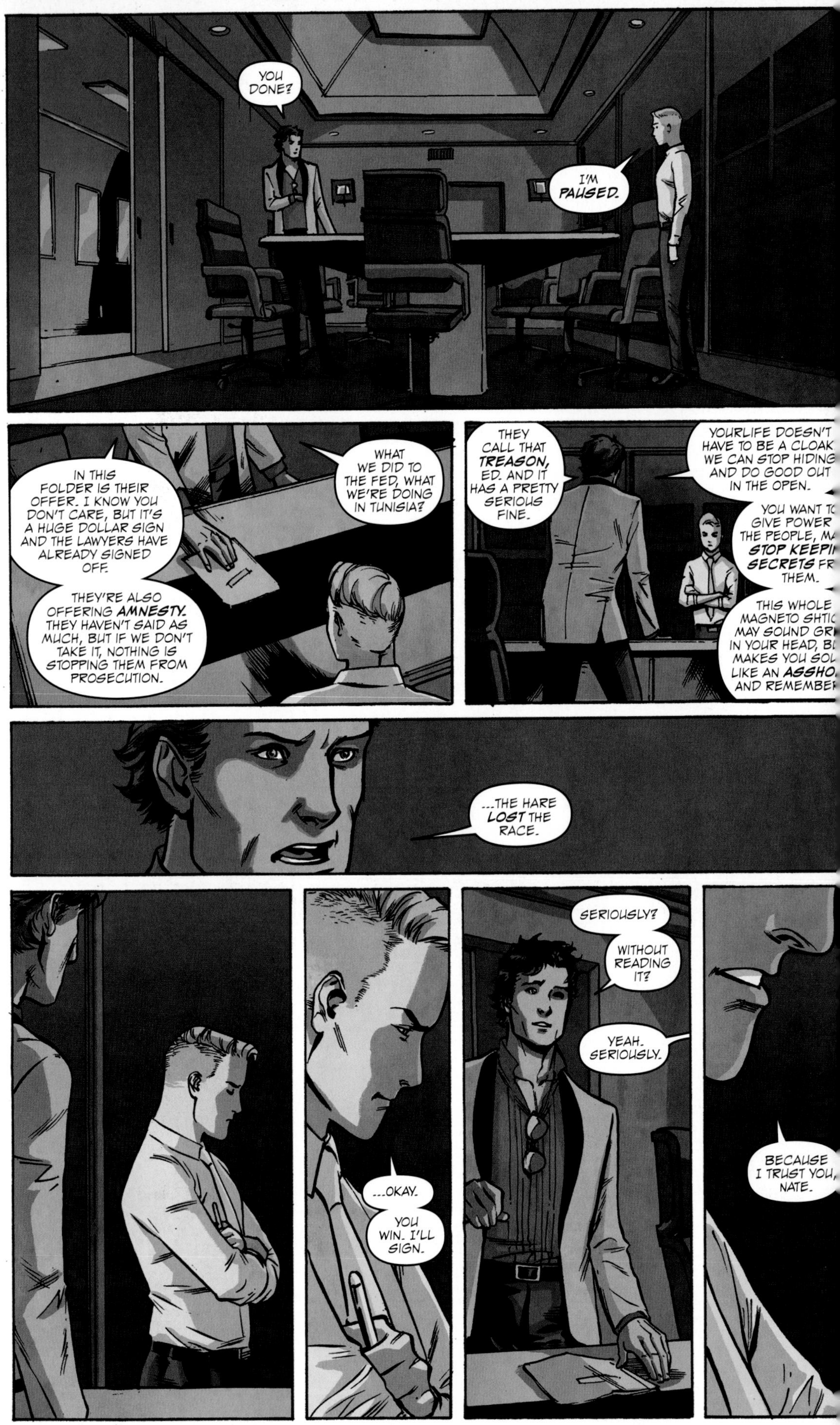

YOU DONE?
I'M PAUSED.
IN THIS FOLDER IS THEIR OFFER. I KNOW YOU DON'T CARE, BUT IT'S A HUGE DOLLAR SIGN AND THE LAWYERS HAVE ALREADY SIGNED OFF.
THEY'RE ALSO OFFERING AMNESTY. THEY HAVEN'T SAID AS MUCH, BUT IF WE DON'T TAKE IT, NOTHING IS STOPPING THEM FROM PROSECUTION.
WHAT WE DID TO THE FED, WHAT WE'RE DOING IN TUNISIA?
THEY CALL THAT TREASON, ED. AND IT HAS A PRETTY SERIOUS FINE.
YOURLIFE DOESN'T HAVE TO BE A CLOAK WE CAN STOP HIDING AND DO GOOD OUT IN THE OPEN.
YOU WANT T GIVE POWER THE PEOPLE, M STOP KEEP SECRETS F THEM.
THIS WHOLE MAGNETO SHTI MAY SOUND GR IN YOUR HEAD, B MAKES YOU SO LIKE AN ASSH AND REMEMBE
...THE HARE LOST THE RACE.
...OKAY.
YOU WIN. I'LL SIGN.
SERIOUSLY?
WITHOUT READING IT?
YEAH. SERIOUSLY.
BECAUSE I TRUST YOU, NATE.

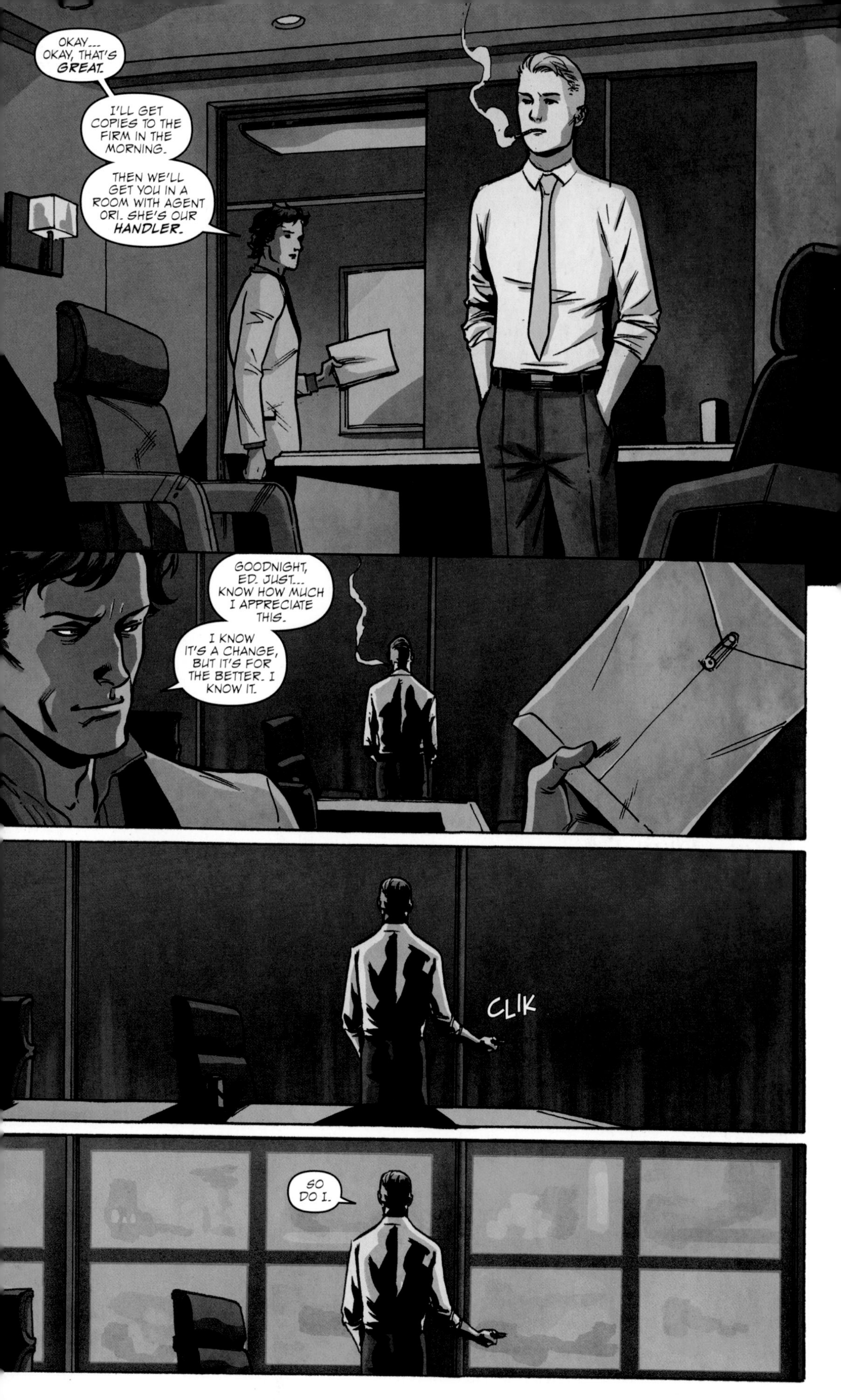
OKAY... OKAY, THAT'S GREAT.
I'LL GET COPIES TO THE FIRM IN THE MORNING.
THEN WE'LL GET YOU IN A ROOM WITH AGENT ORI. SHE'S OUR HANDLER.
GOODNIGHT, ED. JUST... KNOW HOW MUCH I APPRECIATE THIS.
I KNOW IT'S A CHANGE, BUT IT'S FOR THE BETTER. I KNOW IT.
CLIK
SO DO I.

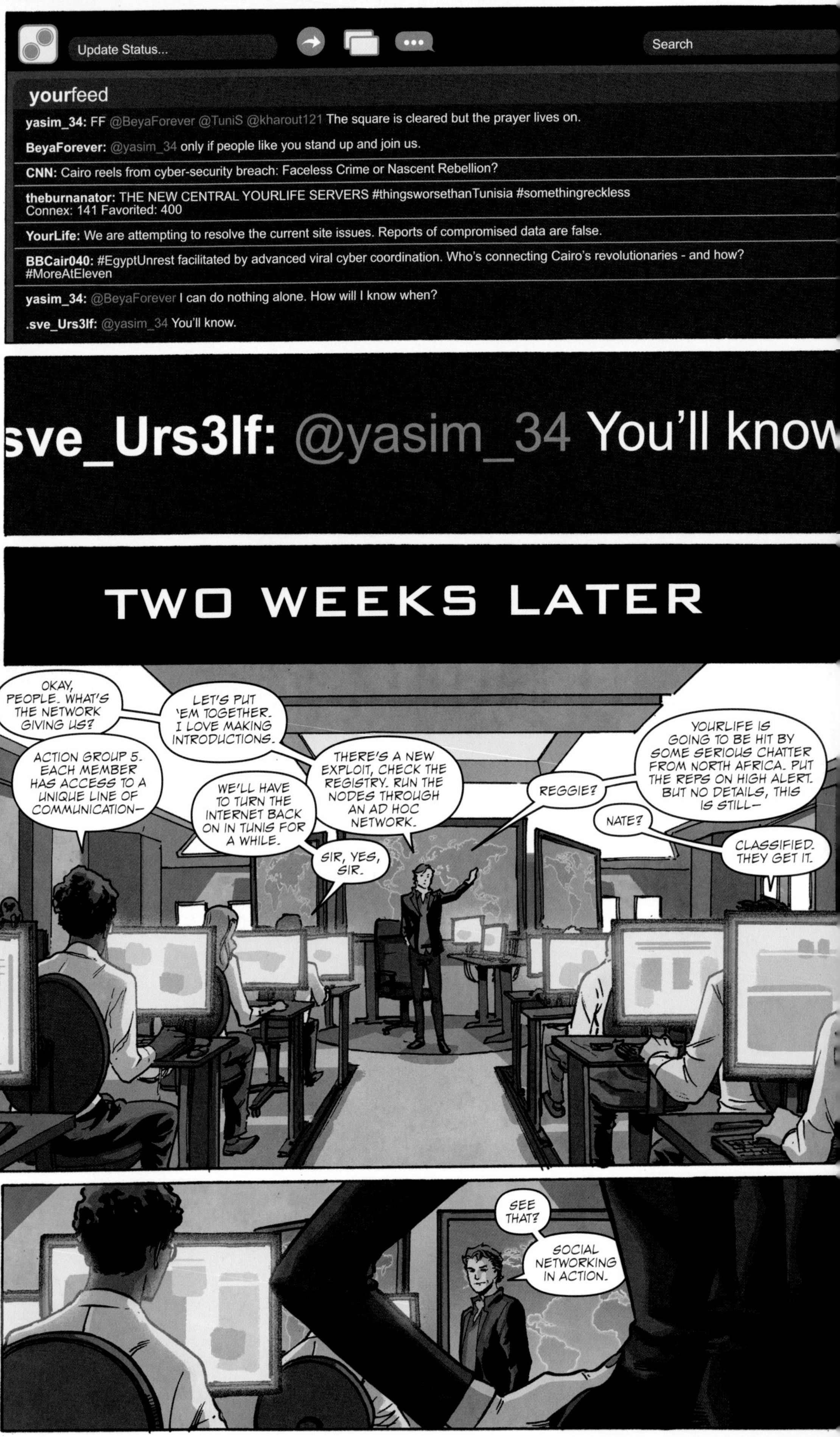
Update Status...
Search
yourfeed
yasim_34: FF @BeyaForever @TuniS @kharout121 The square is cleared but the prayer lives on.
BeyaForever: @yasim_34 only if people like you stand up and join us.
CNN: Cairo reels from cyber-security breach: Faceless Crime or Nascent Rebellion?
theburnanator: THE NEW CENTRAL YOURLIFE SERVERS #thingsworsethanTunisia #somethingreckless
Connex: 141 Favorited: 400
YourLife: We are attempting to resolve the current site issues. Reports of compromised data are false.
BBCair040: #EgyptUnrest facilitated by advanced viral cyber coordination. Who's connecting Cairo's revolutionaries - and how? #MoreAtEleven
yasim_34: @BeyaForever I can do nothing alone. How will I know when?
.sve_Urs3lf: @yasim_34 You'll know.
sve_Urs3lf: @yasim_34 You'll know
TWO WEEKS LATER
OKAY, PEOPLE. WHAT'S THE NETWORK GIVING US?
ACTION GROUP 5. EACH MEMBER HAS ACCESS TO A UNIQUE LINE OF COMMUNICATION—
LET'S PUT 'EM TOGETHER. I LOVE MAKING INTRODUCTIONS.
THERE'S A NEW EXPLOIT, CHECK THE REGISTRY. RUN THE NODES THROUGH AN AD HOC NETWORK.
WE'LL HAVE TO TURN THE INTERNET BACK ON IN TUNIS FOR A WHILE.
SIR, YES, SIR.
REGGIE?
YOURLIFE IS GOING TO BE HIT BY SOME SERIOUS CHATTER FROM NORTH AFRICA. PUT THE REPS ON HIGH ALERT. BUT NO DETAILS, THIS IS STILL—
NATE?
CLASSIFIED. THEY GET IT.
SEE THAT?
SOCIAL NETWORKING IN ACTION.

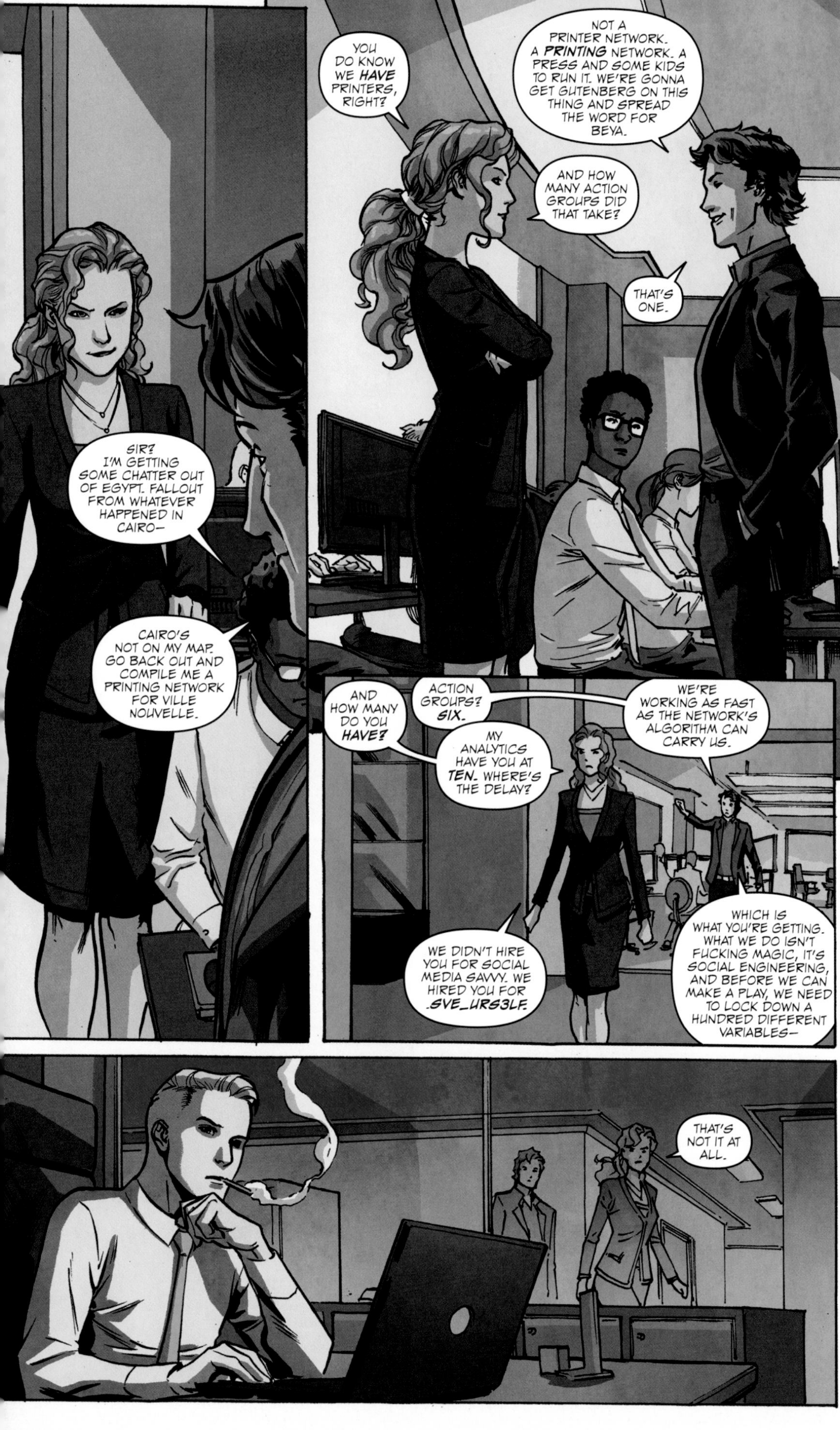

YOU DO KNOW WE HAVE PRINTERS, RIGHT?
NOT A PRINTER NETWORK. A PRINTING NETWORK. A PRESS AND SOME KIDS TO RUN IT. WE'RE GONNA GET GUTENBERG ON THIS THING AND SPREAD THE WORD FOR BEYA.
AND HOW MANY ACTION GROUPS DID THAT TAKE?
THAT'S ONE.
SIR? I'M GETTING SOME CHATTER OUT OF EGYPT. FALLOUT FROM WHATEVER HAPPENED IN CAIRO—
CAIRO'S NOT ON MY MAP. GO BACK OUT AND COMPILE ME A PRINTING NETWORK FOR VILLE NOUVELLE.
AND HOW MANY DO YOU HAVE?
ACTION GROUPS? SIX.
WE'RE WORKING AS FAST AS THE NETWORK'S ALGORITHM CAN CARRY US.
MY ANALYTICS HAVE YOU AT TEN. WHERE'S THE DELAY?
WE DIDN'T HIRE YOU FOR SOCIAL MEDIA SAVVY. WE HIRED YOU FOR .SVE_URS3LF.
WHICH IS WHAT YOU'RE GETTING. WHAT WE DO ISN'T FUCKING MAGIC, IT'S SOCIAL ENGINEERING, AND BEFORE WE CAN MAKE A PLAY, WE NEED TO LOCK DOWN A HUNDRED DIFFERENT VARIABLES—
THAT'S NOT IT AT ALL.

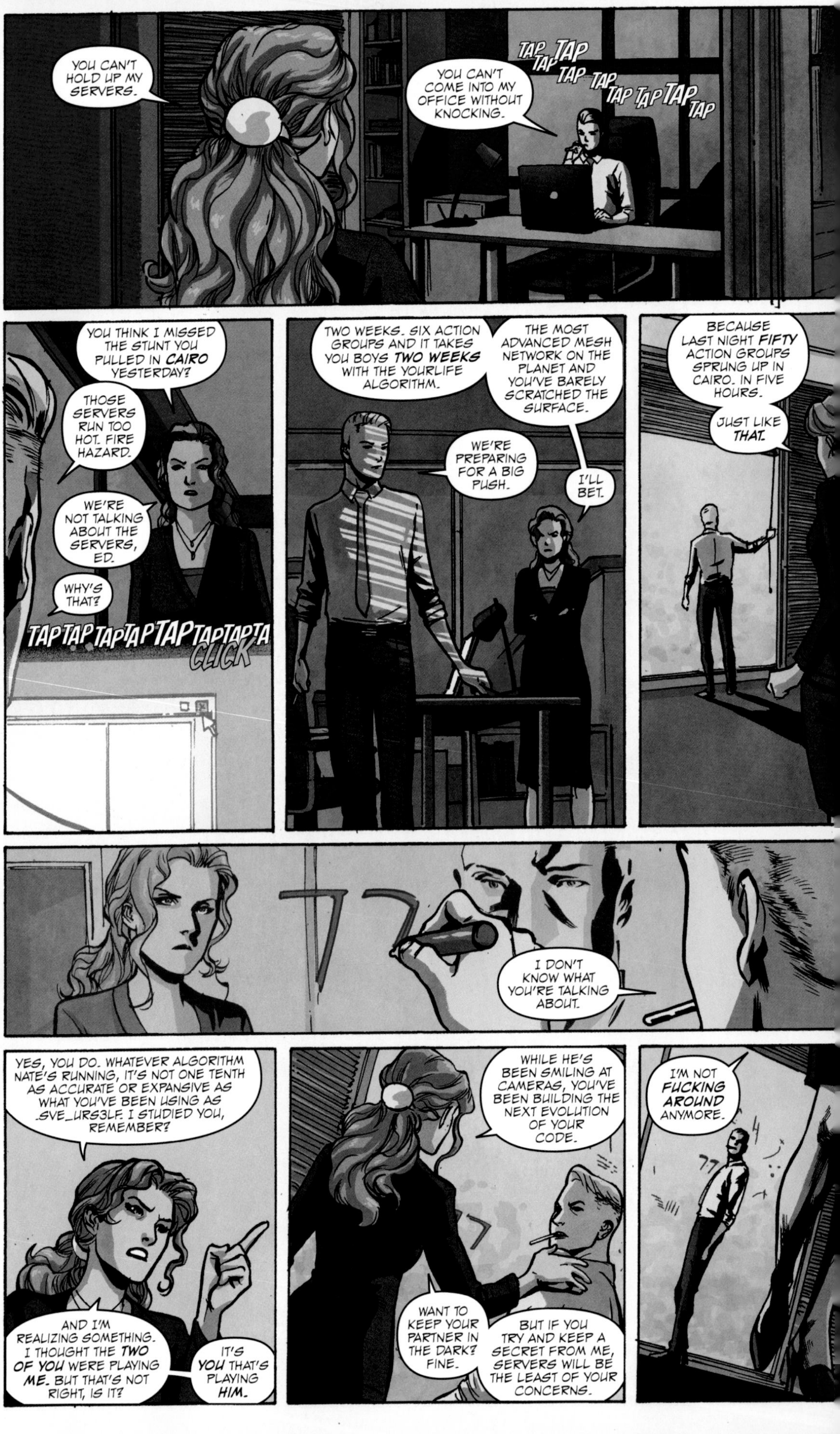
YOU CAN'T HOLD UP MY SERVERS.
YOU CAN'T COME INTO MY OFFICE WITHOUT KNOCKING.
TAP TAP TAP TAP TAP TAP TAP TAP TAP TAP
YOU THINK I MISSED THE STUNT YOU PULLED IN CAIRO YESTERDAY?
THOSE SERVERS RUN TOO HOT. FIRE HAZARD.
WE'RE NOT TALKING ABOUT THE SERVERS, ED.
WHY'S THAT?
TAPTAP TAPTAPTAPTAPTAPTA
CLICK
TWO WEEKS. SIX ACTION GROUPS AND IT TAKES YOU BOYS TWO WEEKS WITH THE YOURLIFE ALGORITHM.
THE MOST ADVANCED MESH NETWORK ON THE PLANET AND YOU'VE BARELY SCRATCHED THE SURFACE.
WE'RE PREPARING FOR A BIG PUSH.
I'LL BET.
BECAUSE LAST NIGHT FIFTY ACTION GROUPS SPRUNG UP IN CAIRO. IN FIVE HOURS.
JUST LIKE THAT.
I DON'T KNOW WHAT YOU'RE TALKING ABOUT.
YES, YOU DO. WHATEVER ALGORITHM NATE'S RUNNING, IT'S NOT ONE TENTH AS ACCURATE OR EXPANSIVE AS WHAT YOU'VE BEEN USING AS .SVE_URS3LF. I STUDIED YOU, REMEMBER?
AND I'M REALIZING SOMETHING. I THOUGHT THE TWO OF YOU WERE PLAYING ME. BUT THAT'S NOT RIGHT, IS IT?
IT'S YOU THAT'S PLAYING HIM.
WHILE HE'S BEEN SMILING AT CAMERAS, YOU'VE BEEN BUILDING THE NEXT EVOLUTION OF YOUR CODE.
WANT TO KEEP YOUR PARTNER IN THE DARK? FINE.
BUT IF YOU TRY AND KEEP A SECRET FROM ME, SERVERS WILL BE THE LEAST OF YOUR CONCERNS.
I'M NOT FUCKING AROUND ANYMORE.

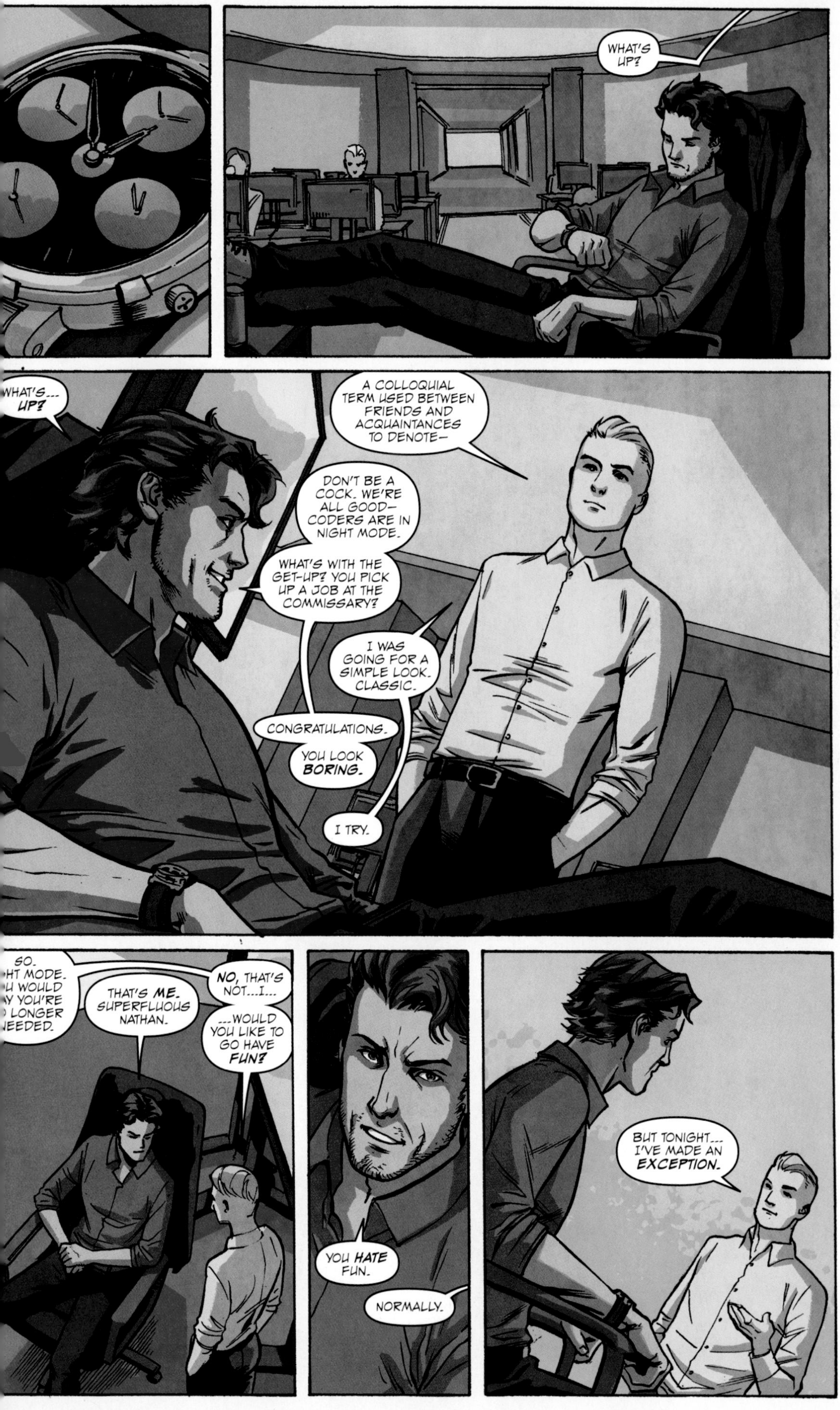
WHAT'S UP?
WHAT'S... UP?
A COLLOQUIAL TERM USED BETWEEN FRIENDS AND ACQUAINTANCES TO DENOTE—
DON'T BE A COCK. WE'RE ALL GOOD— CODERS ARE IN NIGHT MODE.
WHAT'S WITH THE GET-UP? YOU PICK UP A JOB AT THE COMMISSARY?
I WAS GOING FOR A SIMPLE LOOK. CLASSIC.
CONGRATULATIONS.
YOU LOOK BORING.
I TRY.
SO. HT MODE. U WOULD Y YOU'RE LONGER EEDED.
THAT'S ME. SUPERFLUOUS NATHAN.
NO, THAT'S NOT...I...
...WOULD YOU LIKE TO GO HAVE FUN?
YOU HATE FUN.
NORMALLY.
BUT TONIGHT... I'VE MADE AN EXCEPTION.

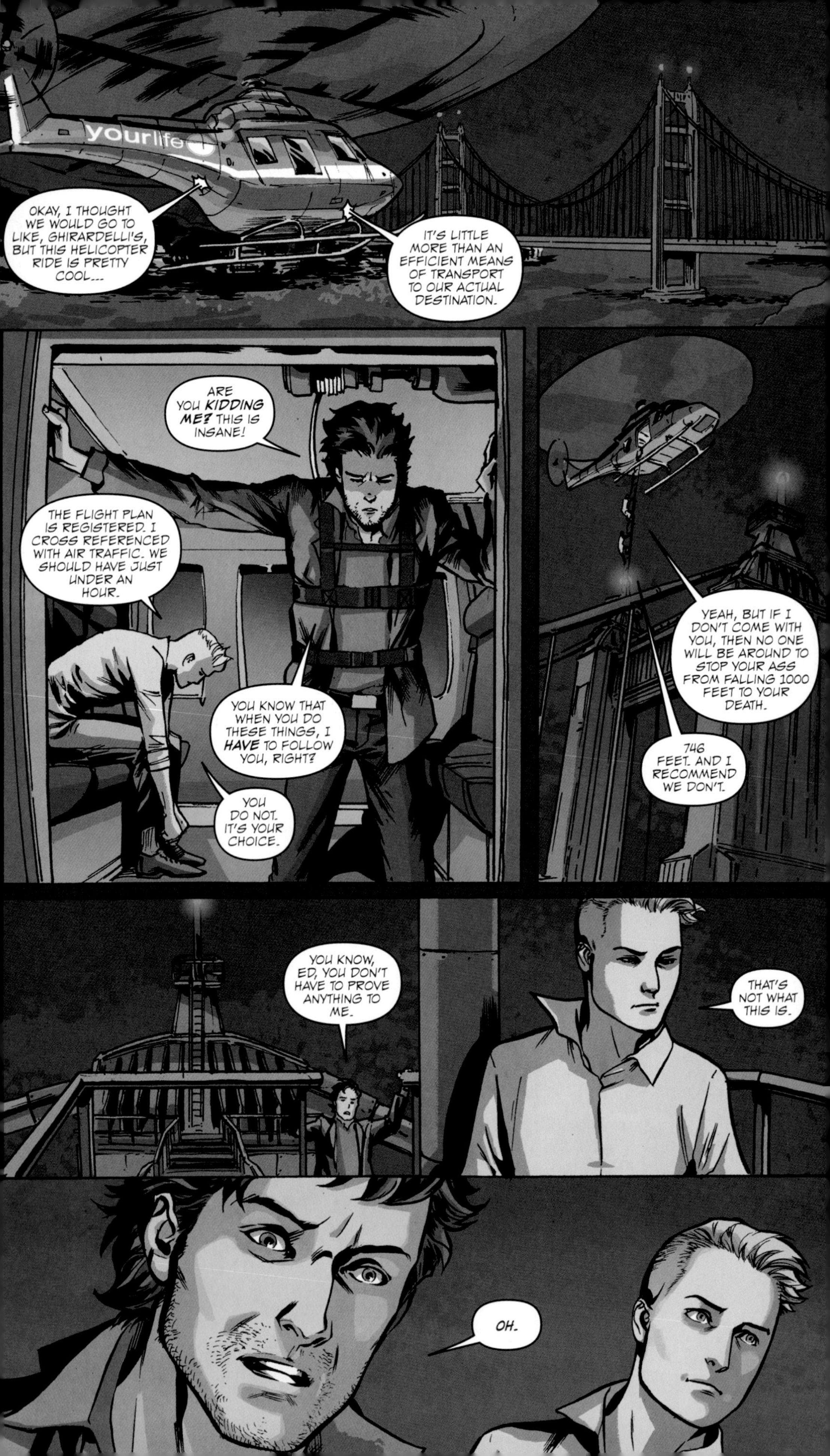
yourlife
OKAY, I THOUGHT WE WOULD GO TO LIKE, GHIRARDELLI'S, BUT THIS HELICOPTER RIDE IS PRETTY COOL...
IT'S LITTLE MORE THAN AN EFFICIENT MEANS OF TRANSPORT TO OUR ACTUAL DESTINATION.
ARE YOU KIDDING ME? THIS IS INSANE!
THE FLIGHT PLAN IS REGISTERED. I CROSS REFERENCED WITH AIR TRAFFIC. WE SHOULD HAVE JUST UNDER AN HOUR.
YOU KNOW THAT WHEN YOU DO THESE THINGS, I HAVE TO FOLLOW YOU, RIGHT?
YOU DO NOT. IT'S YOUR CHOICE.
YEAH, BUT IF I DON'T COME WITH YOU, THEN NO ONE WILL BE AROUND TO STOP YOUR ASS FROM FALLING 1000 FEET TO YOUR DEATH.
746 FEET. AND I RECOMMEND WE DON'T.
YOU KNOW, ED, YOU DON'T HAVE TO PROVE ANYTHING TO ME.
THAT'S NOT WHAT THIS IS.
OH.

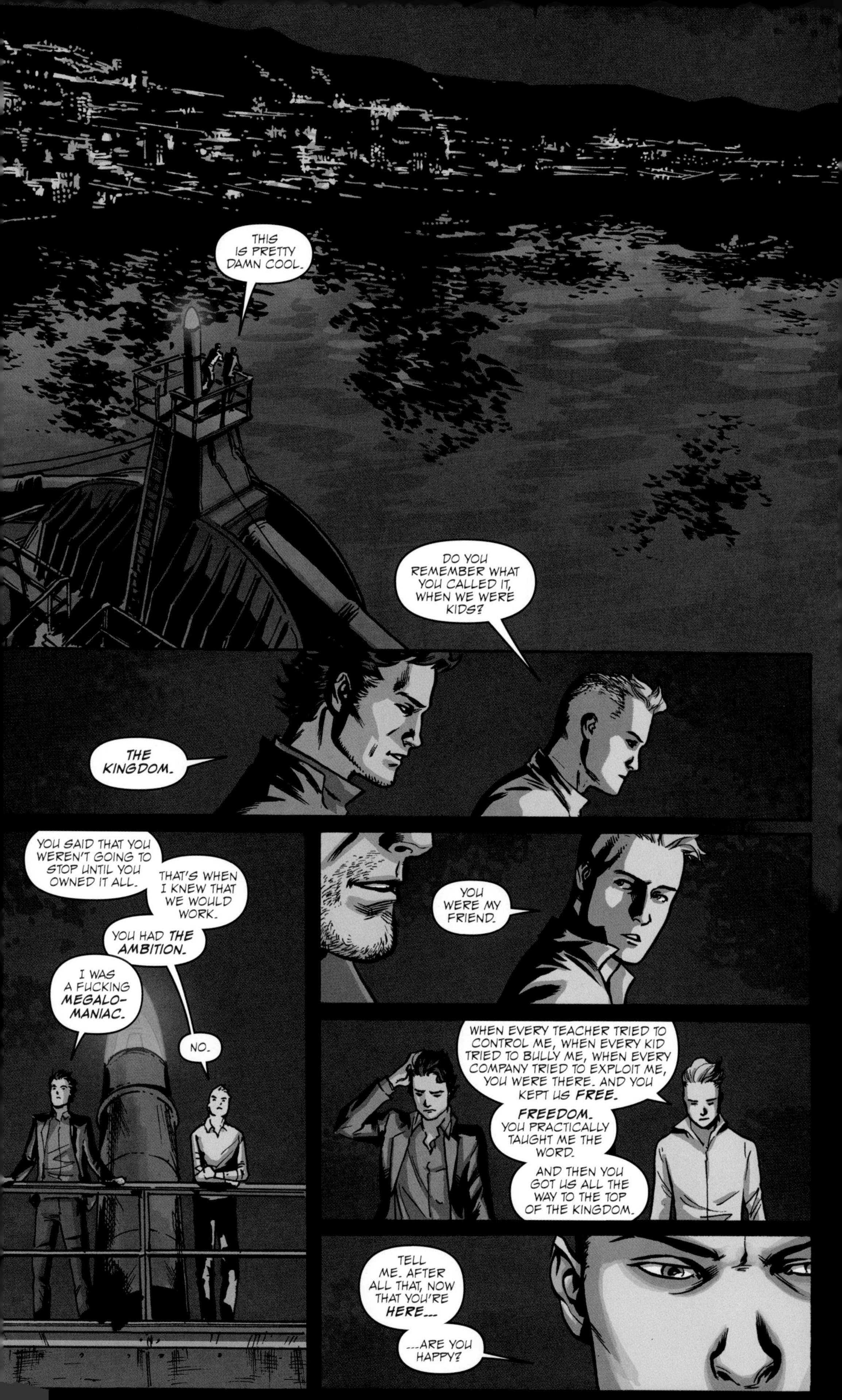
THIS IS PRETTY DAMN COOL.
DO YOU REMEMBER WHAT YOU CALLED IT, WHEN WE WERE KIDS?
THE KINGDOM.
YOU SAID THAT YOU WEREN'T GOING TO STOP UNTIL YOU OWNED IT ALL.
THAT'S WHEN I KNEW THAT WE WOULD WORK.
YOU HAD THE AMBITION.
I WAS A FUCKING MEGALO-MANIAC.
NO.
YOU WERE MY FRIEND.
WHEN EVERY TEACHER TRIED TO CONTROL ME, WHEN EVERY KID TRIED TO BULLY ME, WHEN EVERY COMPANY TRIED TO EXPLOIT ME, YOU WERE THERE. AND YOU KEPT US FREE.
FREEDOM. YOU PRACTICALLY TAUGHT ME THE WORD.
AND THEN YOU GOT US ALL THE WAY TO THE TOP OF THE KINGDOM.
TELL ME. AFTER ALL THAT, NOW THAT YOU'RE HERE...
...ARE YOU HAPPY?

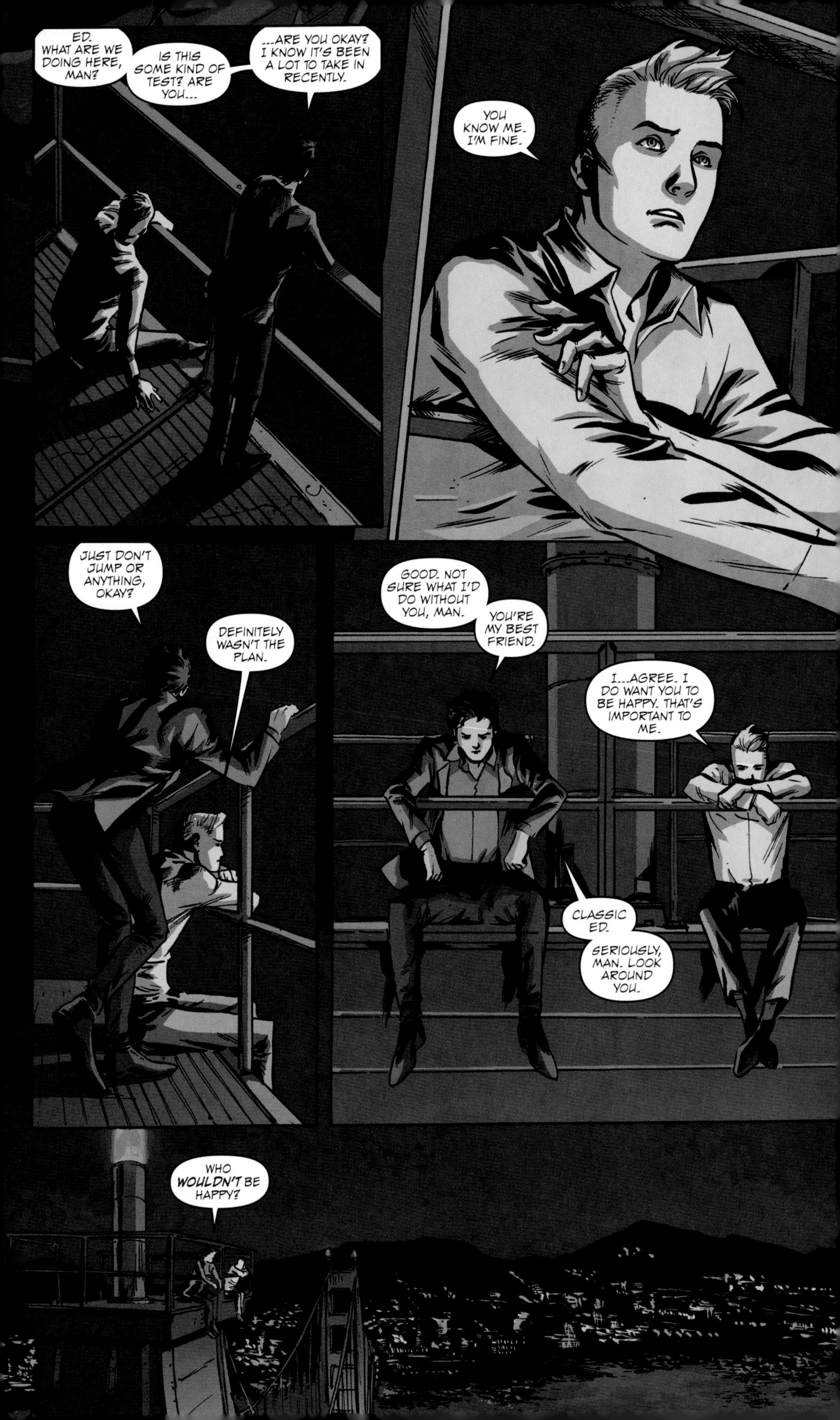

ED. WHAT ARE WE DOING HERE, MAN?
IS THIS SOME KIND OF TEST? ARE YOU...
...ARE YOU OKAY? I KNOW IT'S BEEN A LOT TO TAKE IN RECENTLY.
YOU KNOW ME. I'M FINE.
JUST DON'T JUMP OR ANYTHING, OKAY?
DEFINITELY WASN'T THE PLAN.
GOOD. NOT SURE WHAT I'D DO WITHOUT YOU, MAN.
YOU'RE MY BEST FRIEND.
CLASSIC ED.
I...AGREE. I DO WANT YOU TO BE HAPPY. THAT'S IMPORTANT TO ME.
SERIOUSLY, MAN. LOOK AROUND YOU.
WHO WOULDN'T BE HAPPY?

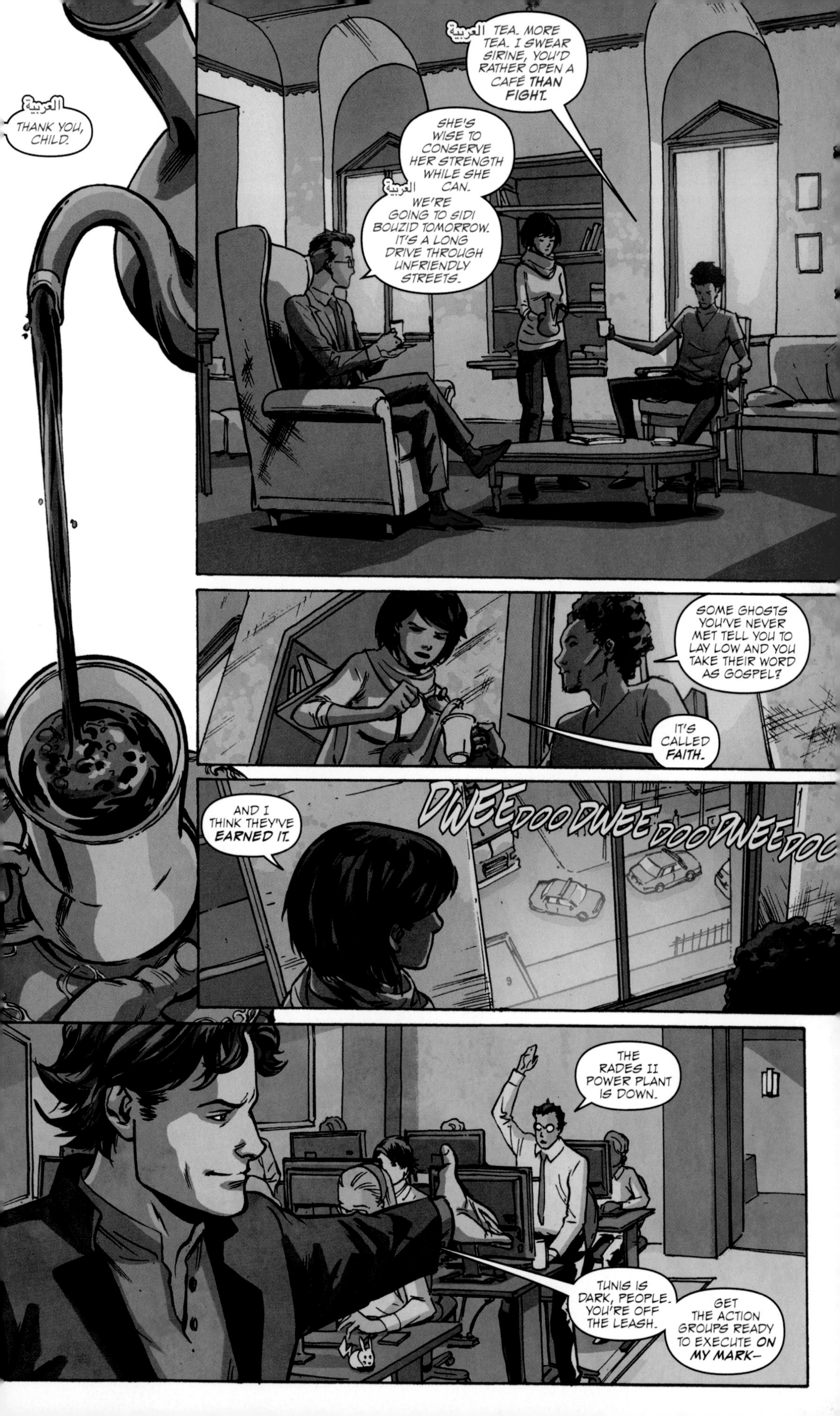
العربية
THANK YOU, CHILD.
العربية
TEA. MORE TEA. I SWEAR SIRINE, YOU'D RATHER OPEN A CAFÉ THAN FIGHT.
SHE'S WISE TO CONSERVE HER STRENGTH WHILE SHE CAN.
العربية
WE'RE GOING TO SIDI BOUZID TOMORROW. IT'S A LONG DRIVE THROUGH UNFRIENDLY STREETS.
SOME GHOSTS YOU'VE NEVER MET TELL YOU TO LAY LOW AND YOU TAKE THEIR WORD AS GOSPEL?
IT'S CALLED FAITH.
AND I THINK THEY'VE EARNED IT.
DWEEDOODWEEDOODWEEDOO
THE RADES II POWER PLANT IS DOWN.
TUNIS IS DARK, PEOPLE. YOU'RE OFF THE LEASH.
GET THE ACTION GROUPS READY TO EXECUTE ON MY MARK—

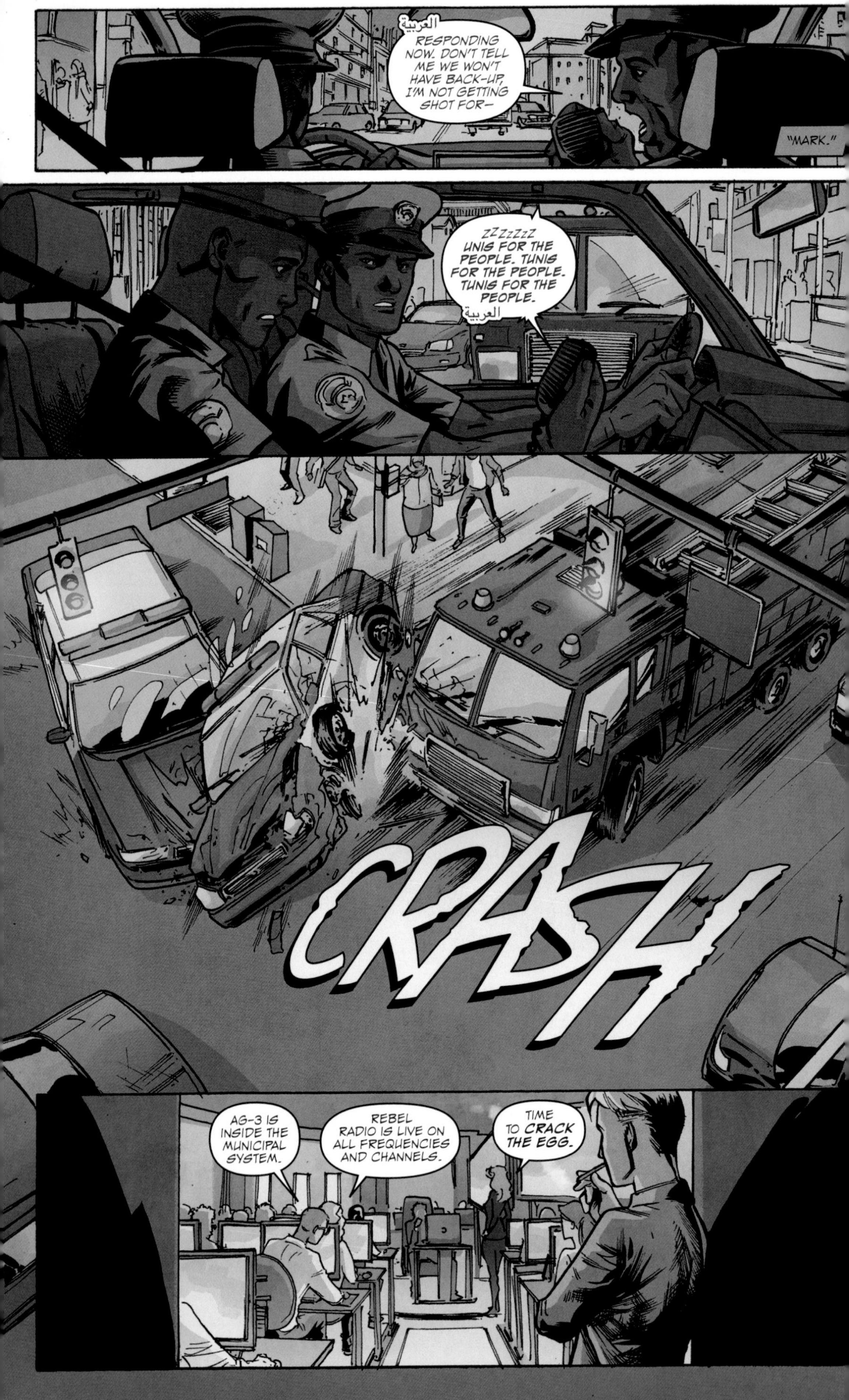

العربية
RESPONDING NOW. DON'T TELL ME WE WON'T HAVE BACK-UP, I'M NOT GETTING SHOT FOR–
"MARK."
ZZZzZzZ UNIS FOR THE PEOPLE. TUNIS FOR THE PEOPLE. TUNIS FOR THE PEOPLE.
العربية
CRASH
AG-3 IS INSIDE THE MUNICIPAL SYSTEM.
REBEL RADIO IS LIVE ON ALL FREQUENCIES AND CHANNELS.
TIME TO CRACK THE EGG.

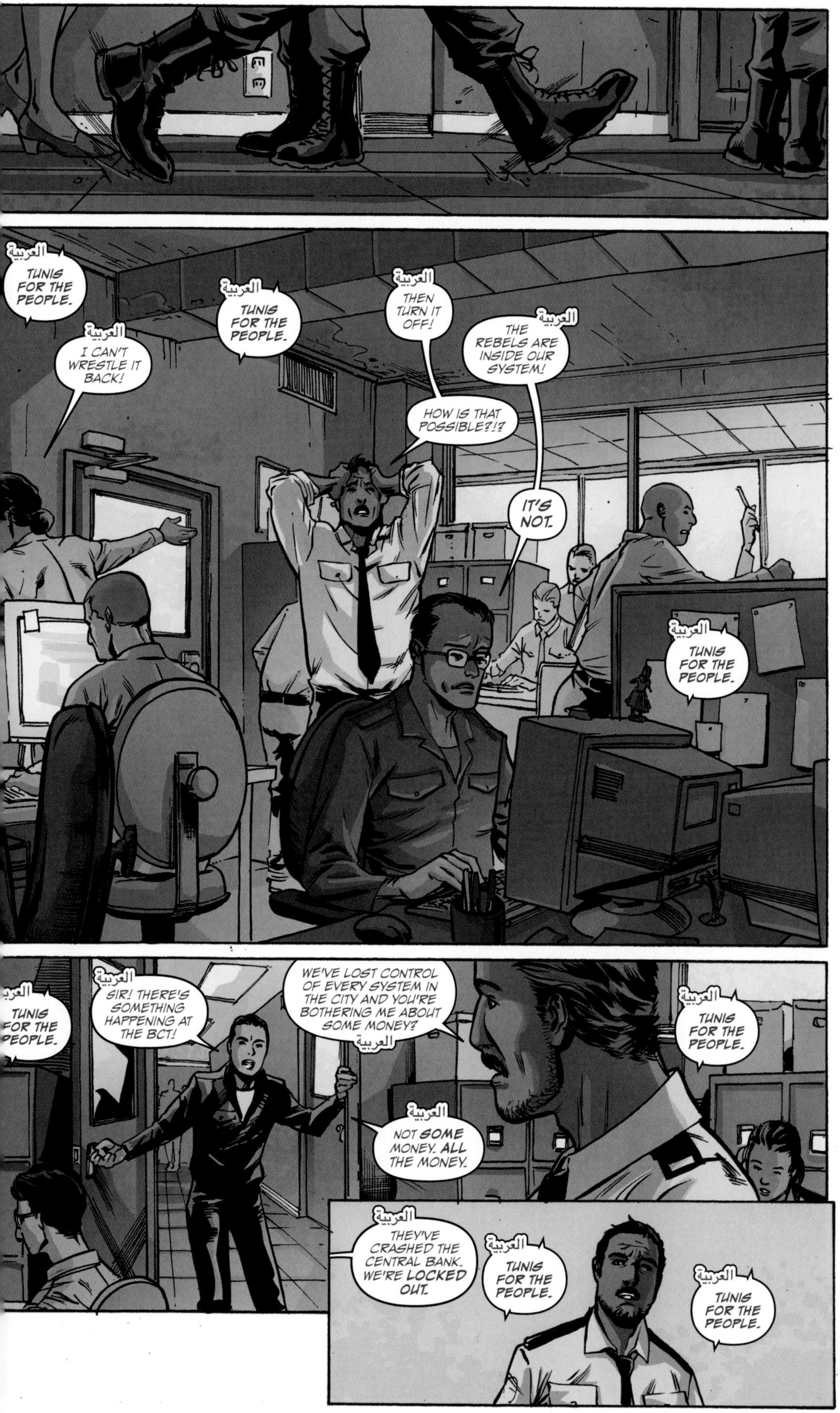
العربية TUNIS FOR THE PEOPLE.
العربية I CAN'T WRESTLE IT BACK!
العربية TUNIS FOR THE PEOPLE.
العربية THEN TURN IT OFF!
HOW IS THAT POSSIBLE?!?
العربية THE REBELS ARE INSIDE OUR SYSTEM!
IT'S NOT.
العربية TUNIS FOR THE PEOPLE.
العربية TUNIS FOR THE PEOPLE.
العربية SIR! THERE'S SOMETHING HAPPENING AT THE BCT!
WE'VE LOST CONTROL OF EVERY SYSTEM IN THE CITY AND YOU'RE BOTHERING ME ABOUT SOME MONEY? العربية
العربية TUNIS FOR THE PEOPLE.
العربية NOT SOME MONEY. ALL THE MONEY.
العربية THEY'VE CRASHED THE CENTRAL BANK. WE'RE LOCKED OUT.
العربية TUNIS FOR THE PEOPLE.
العربية TUNIS FOR THE PEOPLE.

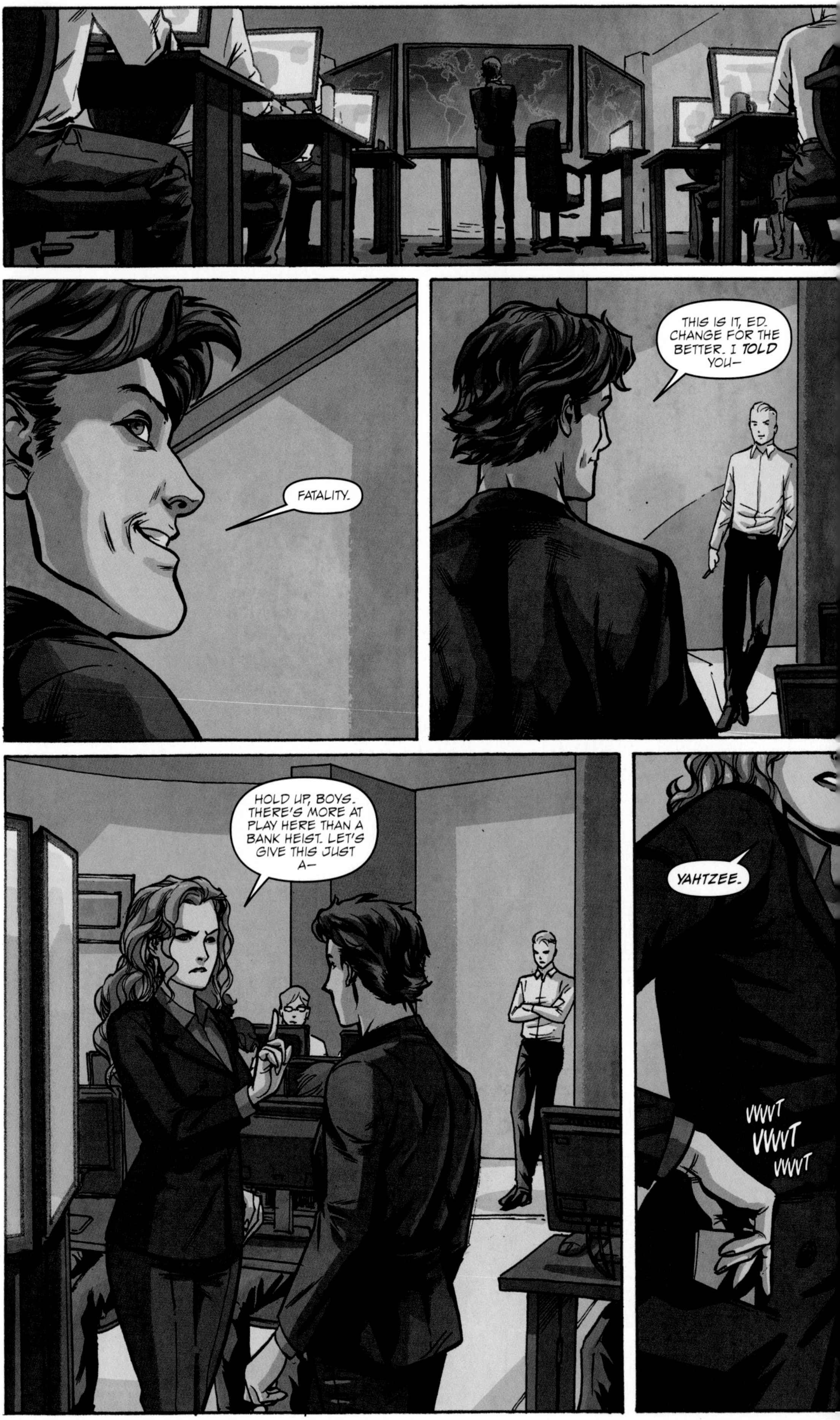
FATALITY.
THIS IS IT, ED. CHANGE FOR THE BETTER. I TOLD YOU—
HOLD UP, BOYS. THERE'S MORE AT PLAY HERE THAN A BANK HEIST. LET'S GIVE THIS JUST A—
YAHTZEE.
VVVVT
VVVVT
VVVVT

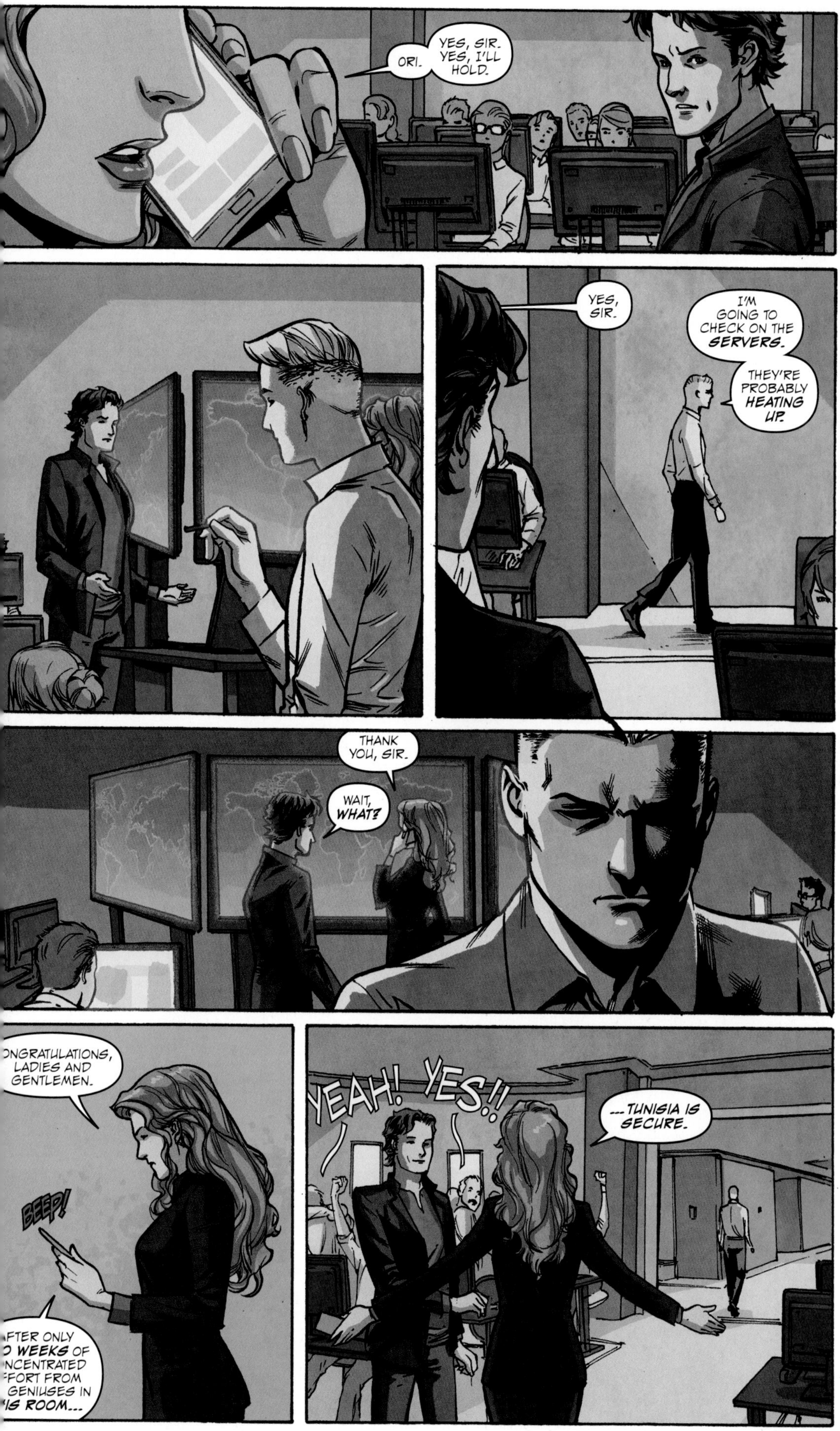
ORI.
YES, SIR. YES, I'LL HOLD.
YES, SIR.
I'M GOING TO CHECK ON THE SERVERS.
THEY'RE PROBABLY HEATING UP.
THANK YOU, SIR.
WAIT, WHAT?
ONGRATULATIONS, LADIES AND GENTLEMEN.
BEEP!
AFTER ONLY O WEEKS OF NCENTRATED FFORT FROM GENIUSES IN IS ROOM...
YEAH!
YES!!
...TUNISIA IS SECURE.

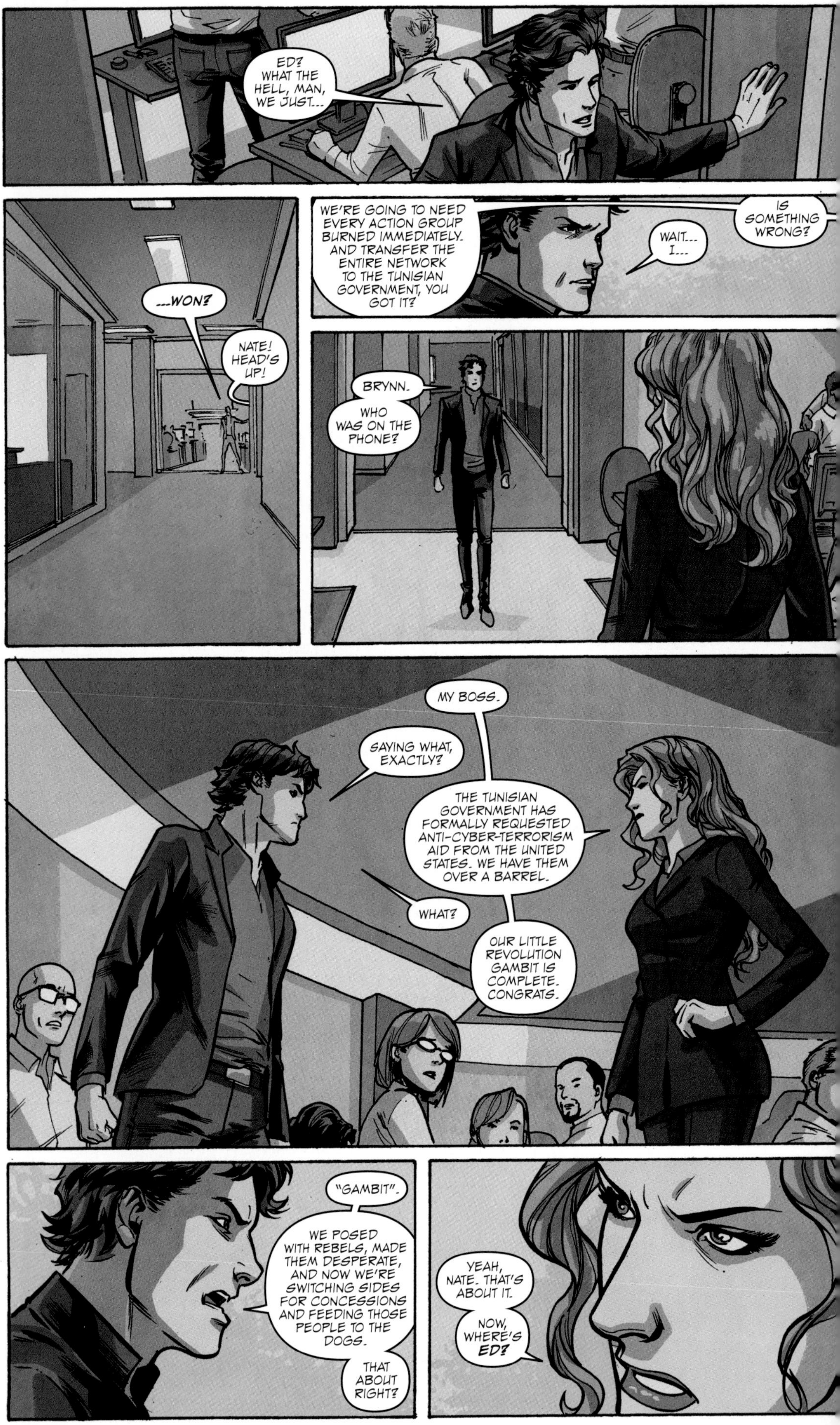
ED? WHAT THE HELL, MAN, WE JUST...
...WON?
NATE! HEAD'S UP!
WE'RE GOING TO NEED EVERY ACTION GROUP BURNED IMMEDIATELY. AND TRANSFER THE ENTIRE NETWORK TO THE TUNISIAN GOVERNMENT, YOU GOT IT?
WAIT... I...
IS SOMETHING WRONG?
BRYNN.
WHO WAS ON THE PHONE?
MY BOSS.
SAYING WHAT, EXACTLY?
THE TUNISIAN GOVERNMENT HAS FORMALLY REQUESTED ANTI-CYBER-TERRORISM AID FROM THE UNITED STATES. WE HAVE THEM OVER A BARREL.
WHAT?
OUR LITTLE REVOLUTION GAMBIT IS COMPLETE. CONGRATS.
"GAMBIT".
WE POSED WITH REBELS, MADE THEM DESPERATE, AND NOW WE'RE SWITCHING SIDES FOR CONCESSIONS AND FEEDING THOSE PEOPLE TO THE DOGS.
THAT ABOUT RIGHT?
YEAH, NATE. THAT'S ABOUT IT.
NOW, WHERE'S ED?

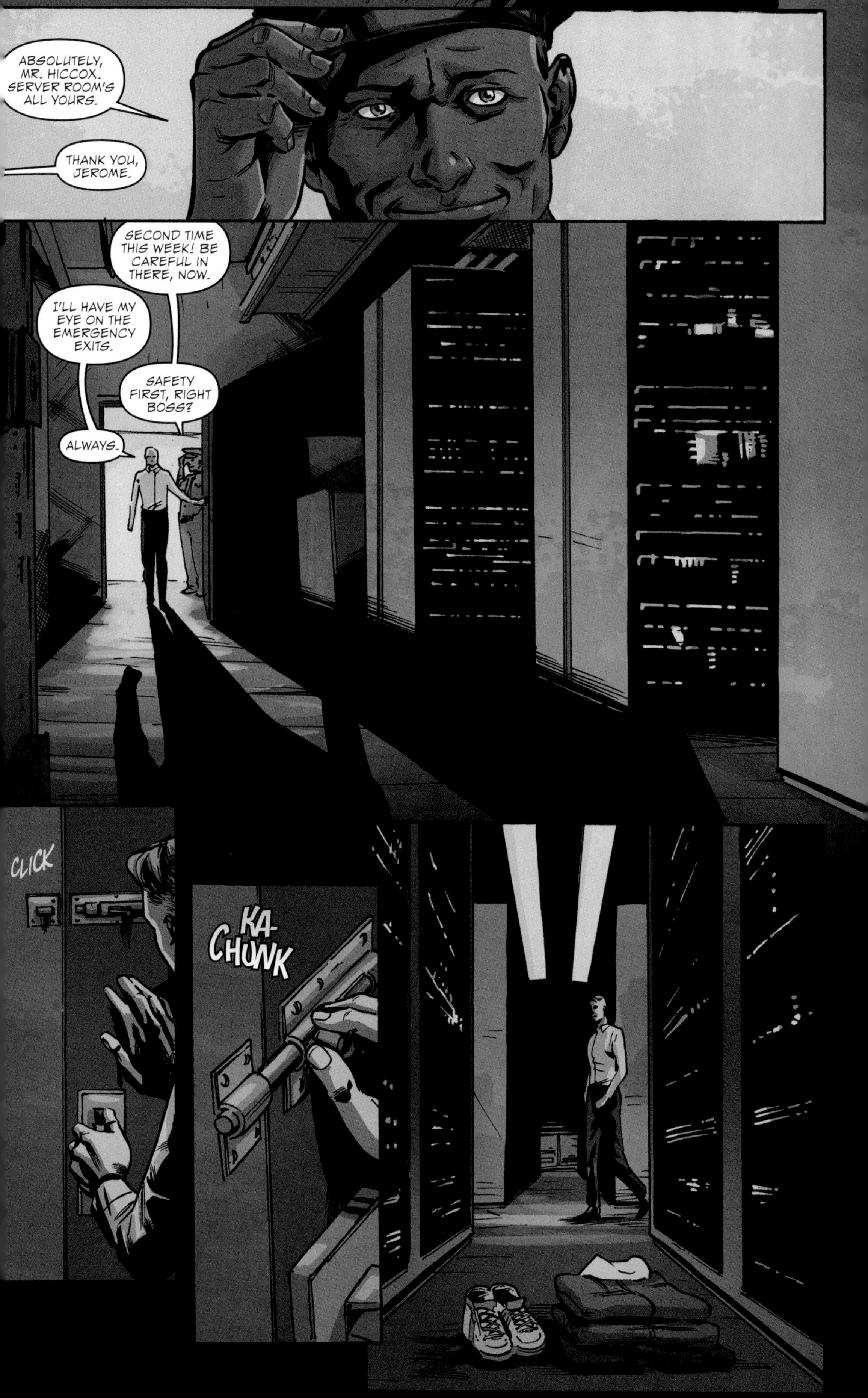

ABSOLUTELY, MR. HICCOX. SERVER ROOM'S ALL YOURS.
THANK YOU, JEROME.
SECOND TIME THIS WEEK! BE CAREFUL IN THERE, NOW.
I'LL HAVE MY EYE ON THE EMERGENCY EXITS.
SAFETY FIRST, RIGHT BOSS?
ALWAYS.
CLICK
KA-CHUNK

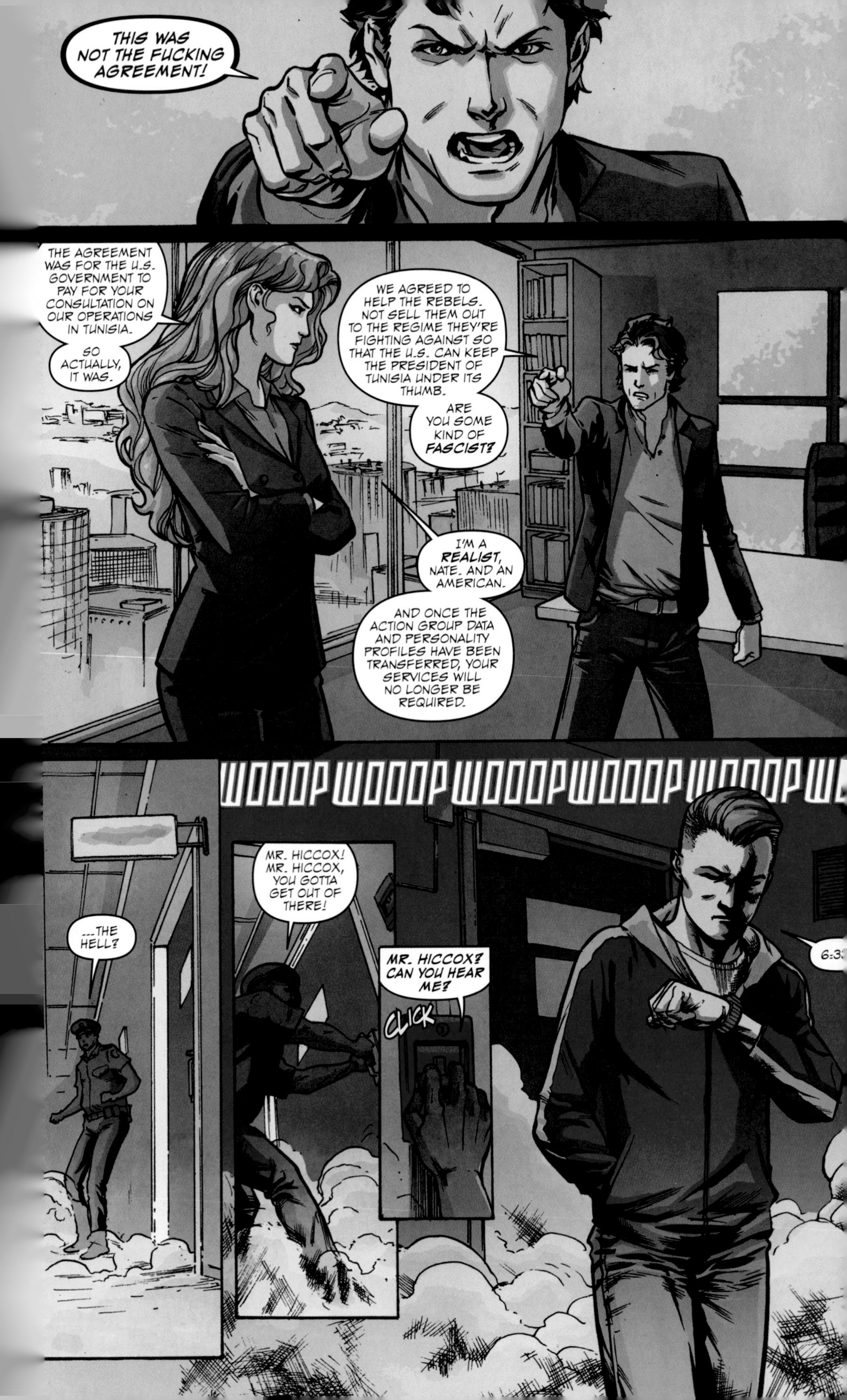
THIS WAS NOT THE FUCKING AGREEMENT!
THE AGREEMENT WAS FOR THE U.S. GOVERNMENT TO PAY FOR YOUR CONSULTATION ON OUR OPERATIONS IN TUNISIA.
SO ACTUALLY, IT WAS.
WE AGREED TO HELP THE REBELS. NOT SELL THEM OUT TO THE REGIME THEY'RE FIGHTING AGAINST SO THAT THE U.S. CAN KEEP THE PRESIDENT OF TUNISIA UNDER ITS THUMB.
ARE YOU SOME KIND OF FASCIST?
I'M A REALIST, NATE. AND AN AMERICAN.
AND ONCE THE ACTION GROUP DATA AND PERSONALITY PROFILES HAVE BEEN TRANSFERRED, YOUR SERVICES WILL NO LONGER BE REQUIRED.
WOOOPWOOOPWOOOPWOOOPWOOOPW
...THE HELL?
MR. HICCOX! MR. HICCOX, YOU GOTTA GET OUT OF THERE!
MR. HICCOX? CAN YOU HEAR ME?
CLICK

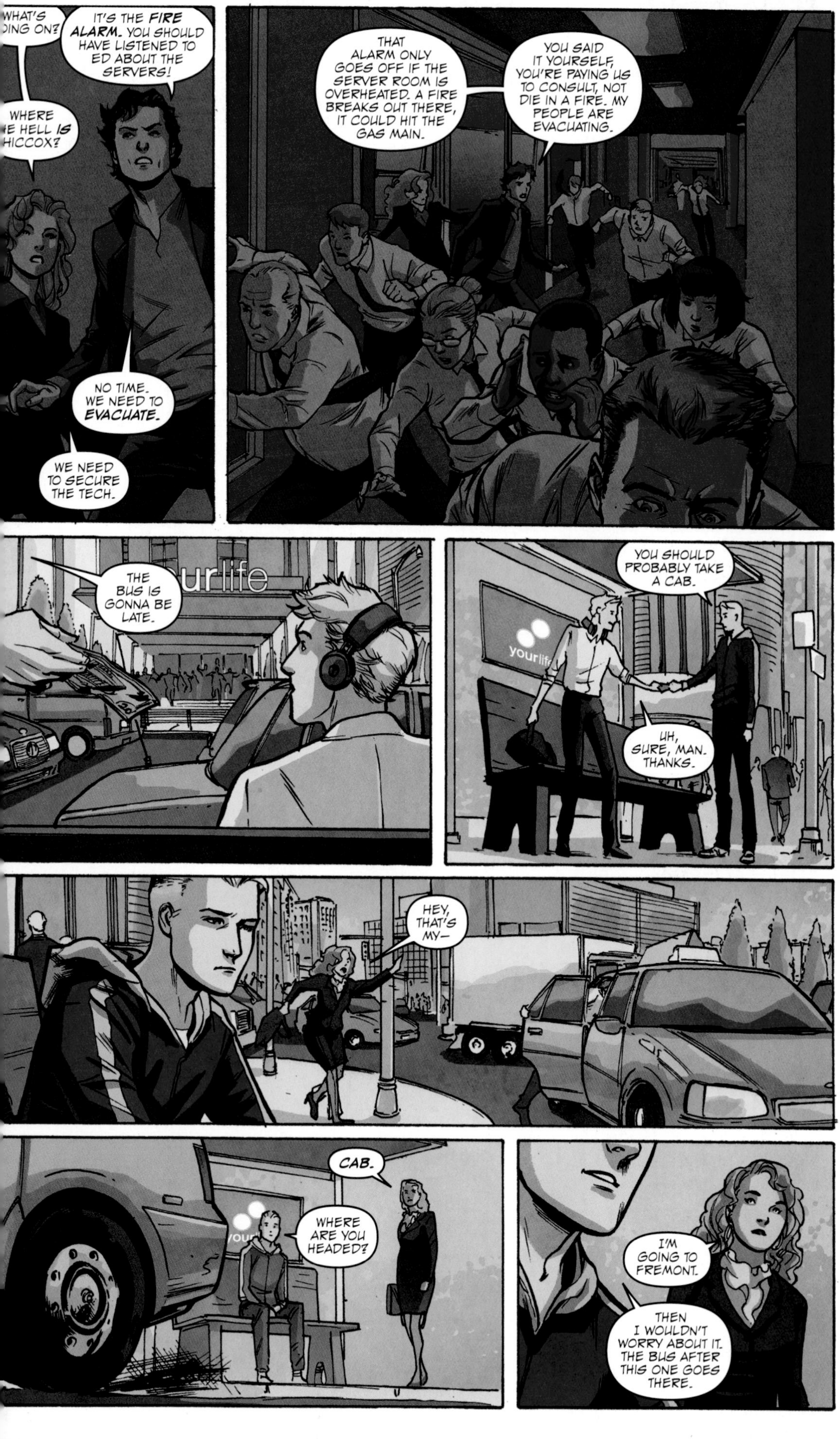
WHAT'S
OING ON?
IT'S THE FIRE ALARM. YOU SHOULD HAVE LISTENED TO ED ABOUT THE SERVERS!
WHERE
E HELL IS
HICCOX?
NO TIME. WE NEED TO EVACUATE.
WE NEED TO SECURE THE TECH.
THAT ALARM ONLY GOES OFF IF THE SERVER ROOM IS OVERHEATED. A FIRE BREAKS OUT THERE, IT COULD HIT THE GAS MAIN.
YOU SAID IT YOURSELF, YOU'RE PAYING US TO CONSULT, NOT DIE IN A FIRE. MY PEOPLE ARE EVACUATING.
urlife
THE BUS IS GONNA BE LATE.
yourlife
YOU SHOULD PROBABLY TAKE A CAB.
UH, SURE, MAN. THANKS.
HEY, THAT'S MY—
CAB.
WHERE ARE YOU HEADED?
I'M GOING TO FREMONT.
THEN I WOULDN'T WORRY ABOUT IT. THE BUS AFTER THIS ONE GOES THERE.

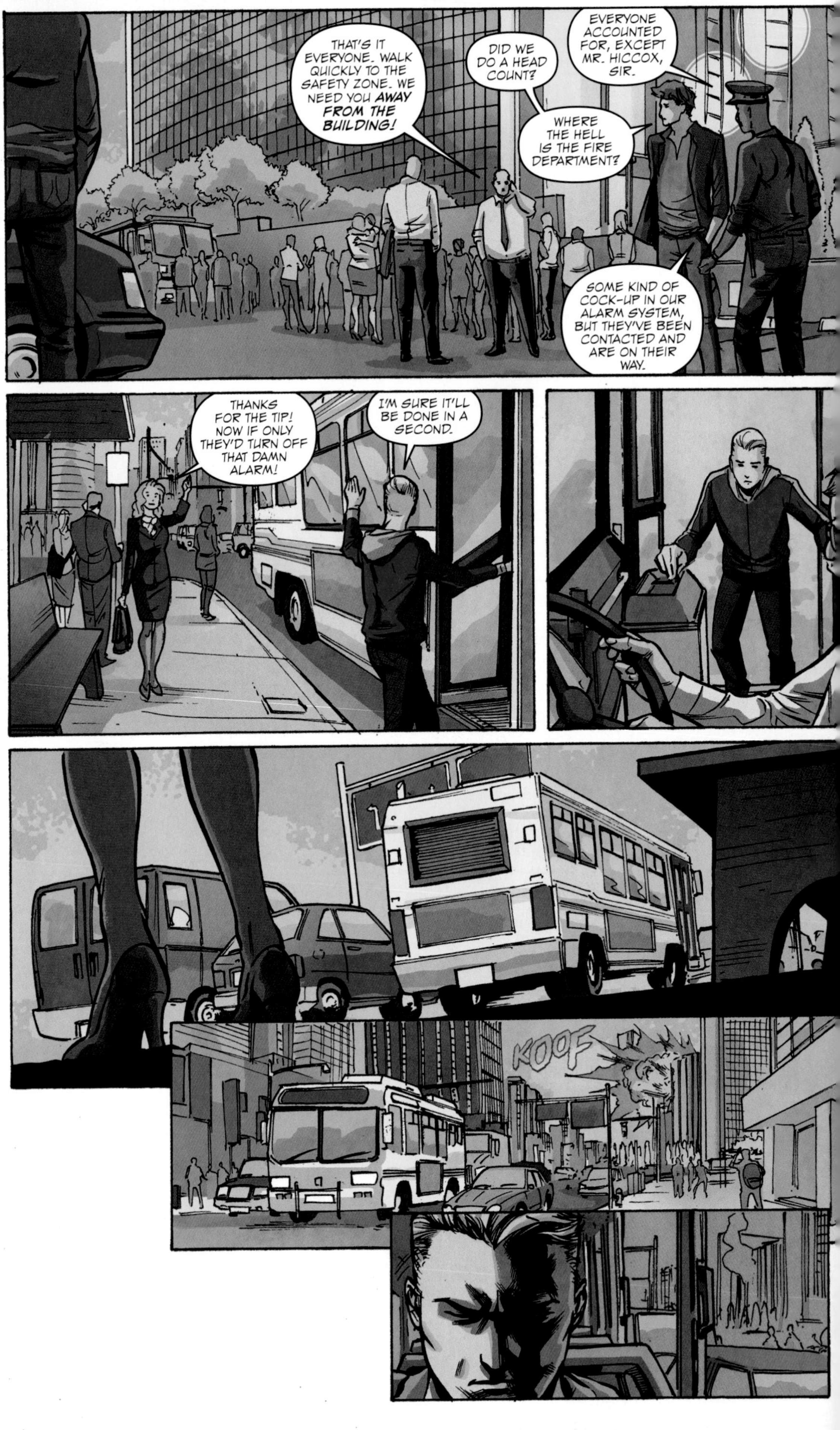
THAT'S IT EVERYONE. WALK QUICKLY TO THE SAFETY ZONE. WE NEED YOU **AWAY FROM THE BUILDING!**
DID WE DO A HEAD COUNT?
EVERYONE ACCOUNTED FOR, EXCEPT MR. HICCOX, SIR.
WHERE THE HELL IS THE FIRE DEPARTMENT?
SOME KIND OF COCK-UP IN OUR ALARM SYSTEM, BUT THEY'VE BEEN CONTACTED AND ARE ON THEIR WAY.
THANKS FOR THE TIP! NOW IF ONLY THEY'D TURN OFF THAT DAMN ALARM!
I'M SURE IT'LL BE DONE IN A SECOND.
KOOF

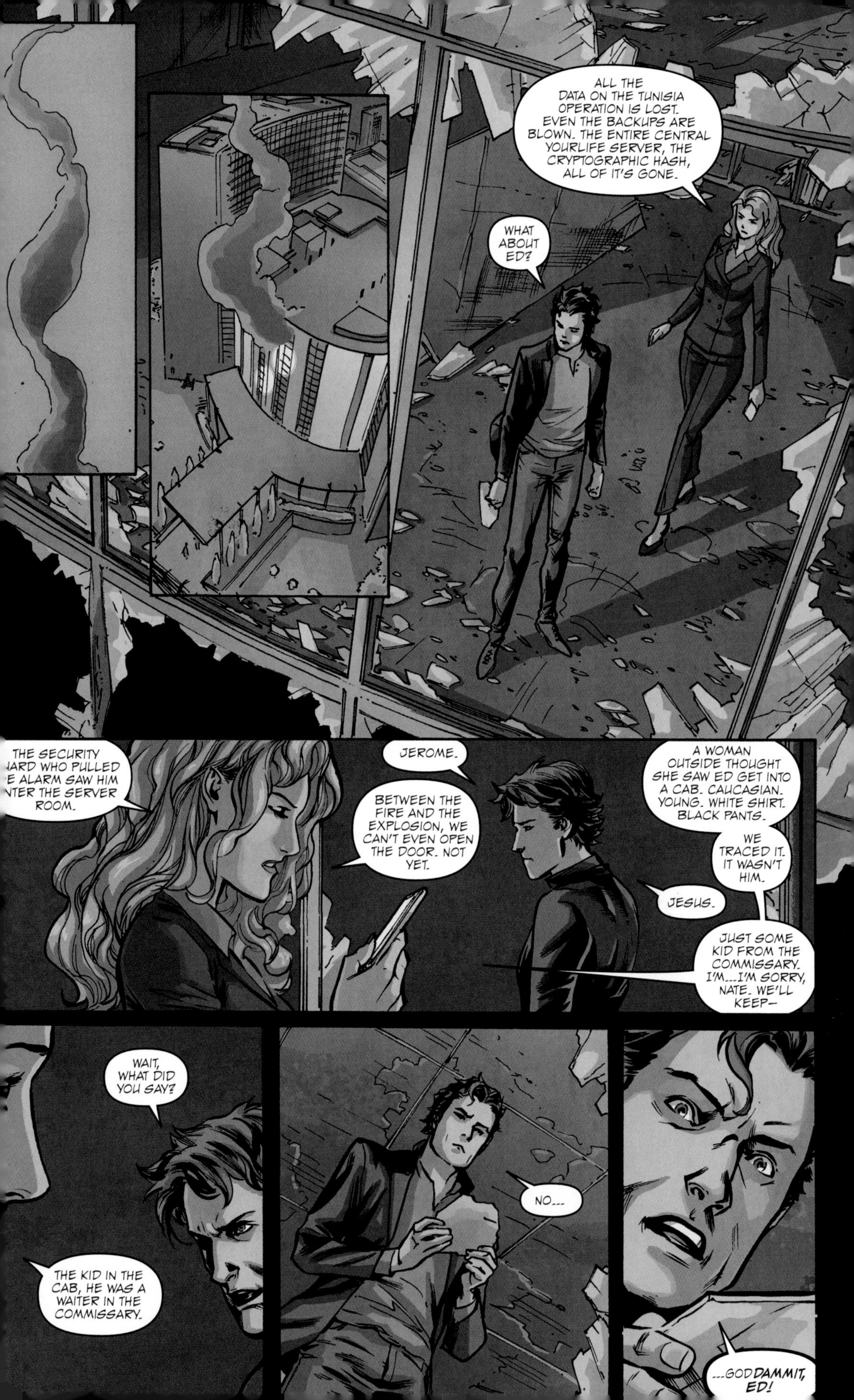
ALL THE DATA ON THE TUNISIA OPERATION IS LOST. EVEN THE BACKUPS ARE BLOWN. THE ENTIRE CENTRAL YOURLIFE SERVER, THE CRYPTOGRAPHIC HASH, ALL OF IT'S GONE.
WHAT ABOUT ED?
THE SECURITY ARD WHO PULLED E ALARM SAW HIM NTER THE SERVER ROOM.
JEROME.
BETWEEN THE FIRE AND THE EXPLOSION, WE CAN'T EVEN OPEN THE DOOR. NOT YET.
A WOMAN OUTSIDE THOUGHT SHE SAW ED GET INTO A CAB. CAUCASIAN. YOUNG. WHITE SHIRT. BLACK PANTS.
WE TRACED IT. IT WASN'T HIM.
JESUS.
JUST SOME KID FROM THE COMMISSARY. I'M...I'M SORRY, NATE. WE'LL KEEP–
WAIT, WHAT DID YOU SAY?
THE KID IN THE CAB, HE WAS A WAITER IN THE COMMISSARY.
NO...
...GOD*DAMMIT*, *ED!*

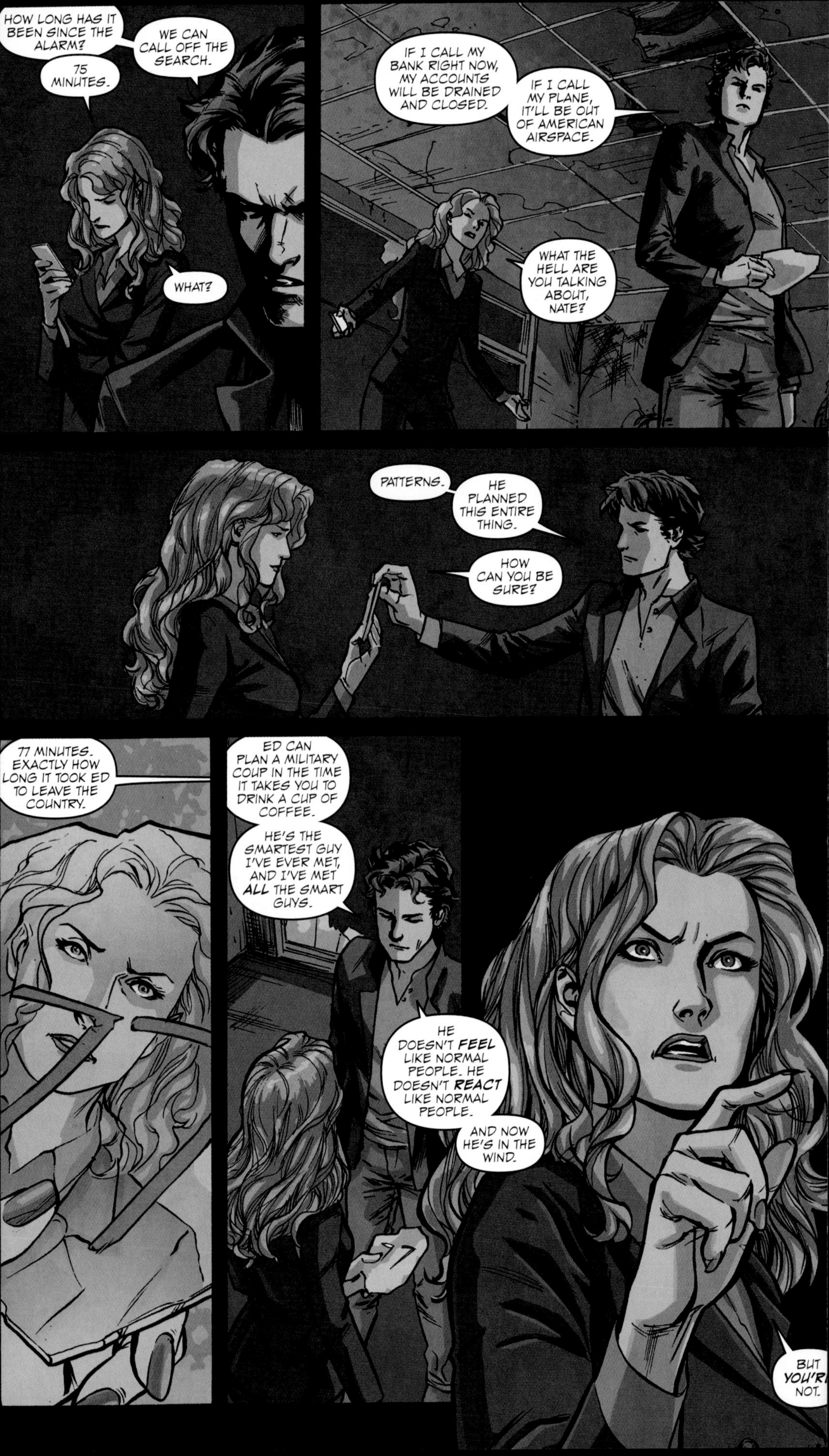

HOW LONG HAS IT BEEN SINCE THE ALARM?
75 MINUTES.
WE CAN CALL OFF THE SEARCH.
WHAT?
IF I CALL MY BANK RIGHT NOW, MY ACCOUNTS WILL BE DRAINED AND CLOSED.
IF I CALL MY PLANE, IT'LL BE OUT OF AMERICAN AIRSPACE.
WHAT THE HELL ARE YOU TALKING ABOUT, NATE?
PATTERNS.
HE PLANNED THIS ENTIRE THING.
HOW CAN YOU BE SURE?
77 MINUTES. EXACTLY HOW LONG IT TOOK ED TO LEAVE THE COUNTRY.
ED CAN PLAN A MILITARY COUP IN THE TIME IT TAKES YOU TO DRINK A CUP OF COFFEE.
HE'S THE SMARTEST GUY I'VE EVER MET, AND I'VE MET ALL THE SMART GUYS.
HE DOESN'T FEEL LIKE NORMAL PEOPLE. HE DOESN'T REACT LIKE NORMAL PEOPLE.
AND NOW HE'S IN THE WIND.
BUT YOU'R NOT.

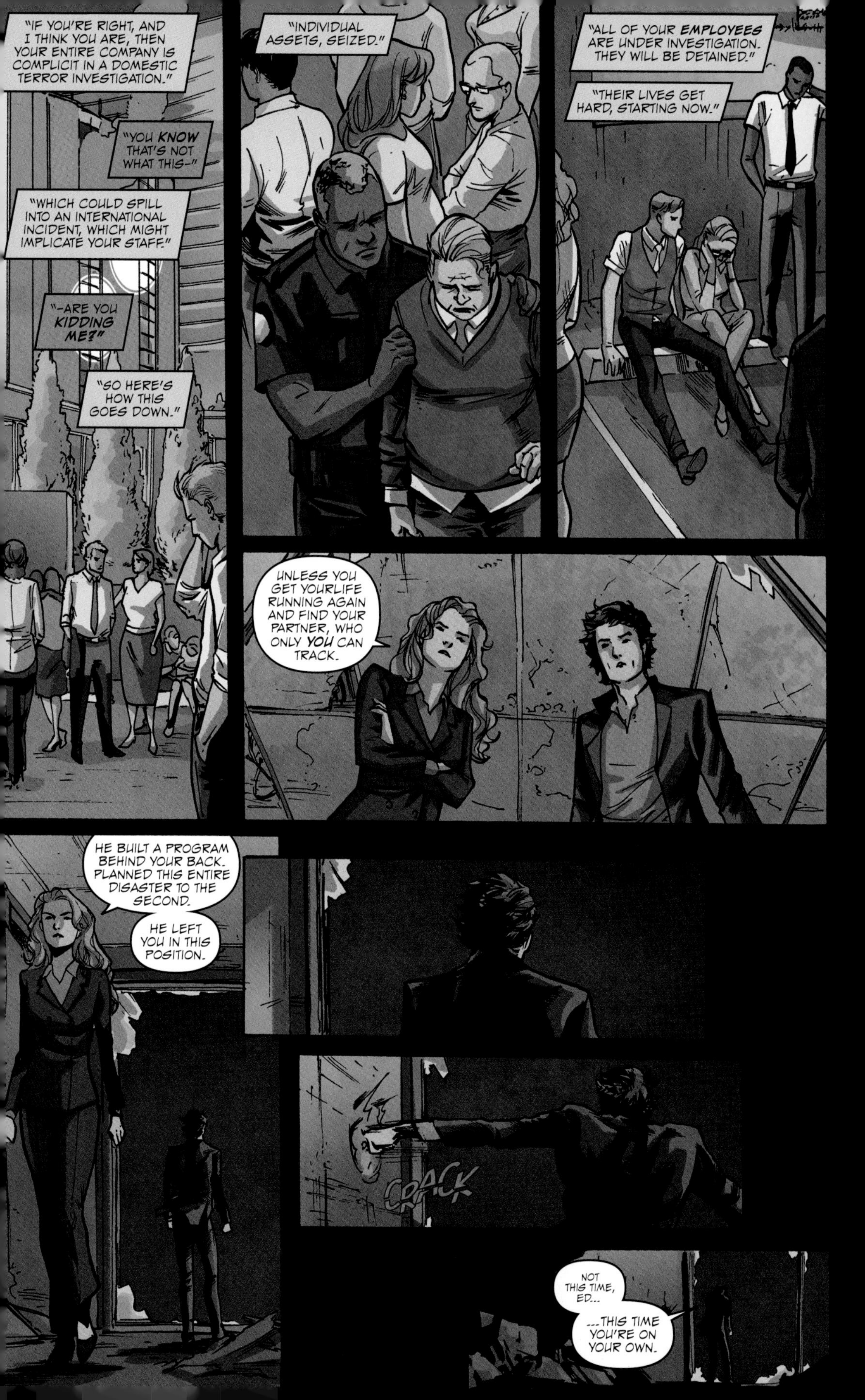
"IF YOU'RE RIGHT, AND I THINK YOU ARE, THEN YOUR ENTIRE COMPANY IS COMPLICIT IN A DOMESTIC TERROR INVESTIGATION."
"YOU KNOW THAT'S NOT WHAT THIS–"
"WHICH COULD SPILL INTO AN INTERNATIONAL INCIDENT, WHICH MIGHT IMPLICATE YOUR STAFF."
"–ARE YOU KIDDING ME?"
"SO HERE'S HOW THIS GOES DOWN."
"INDIVIDUAL ASSETS, SEIZED."
"ALL OF YOUR EMPLOYEES ARE UNDER INVESTIGATION. THEY WILL BE DETAINED."
"THEIR LIVES GET HARD, STARTING NOW."
UNLESS YOU GET YOURLIFE RUNNING AGAIN AND FIND YOUR PARTNER, WHO ONLY YOU CAN TRACK.
HE BUILT A PROGRAM BEHIND YOUR BACK. PLANNED THIS ENTIRE DISASTER TO THE SECOND.
HE LEFT YOU IN THIS POSITION.
CRACK
NOT THIS TIME, ED...
...THIS TIME YOU'RE ON YOUR OWN.

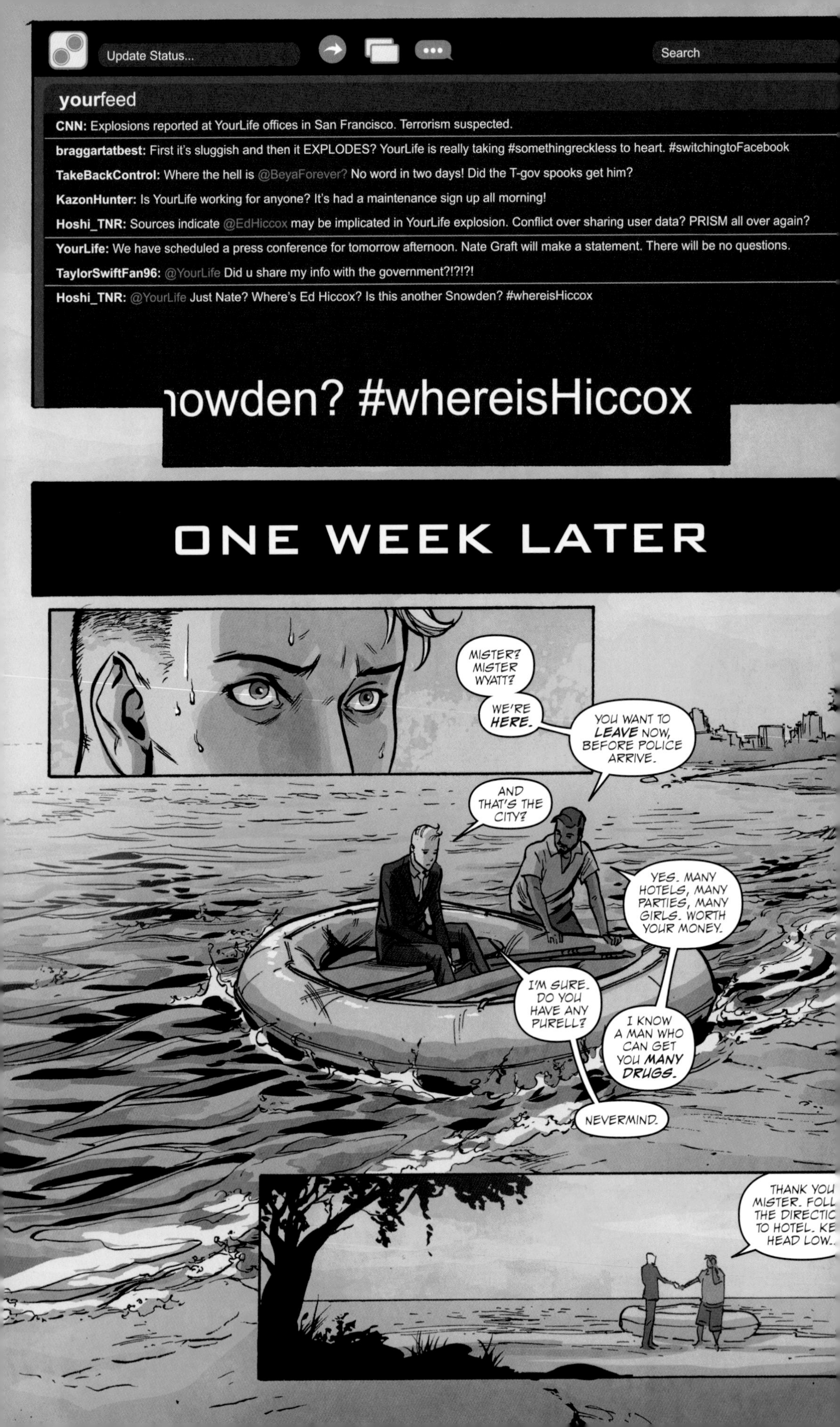
Update Status...
Search
yourfeed
CNN: Explosions reported at YourLife offices in San Francisco. Terrorism suspected.
braggartatbest: First it's sluggish and then it EXPLODES? YourLife is really taking #somethingreckless to heart. #switchingtoFacebook
TakeBackControl: Where the hell is @BeyaForever? No word in two days! Did the T-gov spooks get him?
KazonHunter: Is YourLife working for anyone? It's had a maintenance sign up all morning!
Hoshi_TNR: Sources indicate @EdHiccox may be implicated in YourLife explosion. Conflict over sharing user data? PRISM all over again?
YourLife: We have scheduled a press conference for tomorrow afternoon. Nate Graft will make a statement. There will be no questions.
TaylorSwiftFan96: @YourLife Did u share my info with the government?!?!?!
Hoshi_TNR: @YourLife Just Nate? Where's Ed Hiccox? Is this another Snowden? #whereisHiccox
owden? #whereisHiccox
ONE WEEK LATER
MISTER? MISTER WYATT?
WE'RE HERE.
YOU WANT TO LEAVE NOW, BEFORE POLICE ARRIVE.
AND THAT'S THE CITY?
YES. MANY HOTELS, MANY PARTIES, MANY GIRLS. WORTH YOUR MONEY.
I'M SURE. DO YOU HAVE ANY PURELL?
I KNOW A MAN WHO CAN GET YOU MANY DRUGS.
NEVERMIND.
THANK YOU MISTER. FOLL THE DIRECTIC TO HOTEL. KE HEAD LOW.

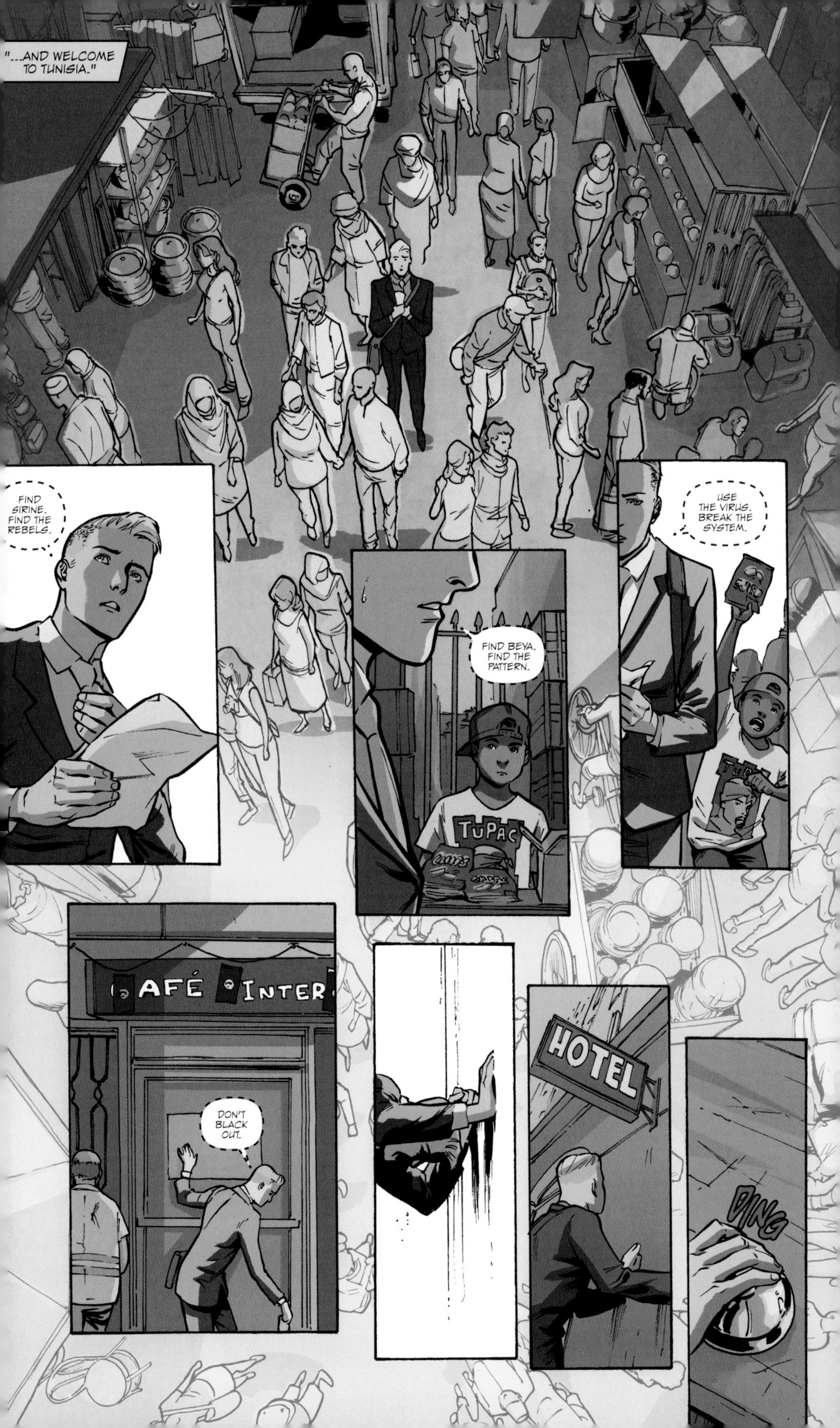
"...AND WELCOME TO TUNISIA."
FIND SIRINE. FIND THE REBELS.
FIND BEYA. FIND THE PATTERN.
TUPAC
USE THE VIRUS. BREAK THE SYSTEM.
CAFÉ INTER
DON'T BLACK OUT.
HOTEL
DING

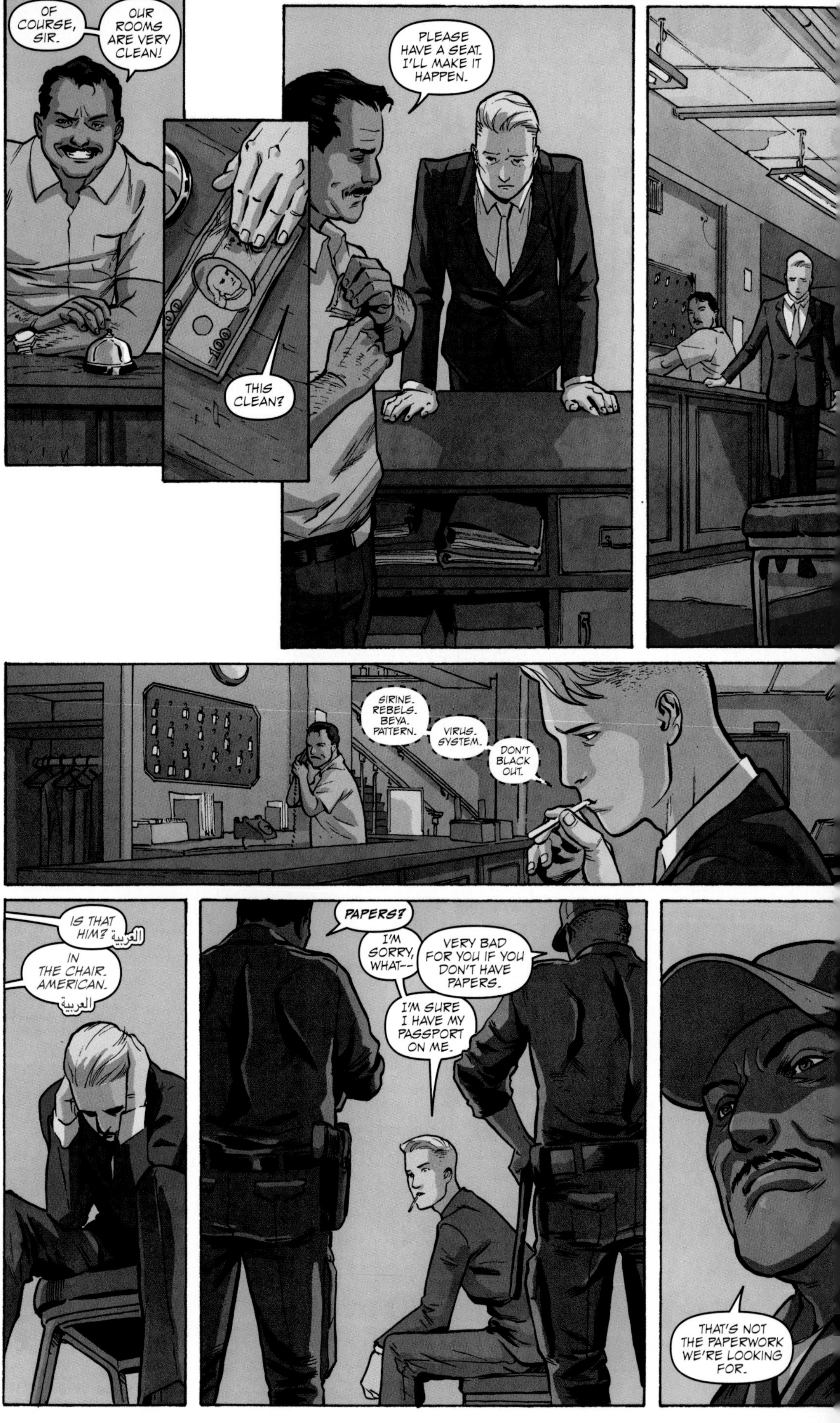

OF COURSE, SIR.
OUR ROOMS ARE VERY CLEAN!
THIS CLEAN?
PLEASE HAVE A SEAT. I'LL MAKE IT HAPPEN.
SIRINE. REBELS. BEYA. PATTERN.
VIRUS. SYSTEM.
DON'T BLACK OUT.
IS THAT HIM? العربية
IN THE CHAIR. AMERICAN. العربية
PAPERS?
I'M SORRY, WHAT--
VERY BAD FOR YOU IF YOU DON'T HAVE PAPERS.
I'M SURE I HAVE MY PASSPORT ON ME.
THAT'S NOT THE PAPERWORK WE'RE LOOKING FOR.

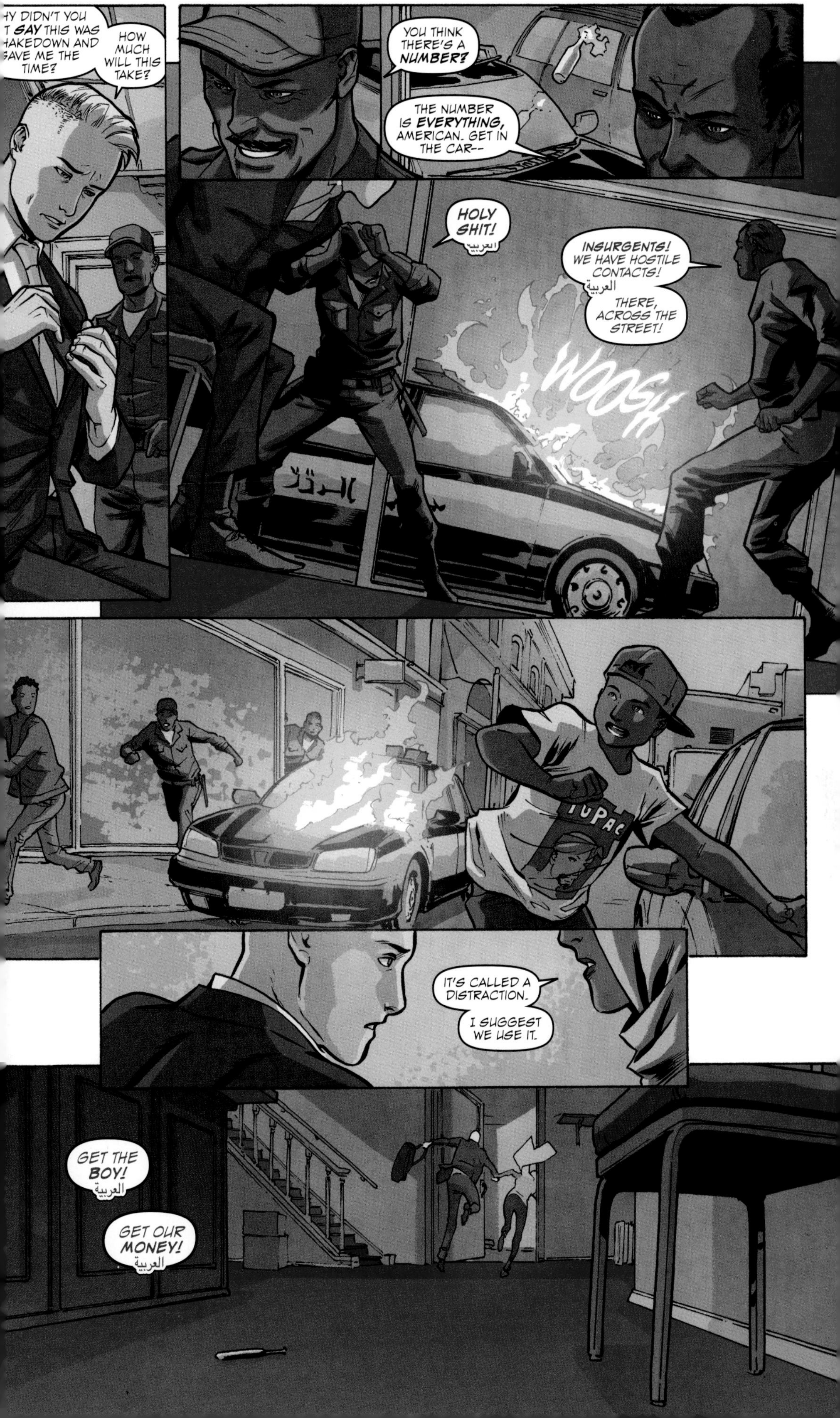

HY DIDN'T YOU
T SAY THIS WAS
HAKEDOWN AND
SAVE ME THE
TIME?
HOW
MUCH
WILL THIS
TAKE?
YOU THINK
THERE'S A
NUMBER?
THE NUMBER
IS EVERYTHING,
AMERICAN. GET IN
THE CAR--
HOLY
SHIT!
العربية
INSURGENTS!
WE HAVE HOSTILE
CONTACTS!
العربية
THERE,
ACROSS THE
STREET!
WOOSH
IT'S CALLED A
DISTRACTION.
I SUGGEST
WE USE IT.
GET THE
BOY!
العربية
GET OUR
MONEY!
العربية

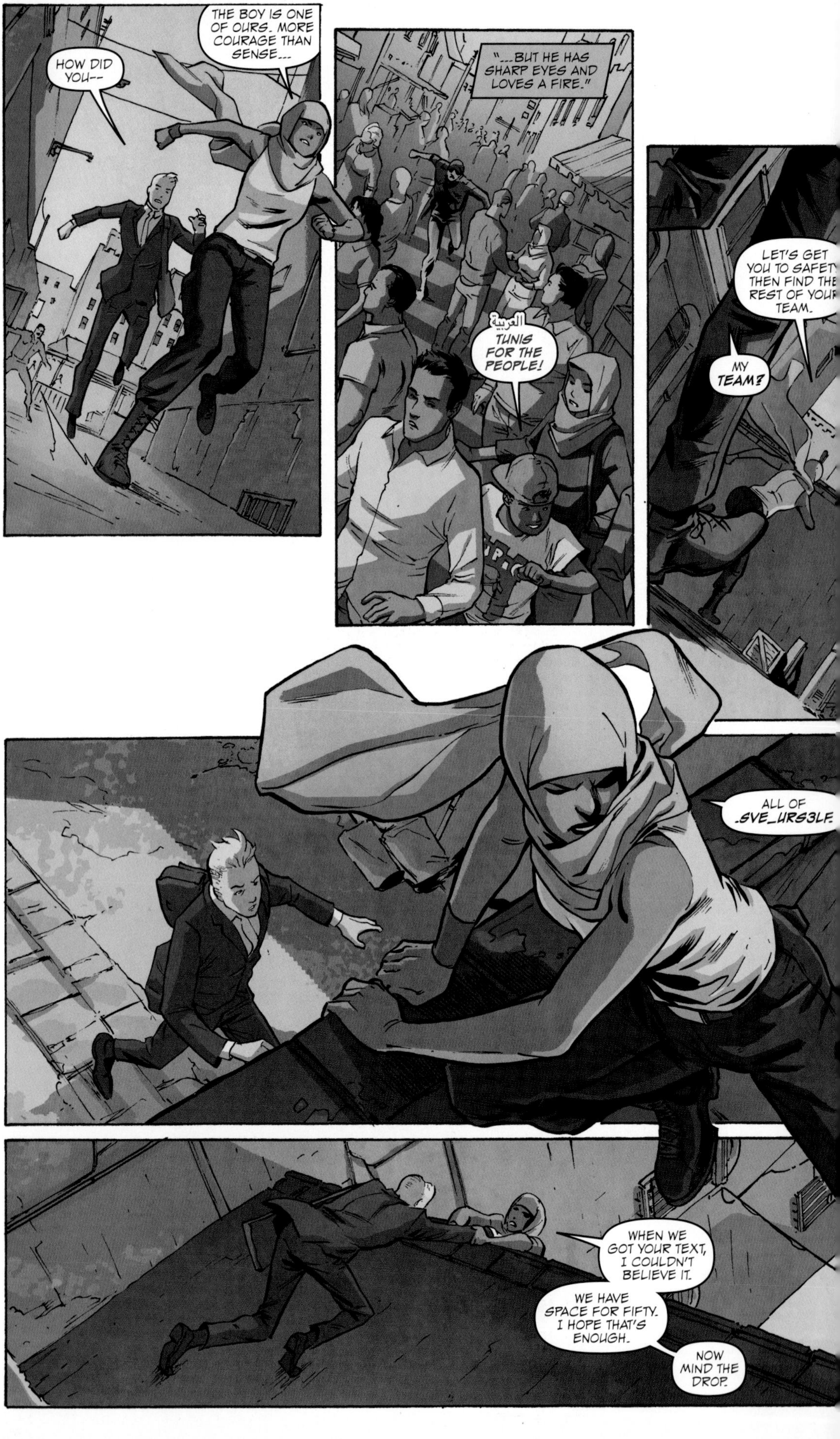
THE BOY IS ONE OF OURS. MORE COURAGE THAN SENSE...
HOW DID YOU--
"...BUT HE HAS SHARP EYES AND LOVES A FIRE."
العربية
TUNIS FOR THE PEOPLE!
LET'S GET YOU TO SAFETY THEN FIND THE REST OF YOUR TEAM.
MY TEAM?
ALL OF .SVE_URS3LF.
WHEN WE GOT YOUR TEXT, I COULDN'T BELIEVE IT.
WE HAVE SPACE FOR FIFTY. I HOPE THAT'S ENOUGH.
NOW MIND THE DROP.

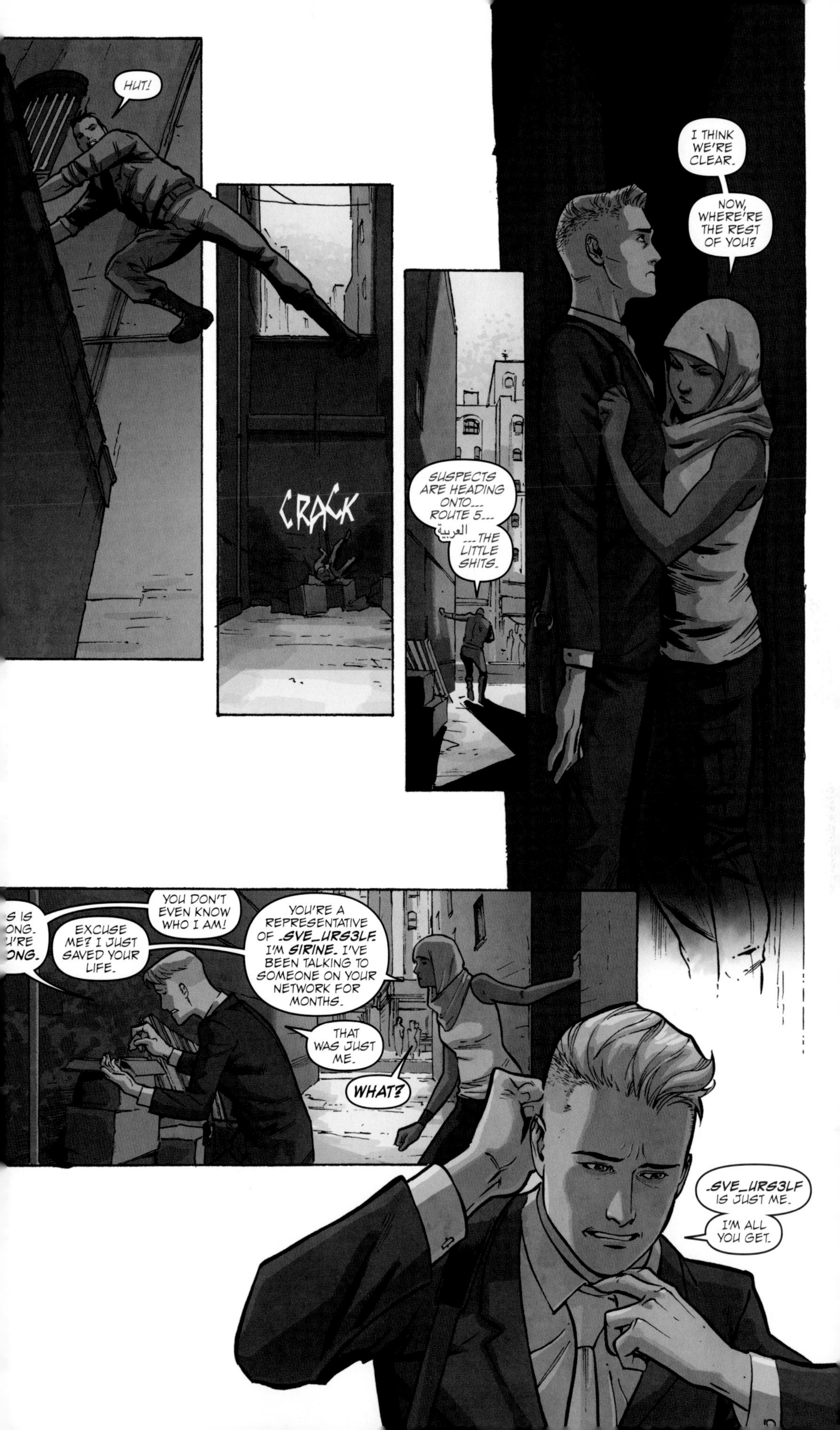
HUT!
CRACK
SUSPECTS ARE HEADING ONTO... ROUTE 5...
العربية
...THE LITTLE SHITS.
I THINK WE'RE CLEAR.
NOW, WHERE'RE THE REST OF YOU?
EXCUSE ME? I JUST SAVED YOUR LIFE.
YOU DON'T EVEN KNOW WHO I AM!
YOU'RE A REPRESENTATIVE OF .SVE_URS3LF. I'M SIRINE. I'VE BEEN TALKING TO SOMEONE ON YOUR NETWORK FOR MONTHS.
THAT WAS JUST ME.
WHAT?
.SVE_URS3LF IS JUST ME.
I'M ALL YOU GET.

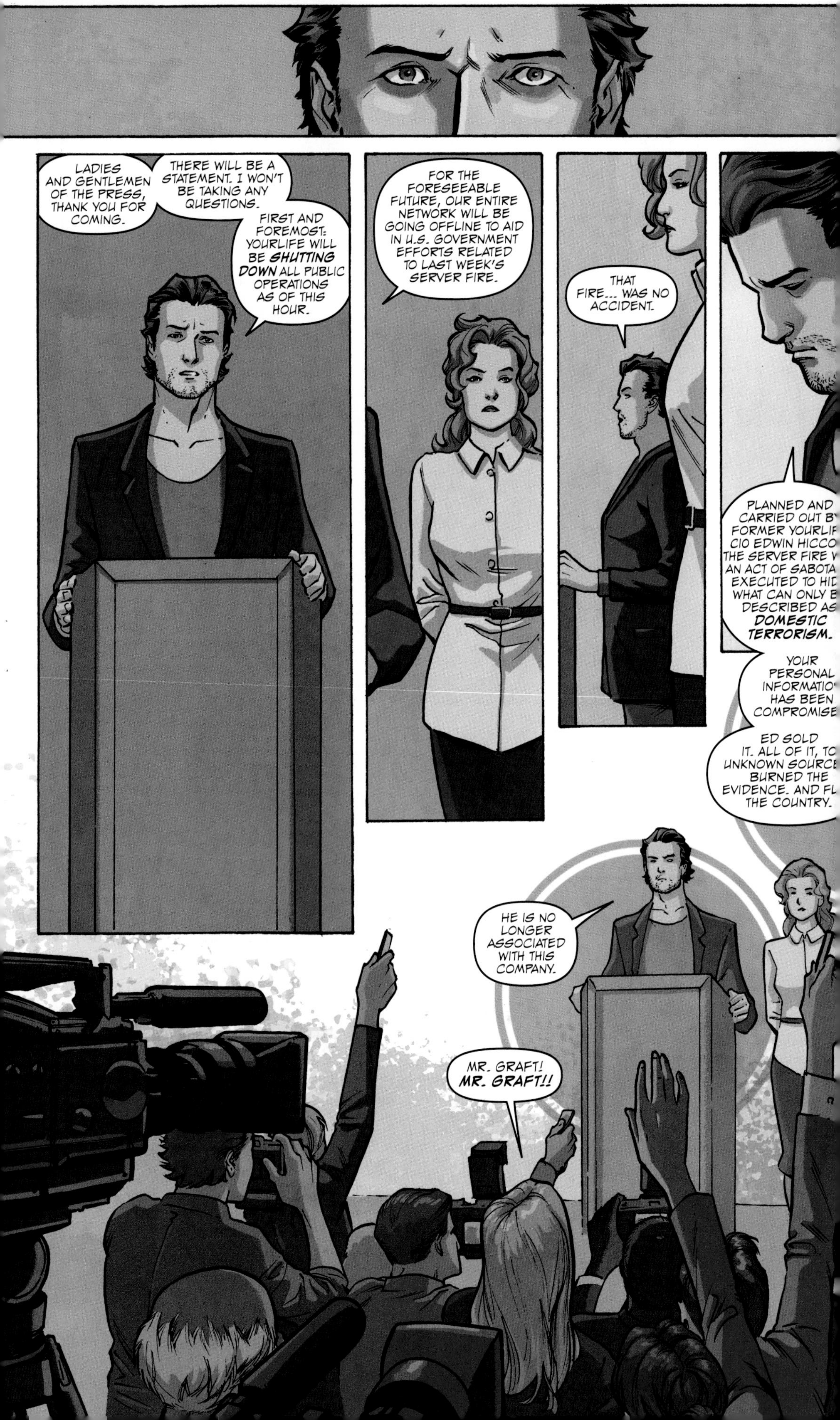

LADIES AND GENTLEMEN OF THE PRESS, THANK YOU FOR COMING.
THERE WILL BE A STATEMENT. I WON'T BE TAKING ANY QUESTIONS.
FIRST AND FOREMOST: YOURLIFE WILL BE **SHUTTING DOWN** ALL PUBLIC OPERATIONS AS OF THIS HOUR.
FOR THE FORESEEABLE FUTURE, OUR ENTIRE NETWORK WILL BE GOING OFFLINE TO AID IN U.S. GOVERNMENT EFFORTS RELATED TO LAST WEEK'S SERVER FIRE.
THAT FIRE... WAS NO ACCIDENT.
PLANNED AND CARRIED OUT BY FORMER YOURLIF CIO EDWIN HICCO THE SERVER FIRE W AN ACT OF SABOTA EXECUTED TO HID WHAT CAN ONLY B DESCRIBED AS **DOMESTIC TERRORISM.**
YOUR PERSONAL INFORMATIO HAS BEEN COMPROMISE
ED SOLD IT. ALL OF IT, TO UNKNOWN SOURCE BURNED THE EVIDENCE. AND FL THE COUNTRY.
HE IS NO LONGER ASSOCIATED WITH THIS COMPANY.
MR. GRAFT! **MR. GRAFT!!**

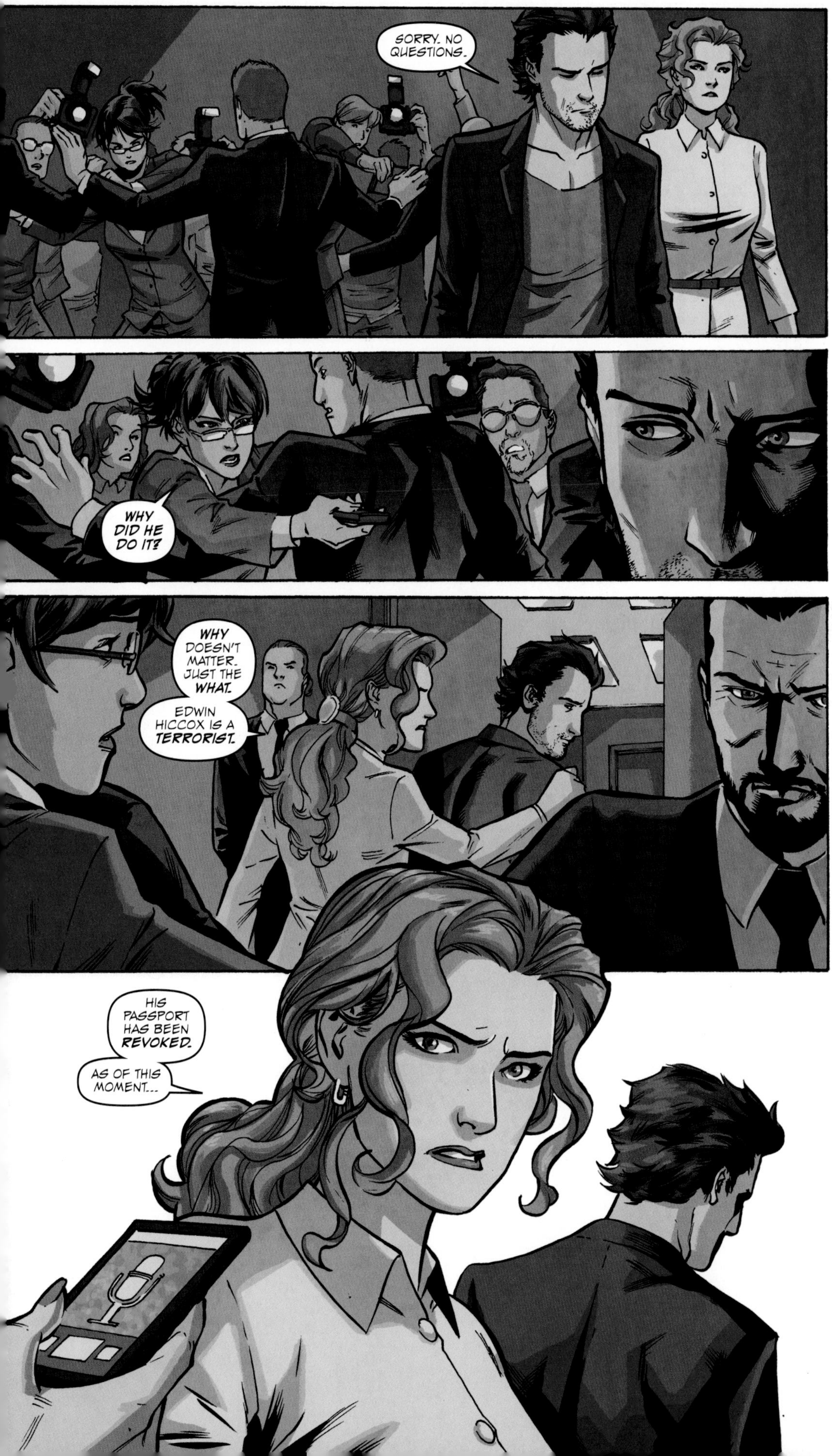
SORRY. NO QUESTIONS.
WHY DID HE DO IT?
WHY DOESN'T MATTER. JUST THE WHAT.
EDWIN HICCOX IS A TERRORIST.
HIS PASSPORT HAS BEEN REVOKED.
AS OF THIS MOMENT...

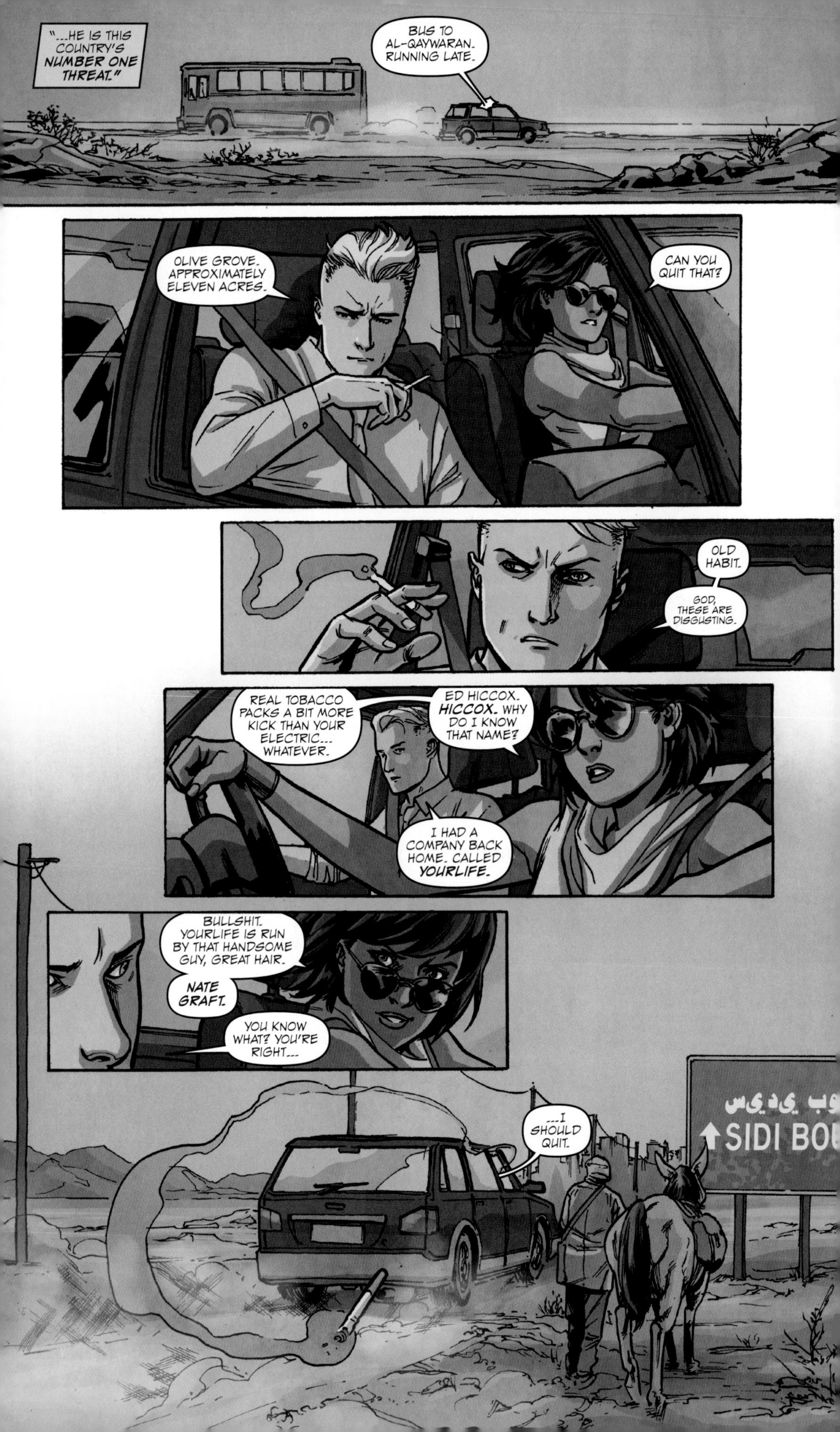
"...HE IS THIS COUNTRY'S NUMBER ONE THREAT."
BUS TO AL-QAYWARAN. RUNNING LATE.
OLIVE GROVE. APPROXIMATELY ELEVEN ACRES.
CAN YOU QUIT THAT?
OLD HABIT.
GOD, THESE ARE DISGUSTING.
REAL TOBACCO PACKS A BIT MORE KICK THAN YOUR ELECTRIC... WHATEVER.
ED HICCOX. HICCOX. WHY DO I KNOW THAT NAME?
I HAD A COMPANY BACK HOME. CALLED YOURLIFE.
BULLSHIT. YOURLIFE IS RUN BY THAT HANDSOME GUY, GREAT HAIR.
NATE GRAFT.
YOU KNOW WHAT? YOU'RE RIGHT...
...I SHOULD QUIT.
SIDI BOU

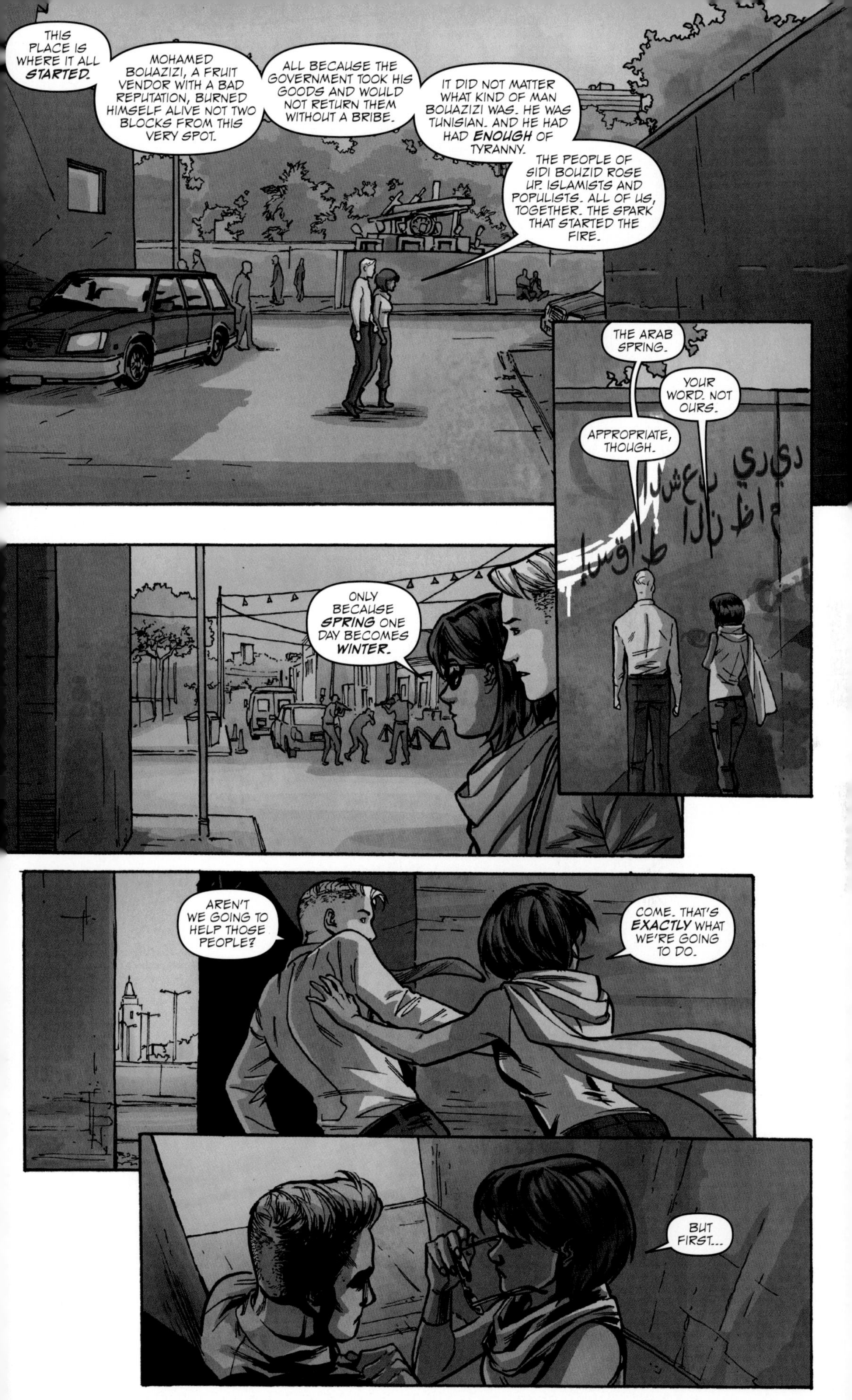

THIS PLACE IS WHERE IT ALL **STARTED.**
MOHAMED BOUAZIZI, A FRUIT VENDOR WITH A BAD REPUTATION, BURNED HIMSELF ALIVE NOT TWO BLOCKS FROM THIS VERY SPOT.
ALL BECAUSE THE GOVERNMENT TOOK HIS GOODS AND WOULD NOT RETURN THEM WITHOUT A BRIBE.
IT DID NOT MATTER WHAT KIND OF MAN BOUAZIZI WAS. HE WAS TUNISIAN. AND HE HAD HAD **ENOUGH** OF TYRANNY.
THE PEOPLE OF SIDI BOUZID ROSE UP. ISLAMISTS AND POPULISTS. ALL OF US, TOGETHER. THE SPARK THAT STARTED THE FIRE.
THE ARAB SPRING.
YOUR WORD. NOT OURS.
APPROPRIATE, THOUGH.
ONLY BECAUSE **SPRING** ONE DAY BECOMES **WINTER.**
AREN'T WE GOING TO HELP THOSE PEOPLE?
COME. THAT'S **EXACTLY** WHAT WE'RE GOING TO DO.
BUT FIRST...

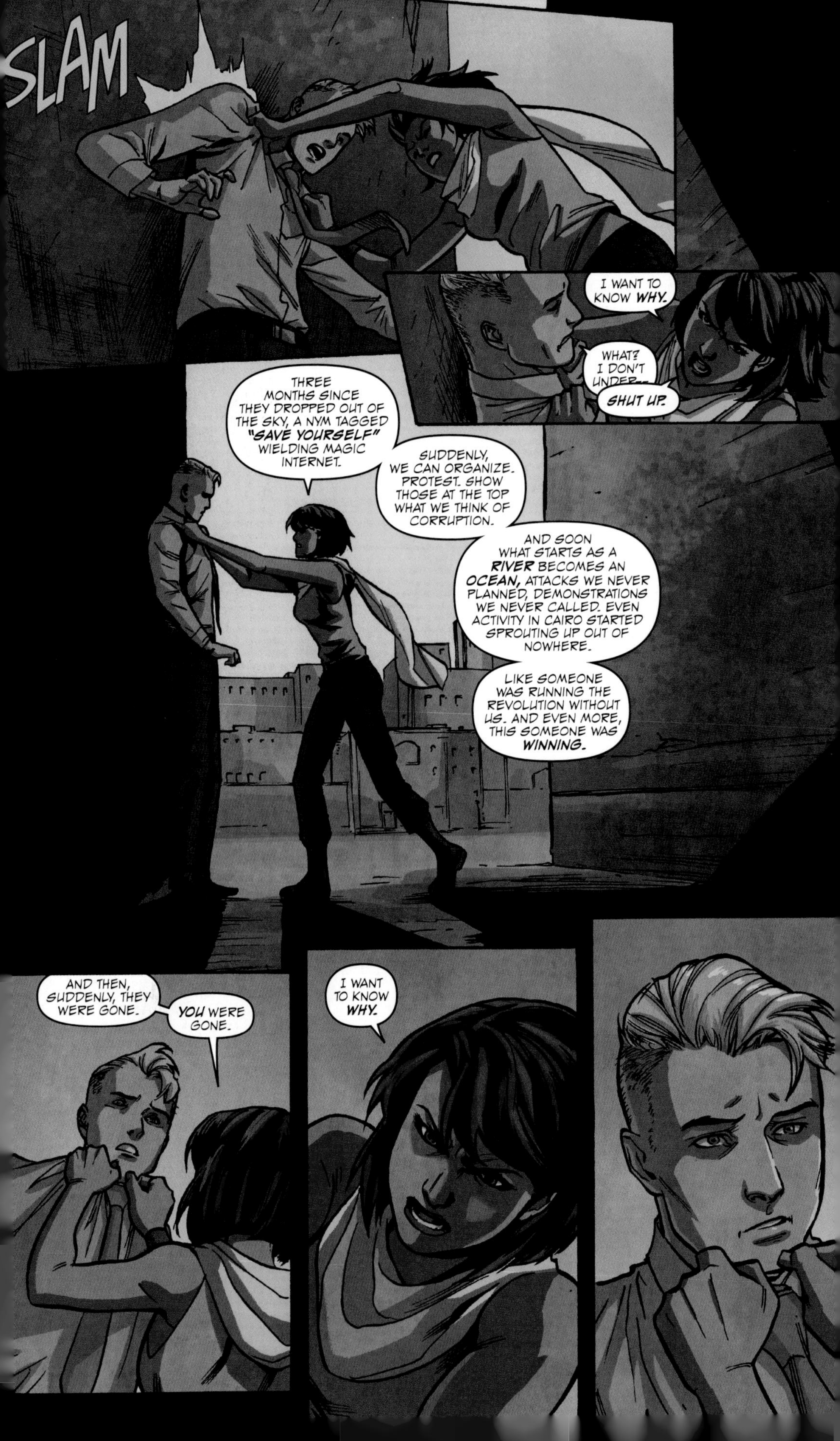
SLAM
I WANT TO KNOW **WHY.**
WHAT? I DON'T UNDER--
SHUT UP.
THREE MONTHS SINCE THEY DROPPED OUT OF THE SKY, A NYM TAGGED **"SAVE YOURSELF"** WIELDING MAGIC INTERNET.
SUDDENLY, WE CAN ORGANIZE. PROTEST. SHOW THOSE AT THE TOP WHAT WE THINK OF CORRUPTION.
AND SOON WHAT STARTS AS A **RIVER** BECOMES AN **OCEAN,** ATTACKS WE NEVER PLANNED, DEMONSTRATIONS WE NEVER CALLED. EVEN ACTIVITY IN CAIRO STARTED SPROUTING UP OUT OF NOWHERE.
LIKE SOMEONE WAS RUNNING THE REVOLUTION WITHOUT US. AND EVEN MORE, THIS SOMEONE WAS **WINNING.**
AND THEN, SUDDENLY, THEY WERE GONE.
YOU WERE GONE.
I WANT TO KNOW **WHY.**

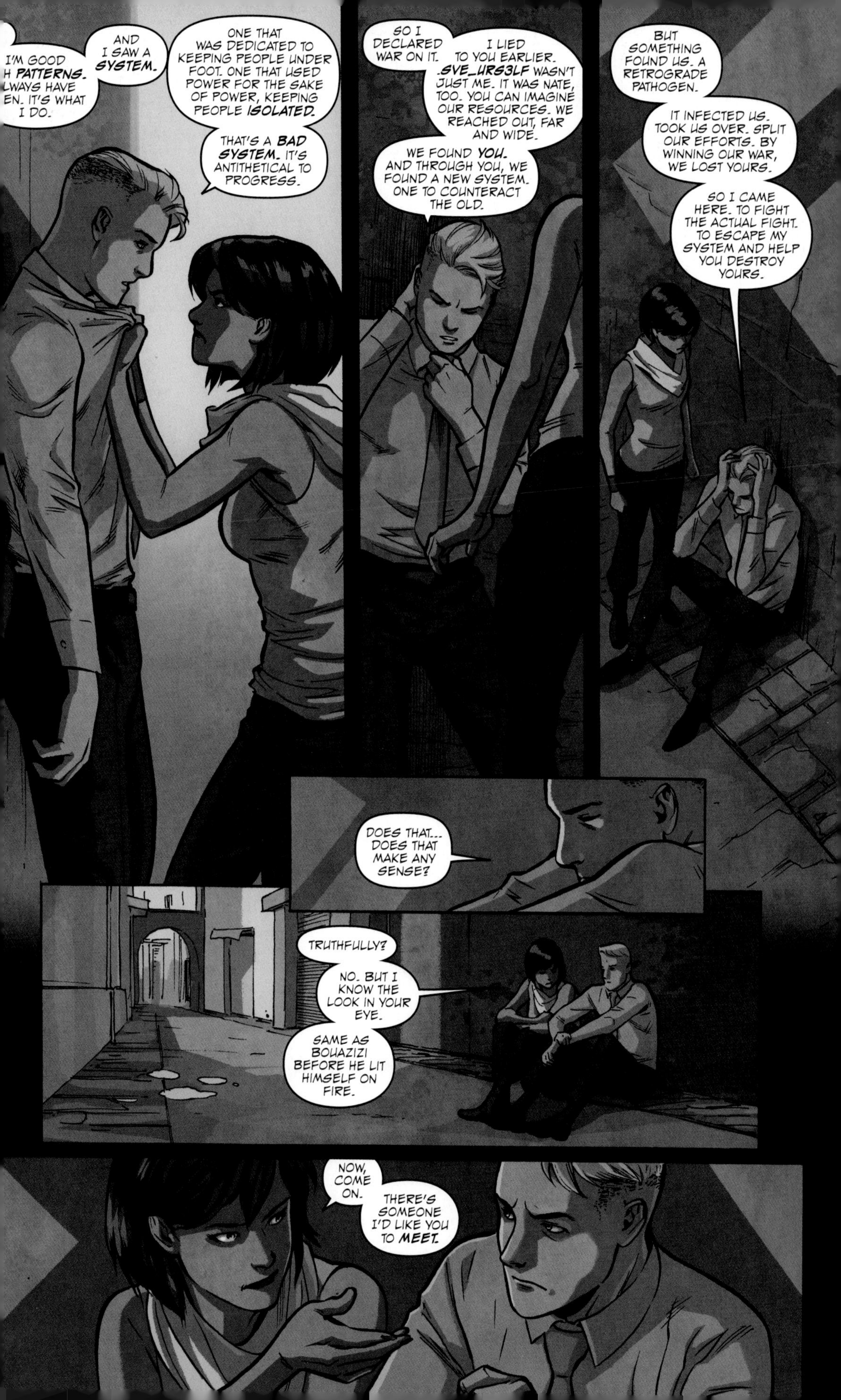
I'M GOOD H PATTERNS. LWAYS HAVE EN. IT'S WHAT I DO.
AND I SAW A SYSTEM.
ONE THAT WAS DEDICATED TO KEEPING PEOPLE UNDER FOOT. ONE THAT USED POWER FOR THE SAKE OF POWER, KEEPING PEOPLE ISOLATED.
THAT'S A BAD SYSTEM. IT'S ANTITHETICAL TO PROGRESS.
SO I DECLARED WAR ON IT.
I LIED TO YOU EARLIER. .SVE_URS3LF WASN'T JUST ME. IT WAS NATE, TOO. YOU CAN IMAGINE OUR RESOURCES. WE REACHED OUT, FAR AND WIDE.
WE FOUND YOU. AND THROUGH YOU, WE FOUND A NEW SYSTEM. ONE TO COUNTERACT THE OLD.
BUT SOMETHING FOUND US. A RETROGRADE PATHOGEN.
IT INFECTED US. TOOK US OVER. SPLIT OUR EFFORTS. BY WINNING OUR WAR, WE LOST YOURS.
SO I CAME HERE. TO FIGHT THE ACTUAL FIGHT. TO ESCAPE MY SYSTEM AND HELP YOU DESTROY YOURS.
DOES THAT... DOES THAT MAKE ANY SENSE?
TRUTHFULLY?
NO. BUT I KNOW THE LOOK IN YOUR EYE.
SAME AS BOUAZIZI BEFORE HE LIT HIMSELF ON FIRE.
NOW, COME ON.
THERE'S SOMEONE I'D LIKE YOU TO MEET.

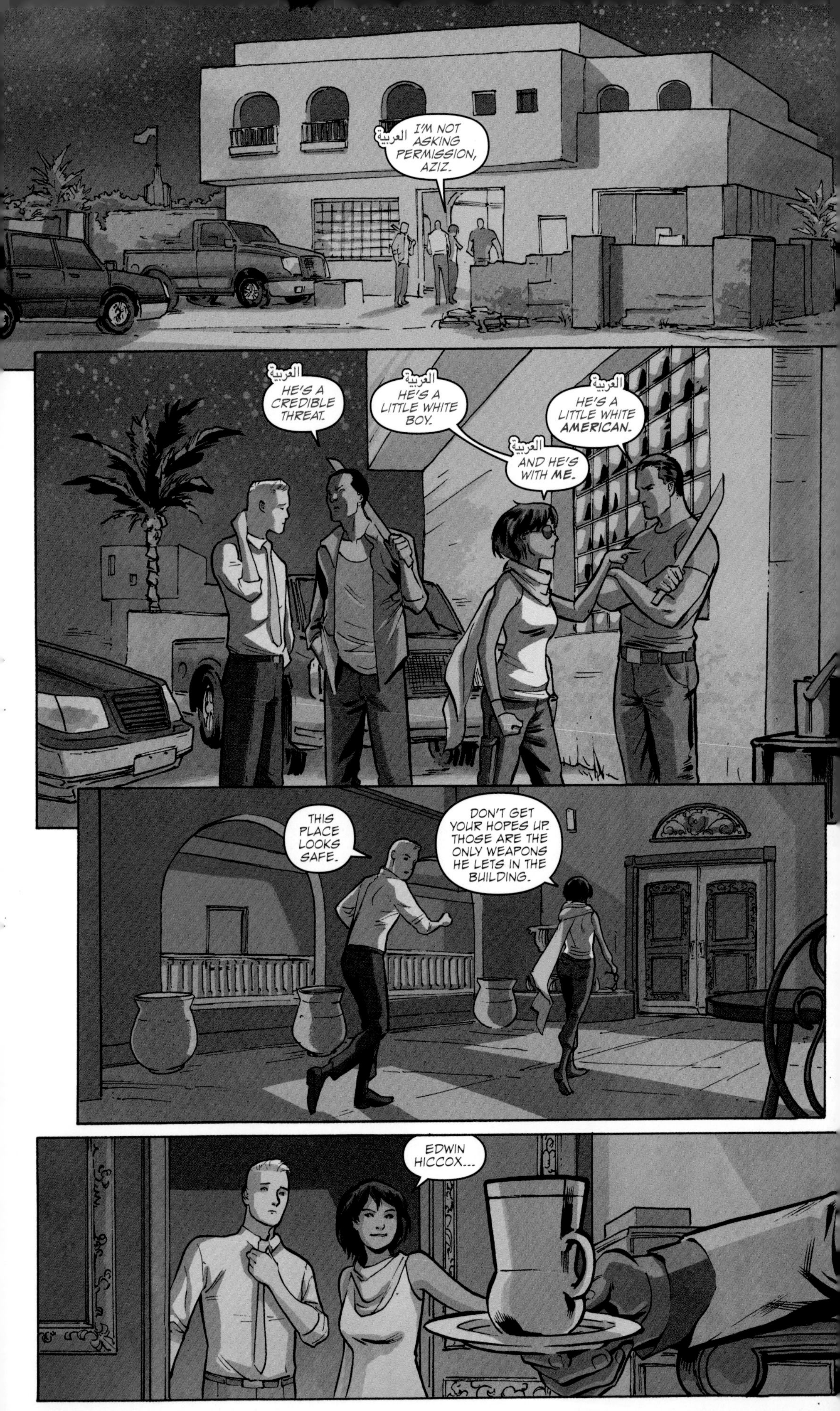
العربية
I'M NOT ASKING PERMISSION, AZIZ.
العربية
HE'S A CREDIBLE THREAT.
العربية
HE'S A LITTLE WHITE BOY.
العربية
HE'S A LITTLE WHITE AMERICAN.
العربية
AND HE'S WITH ME.
THIS PLACE LOOKS SAFE.
DON'T GET YOUR HOPES UP. THOSE ARE THE ONLY WEAPONS HE LETS IN THE BUILDING.
EDWIN HICCOX...

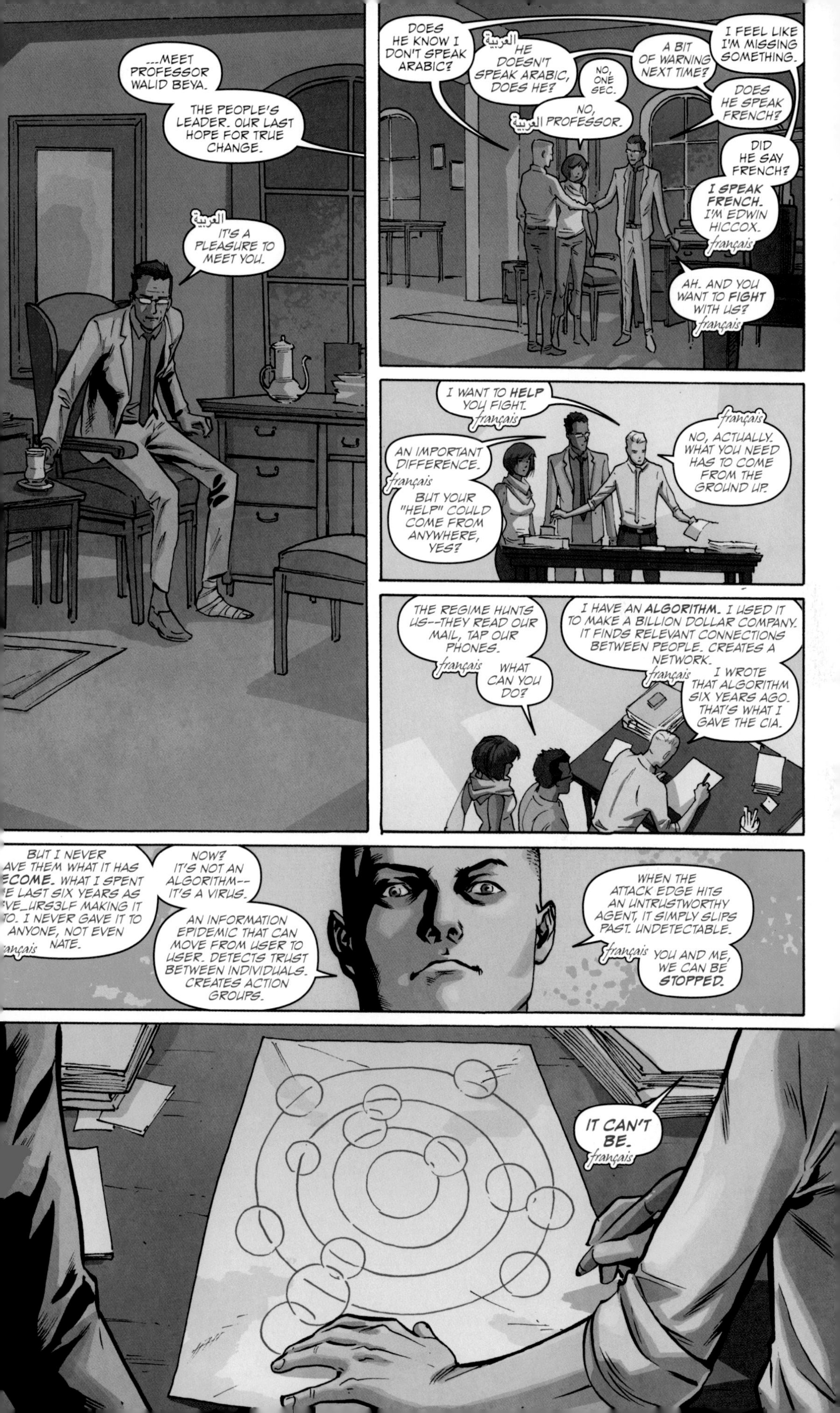

---MEET PROFESSOR WALID BEYA.
THE PEOPLE'S LEADER. OUR LAST HOPE FOR TRUE CHANGE.
العربية
IT'S A PLEASURE TO MEET YOU.
DOES HE KNOW I DON'T SPEAK ARABIC?
العربية
HE DOESN'T SPEAK ARABIC, DOES HE?
NO, ONE SEC.
العربية
NO, PROFESSOR.
I FEEL LIKE I'M MISSING SOMETHING.
A BIT OF WARNING NEXT TIME?
DOES HE SPEAK FRENCH?
DID HE SAY FRENCH?
I SPEAK FRENCH. I'M EDWIN HICCOX.
français
AH. AND YOU WANT TO FIGHT WITH US?
français
I WANT TO HELP YOU FIGHT.
français
AN IMPORTANT DIFFERENCE.
français
BUT YOUR "HELP" COULD COME FROM ANYWHERE, YES?
français
NO, ACTUALLY. WHAT YOU NEED HAS TO COME FROM THE GROUND UP.
THE REGIME HUNTS US--THEY READ OUR MAIL, TAP OUR PHONES.
français
WHAT CAN YOU DO?
I HAVE AN ALGORITHM. I USED IT TO MAKE A BILLION DOLLAR COMPANY. IT FINDS RELEVANT CONNECTIONS BETWEEN PEOPLE. CREATES A NETWORK.
français
I WROTE THAT ALGORITHM SIX YEARS AGO. THAT'S WHAT I GAVE THE CIA.
BUT I NEVER AVE THEM WHAT IT HAS ECOME. WHAT I SPENT E LAST SIX YEARS AS VE_URS3LF MAKING IT O. I NEVER GAVE IT TO ANYONE, NOT EVEN NATE.
ançais
NOW? IT'S NOT AN ALGORITHM-- IT'S A VIRUS.
AN INFORMATION EPIDEMIC THAT CAN MOVE FROM USER TO USER. DETECTS TRUST BETWEEN INDIVIDUALS. CREATES ACTION GROUPS.
WHEN THE ATTACK EDGE HITS AN UNTRUSTWORTHY AGENT, IT SIMPLY SLIPS PAST. UNDETECTABLE.
français
YOU AND ME, WE CAN BE STOPPED.
IT CAN'T BE.
français

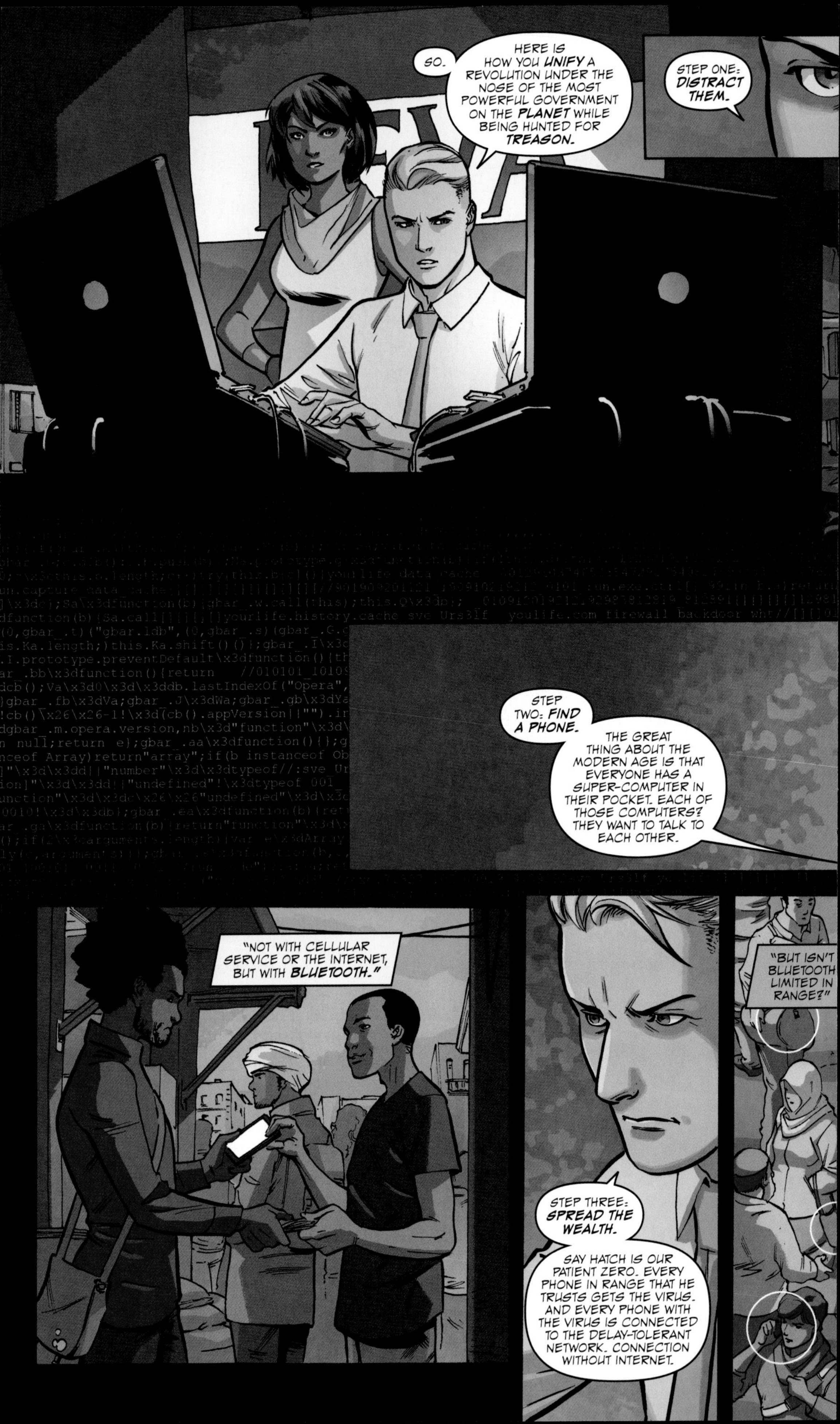
SO.
HERE IS HOW YOU **UNIFY** A REVOLUTION UNDER THE NOSE OF THE MOST POWERFUL GOVERNMENT ON THE **PLANET** WHILE BEING HUNTED FOR **TREASON.**
STEP ONE: **DISTRACT THEM.**
STEP TWO: **FIND A PHONE.**
THE GREAT THING ABOUT THE MODERN AGE IS THAT EVERYONE HAS A SUPER-COMPUTER IN THEIR POCKET. EACH OF THOSE COMPUTERS? THEY WANT TO TALK TO EACH OTHER.
"NOT WITH CELLULAR SERVICE OR THE INTERNET, BUT WITH **BLUETOOTH.**"
STEP THREE: **SPREAD THE WEALTH.**
SAY HATCH IS OUR PATIENT ZERO. EVERY PHONE IN RANGE THAT HE TRUSTS GETS THE VIRUS. AND EVERY PHONE WITH THE VIRUS IS CONNECTED TO THE DELAY-TOLERANT NETWORK. CONNECTION WITHOUT INTERNET.
"BUT ISN'T BLUETOOTH LIMITED IN RANGE?"

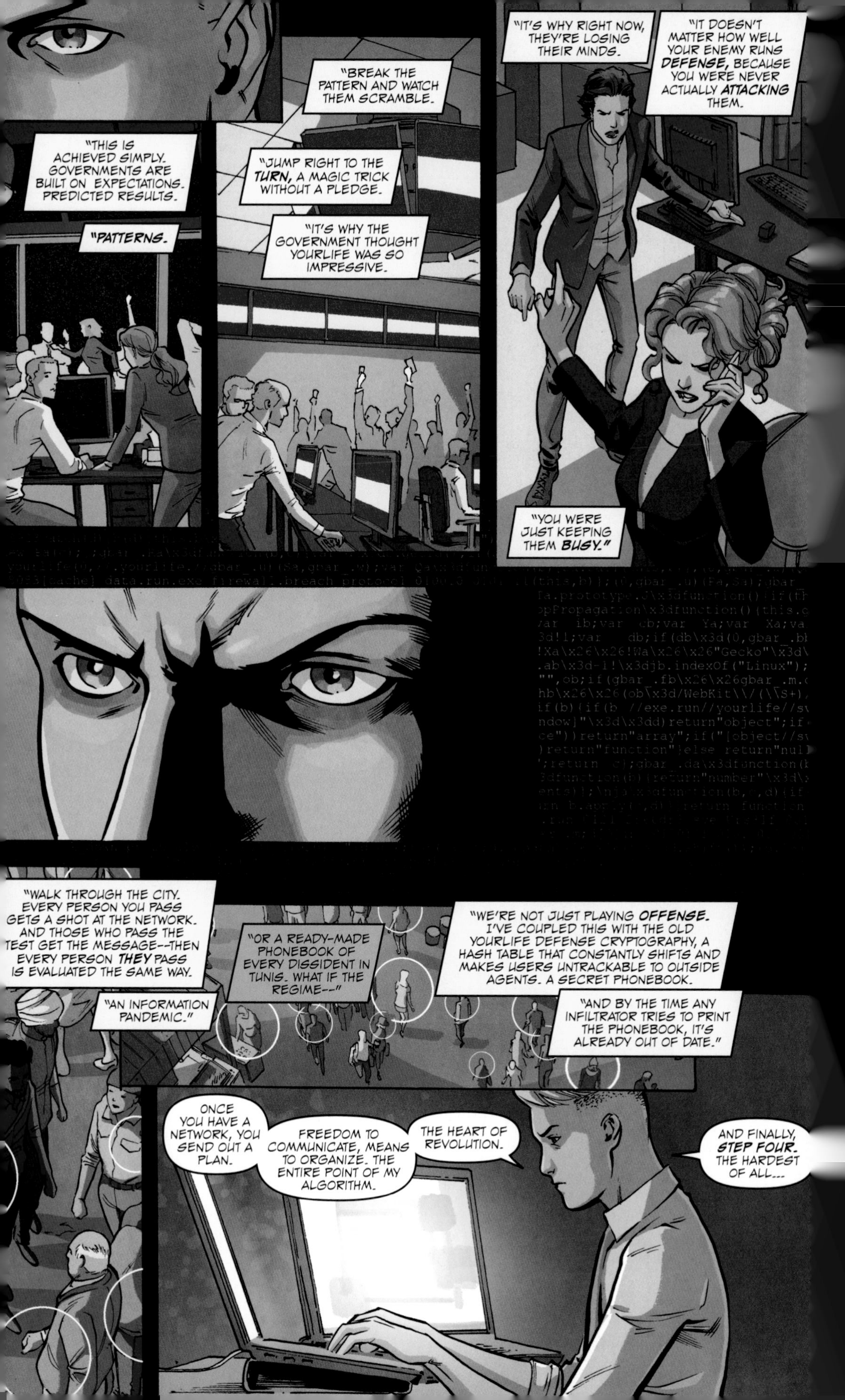
"BREAK THE PATTERN AND WATCH THEM SCRAMBLE.
"THIS IS ACHIEVED SIMPLY. GOVERNMENTS ARE BUILT ON EXPECTATIONS. PREDICTED RESULTS.
"PATTERNS.
"JUMP RIGHT TO THE TURN, A MAGIC TRICK WITHOUT A PLEDGE.
"IT'S WHY THE GOVERNMENT THOUGHT YOURLIFE WAS SO IMPRESSIVE.
"IT'S WHY RIGHT NOW, THEY'RE LOSING THEIR MINDS.
"IT DOESN'T MATTER HOW WELL YOUR ENEMY RUNS DEFENSE, BECAUSE YOU WERE NEVER ACTUALLY ATTACKING THEM.
"YOU WERE JUST KEEPING THEM BUSY."
"WALK THROUGH THE CITY. EVERY PERSON YOU PASS GETS A SHOT AT THE NETWORK. AND THOSE WHO PASS THE TEST GET THE MESSAGE--THEN EVERY PERSON THEY PASS IS EVALUATED THE SAME WAY.
"AN INFORMATION PANDEMIC."
"OR A READY-MADE PHONEBOOK OF EVERY DISSIDENT IN TUNIS. WHAT IF THE REGIME--"
"WE'RE NOT JUST PLAYING OFFENSE. I'VE COUPLED THIS WITH THE OLD YOURLIFE DEFENSE CRYPTOGRAPHY, A HASH TABLE THAT CONSTANTLY SHIFTS AND MAKES USERS UNTRACKABLE TO OUTSIDE AGENTS. A SECRET PHONEBOOK.
"AND BY THE TIME ANY INFILTRATOR TRIES TO PRINT THE PHONEBOOK, IT'S ALREADY OUT OF DATE."
ONCE YOU HAVE A NETWORK, YOU SEND OUT A PLAN.
FREEDOM TO COMMUNICATE, MEANS TO ORGANIZE. THE ENTIRE POINT OF MY ALGORITHM.
THE HEART OF REVOLUTION.
AND FINALLY, STEP FOUR. THE HARDEST OF ALL...

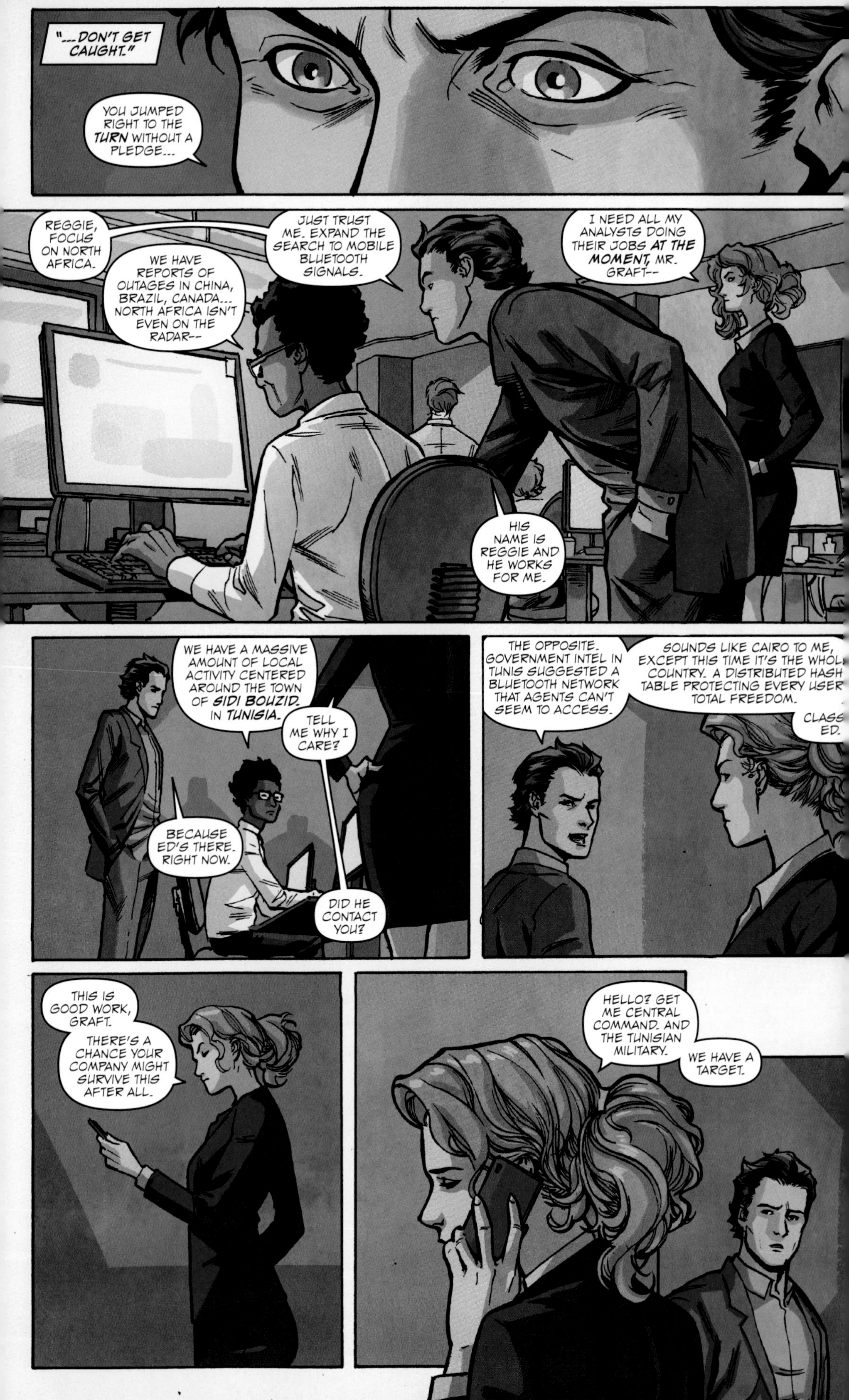
"...DON'T GET CAUGHT."
YOU JUMPED RIGHT TO THE TURN WITHOUT A PLEDGE...
REGGIE, FOCUS ON NORTH AFRICA.
WE HAVE REPORTS OF OUTAGES IN CHINA, BRAZIL, CANADA... NORTH AFRICA ISN'T EVEN ON THE RADAR--
JUST TRUST ME. EXPAND THE SEARCH TO MOBILE BLUETOOTH SIGNALS.
I NEED ALL MY ANALYSTS DOING THEIR JOBS AT THE MOMENT, MR. GRAFT--
HIS NAME IS REGGIE AND HE WORKS FOR ME.
WE HAVE A MASSIVE AMOUNT OF LOCAL ACTIVITY CENTERED AROUND THE TOWN OF SIDI BOUZID IN TUNISIA.
TELL ME WHY I CARE?
BECAUSE ED'S THERE. RIGHT NOW.
DID HE CONTACT YOU?
THE OPPOSITE. GOVERNMENT INTEL IN TUNIS SUGGESTED A BLUETOOTH NETWORK THAT AGENTS CAN'T SEEM TO ACCESS.
SOUNDS LIKE CAIRO TO ME, EXCEPT THIS TIME IT'S THE WHOL COUNTRY. A DISTRIBUTED HASH TABLE PROTECTING EVERY USER TOTAL FREEDOM.
CLASS ED.
THIS IS GOOD WORK, GRAFT.
THERE'S A CHANCE YOUR COMPANY MIGHT SURVIVE THIS AFTER ALL.
HELLO? GET ME CENTRAL COMMAND. AND THE TUNISIAN MILITARY.
WE HAVE A TARGET.

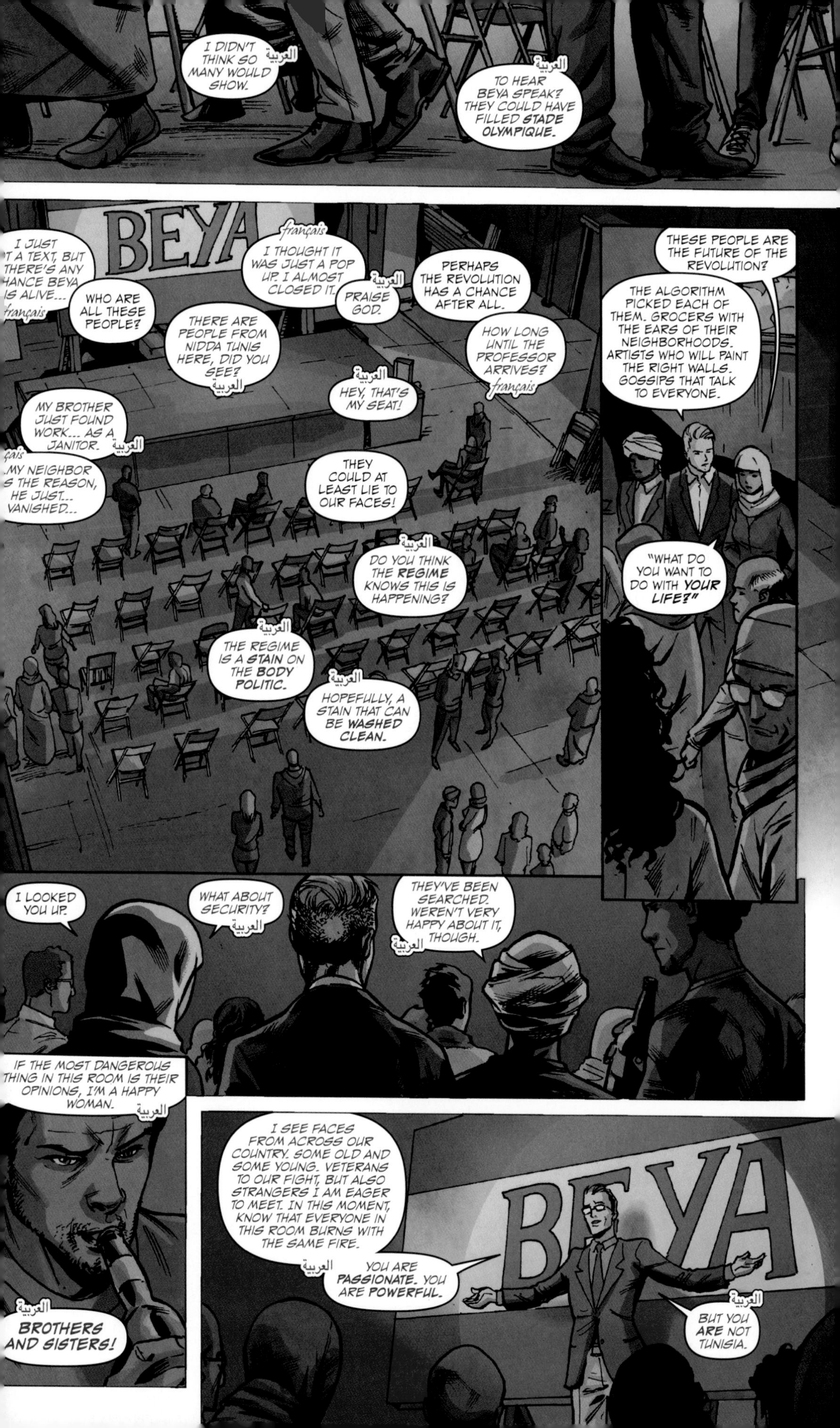

العربية
I DIDN'T THINK SO MANY WOULD SHOW.
العربية
TO HEAR BEYA SPEAK? THEY COULD HAVE FILLED STADE OLYMPIQUE.
BEYA
I JUST 'T A TEXT, BUT THERE'S ANY HANCE BEYA IS ALIVE...
français
WHO ARE ALL THESE PEOPLE?
français
I THOUGHT IT WAS JUST A POP UP. I ALMOST CLOSED IT.
العربية
PRAISE GOD.
PERHAPS THE REVOLUTION HAS A CHANCE AFTER ALL.
THERE ARE PEOPLE FROM NIDDA TUNIS HERE, DID YOU SEE?
العربية
HOW LONG UNTIL THE PROFESSOR ARRIVES?
français
العربية
HEY, THAT'S MY SEAT!
MY BROTHER JUST FOUND WORK... AS A JANITOR.
العربية
çais
.MY NEIGHBOR S THE REASON, HE JUST... VANISHED...
THEY COULD AT LEAST LIE TO OUR FACES!
العربية
DO YOU THINK THE REGIME KNOWS THIS IS HAPPENING?
العربية
THE REGIME IS A STAIN ON THE BODY POLITIC.
العربية
HOPEFULLY, A STAIN THAT CAN BE WASHED CLEAN.
THESE PEOPLE ARE THE FUTURE OF THE REVOLUTION?
THE ALGORITHM PICKED EACH OF THEM. GROCERS WITH THE EARS OF THEIR NEIGHBORHOODS. ARTISTS WHO WILL PAINT THE RIGHT WALLS. GOSSIPS THAT TALK TO EVERYONE.
"WHAT DO YOU WANT TO DO WITH YOUR LIFE?"
I LOOKED YOU UP.
WHAT ABOUT SECURITY?
العربية
THEY'VE BEEN SEARCHED. WEREN'T VERY HAPPY ABOUT IT, THOUGH.
العربية
IF THE MOST DANGEROUS THING IN THIS ROOM IS THEIR OPINIONS, I'M A HAPPY WOMAN.
العربية
العربية
BROTHERS AND SISTERS!
I SEE FACES FROM ACROSS OUR COUNTRY. SOME OLD AND SOME YOUNG. VETERANS TO OUR FIGHT, BUT ALSO STRANGERS I AM EAGER TO MEET. IN THIS MOMENT, KNOW THAT EVERYONE IN THIS ROOM BURNS WITH THE SAME FIRE.
العربية
YOU ARE PASSIONATE. YOU ARE POWERFUL.
BEYA
العربية
BUT YOU ARE NOT TUNISIA.

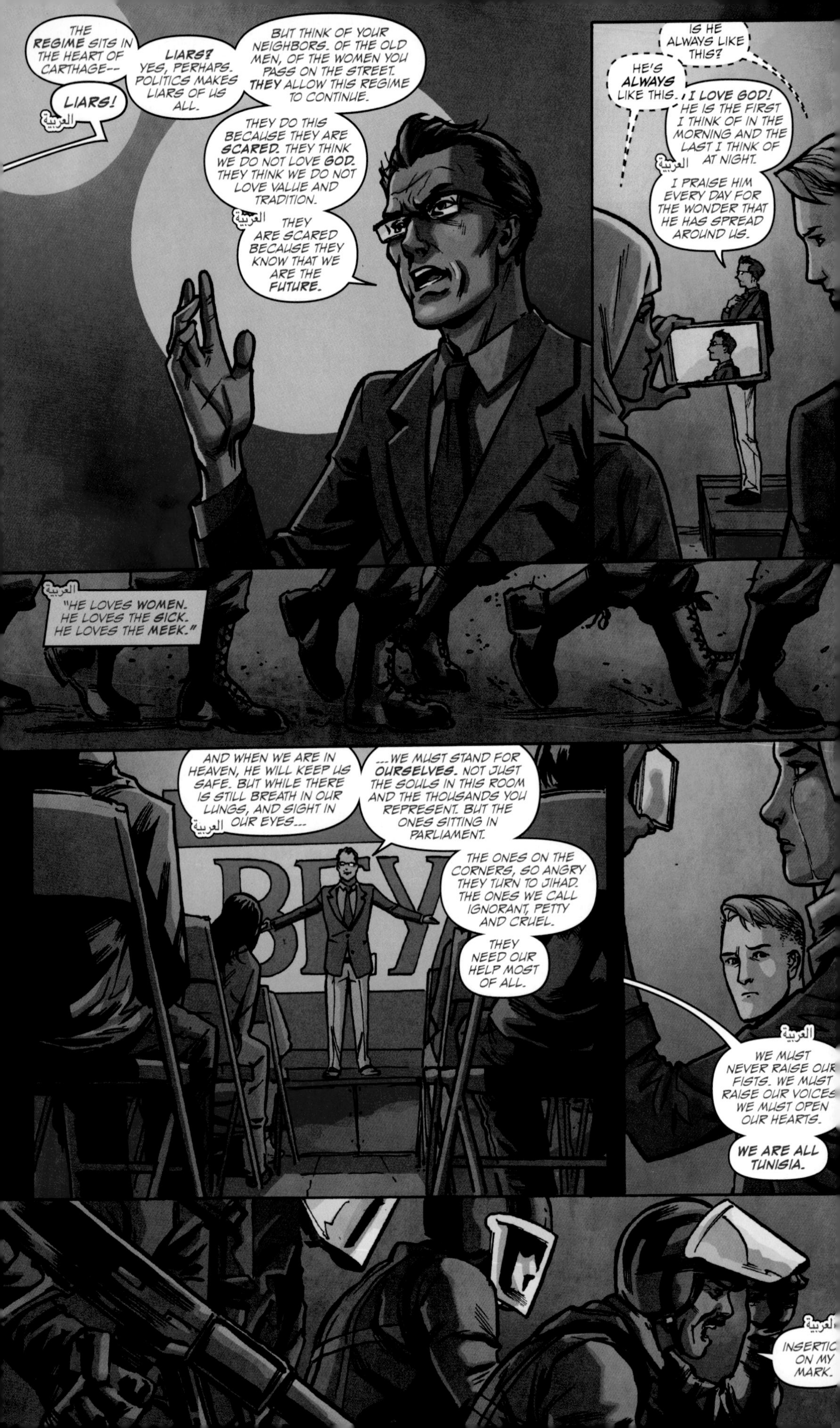
THE REGIME SITS IN THE HEART OF CARTHAGE--
LIARS!
العربية
LIARS? YES, PERHAPS. POLITICS MAKES LIARS OF US ALL.
BUT THINK OF YOUR NEIGHBORS. OF THE OLD MEN, OF THE WOMEN YOU PASS ON THE STREET. THEY ALLOW THIS REGIME TO CONTINUE.
THEY DO THIS BECAUSE THEY ARE SCARED. THEY THINK WE DO NOT LOVE GOD. THEY THINK WE DO NOT LOVE VALUE AND TRADITION.
العربية
THEY ARE SCARED BECAUSE THEY KNOW THAT WE ARE THE FUTURE.
IS HE ALWAYS LIKE THIS?
HE'S ALWAYS LIKE THIS.
I LOVE GOD! HE IS THE FIRST I THINK OF IN THE MORNING AND THE LAST I THINK OF AT NIGHT.
العربية
I PRAISE HIM EVERY DAY FOR THE WONDER THAT HE HAS SPREAD AROUND US.
العربية
"HE LOVES WOMEN. HE LOVES THE SICK. HE LOVES THE MEEK."
AND WHEN WE ARE IN HEAVEN, HE WILL KEEP US SAFE. BUT WHILE THERE IS STILL BREATH IN OUR LUNGS, AND SIGHT IN OUR EYES...
العربية
...WE MUST STAND FOR OURSELVES. NOT JUST THE SOULS IN THIS ROOM AND THE THOUSANDS YOU REPRESENT. BUT THE ONES SITTING IN PARLIAMENT.
THE ONES ON THE CORNERS, SO ANGRY THEY TURN TO JIHAD. THE ONES WE CALL IGNORANT, PETTY AND CRUEL.
THEY NEED OUR HELP MOST OF ALL.
BEY
العربية
WE MUST NEVER RAISE OUR FISTS. WE MUST RAISE OUR VOICES. WE MUST OPEN OUR HEARTS.
WE ARE ALL TUNISIA.
العربية
INSERTIC ON MY MARK.

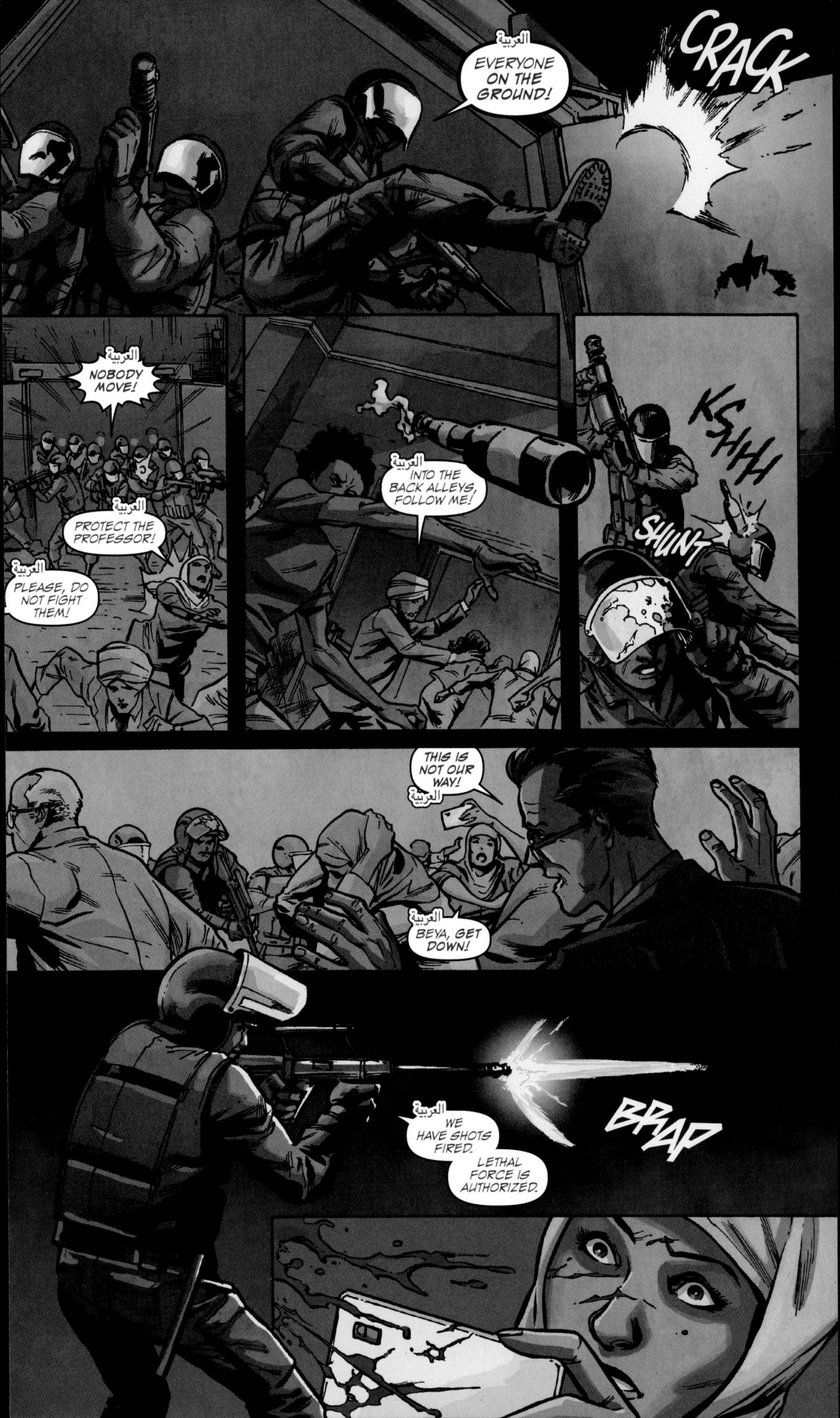

العربية
EVERYONE ON THE GROUND!
CRACK
العربية
NOBODY MOVE!
العربية
PROTECT THE PROFESSOR!
العربية
PLEASE, DO NOT FIGHT THEM!
العربية
INTO THE BACK ALLEYS, FOLLOW ME!
KSHHH
SHUNT
THIS IS NOT OUR WAY!
العربية
العربية
BEYA, GET DOWN!
العربية
WE HAVE SHOTS FIRED.
LETHAL FORCE IS AUTHORIZED.
BRAP

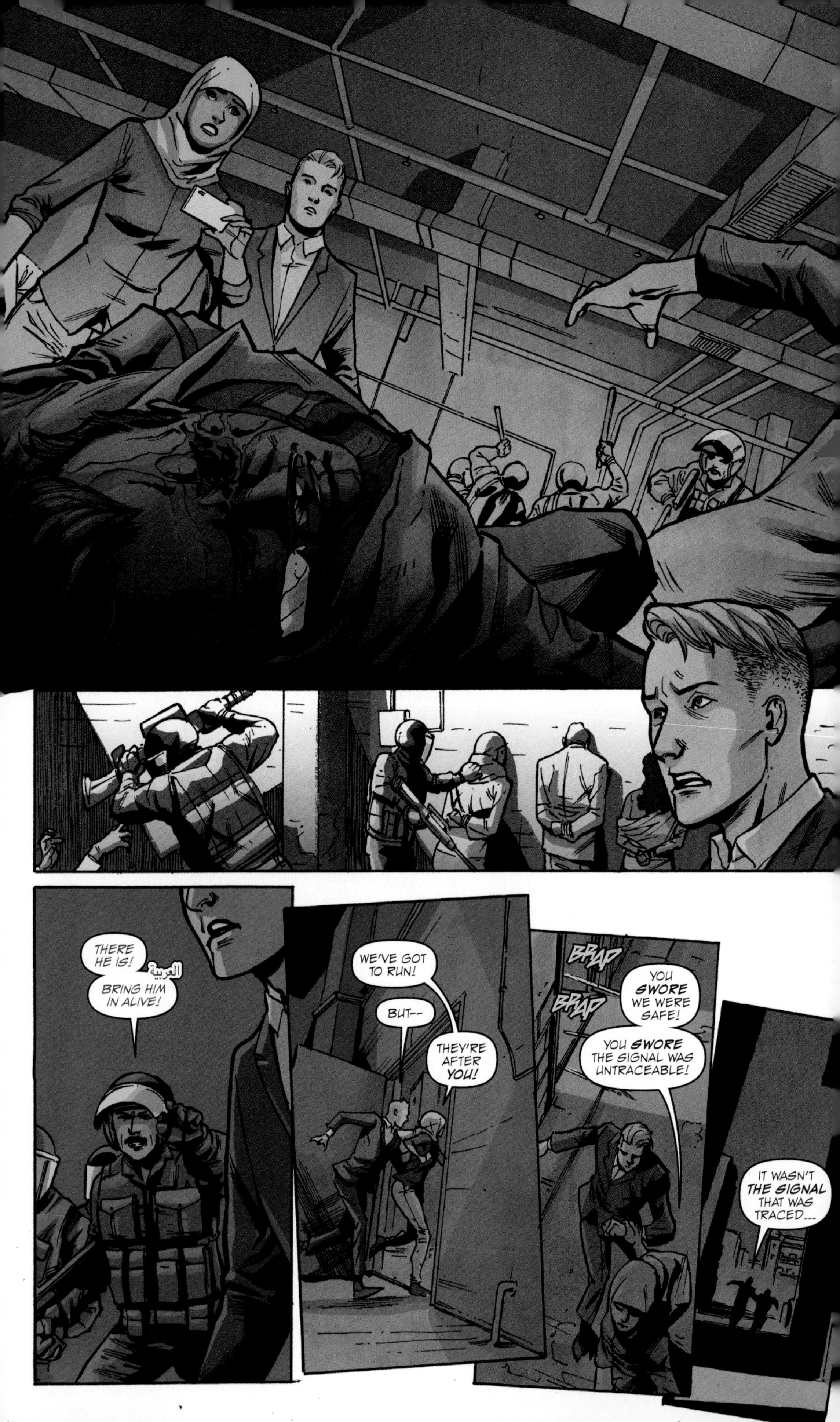
THERE HE IS!
العربية
BRING HIM IN ALIVE!
WE'VE GOT TO RUN!
BUT--
THEY'RE AFTER YOU!
BRAP
BRAP
YOU SWORE WE WERE SAFE!
YOU SWORE THE SIGNAL WAS UNTRACEABLE!
IT WASN'T THE SIGNAL THAT WAS TRACED...

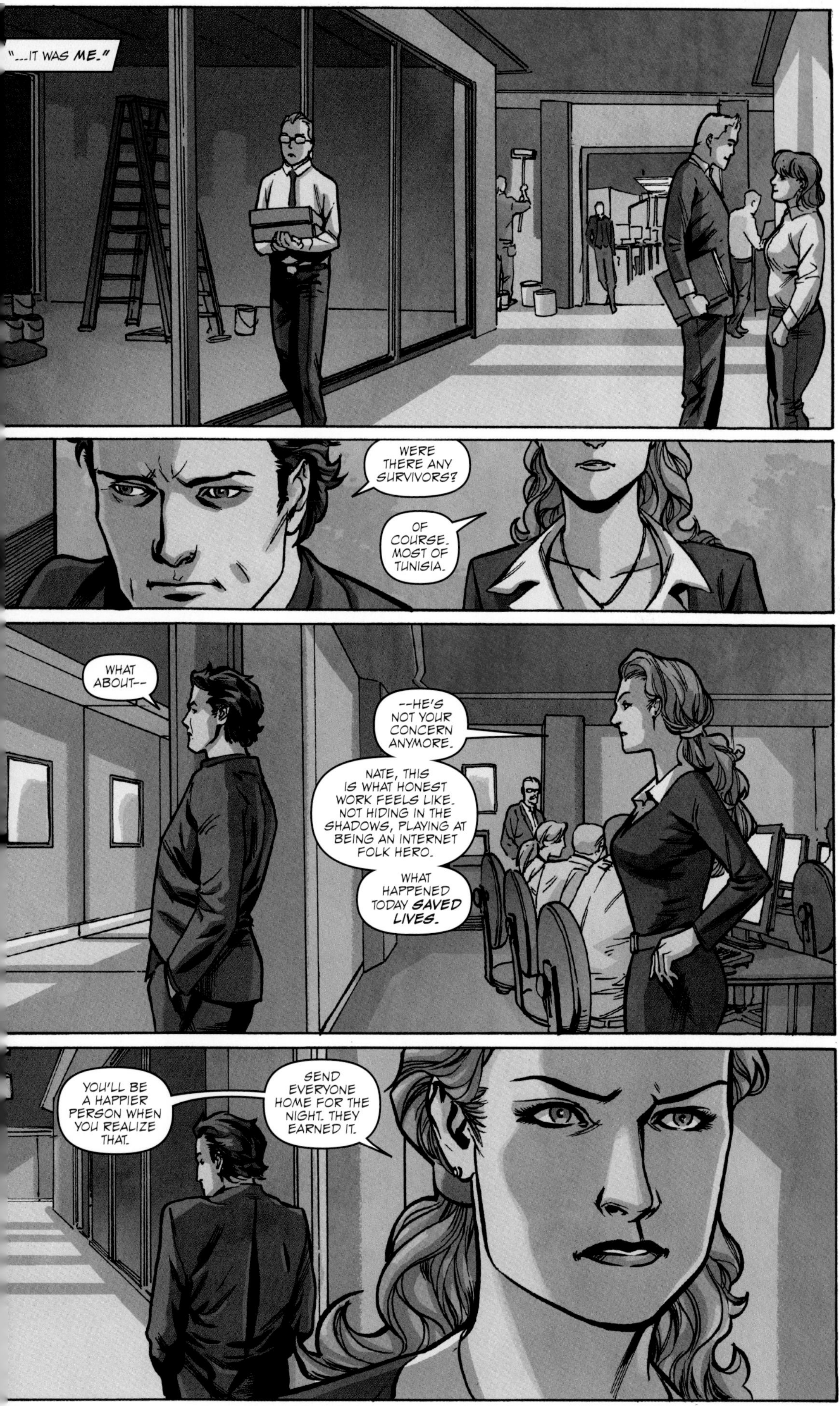
"...IT WAS ME."
WERE THERE ANY SURVIVORS?
OF COURSE. MOST OF TUNISIA.
WHAT ABOUT--
--HE'S NOT YOUR CONCERN ANYMORE.
NATE, THIS IS WHAT HONEST WORK FEELS LIKE. NOT HIDING IN THE SHADOWS, PLAYING AT BEING AN INTERNET FOLK HERO.
WHAT HAPPENED TODAY SAVED LIVES.
SEND EVERYONE HOME FOR THE NIGHT. THEY EARNED IT.
YOU'LL BE A HAPPIER PERSON WHEN YOU REALIZE THAT.

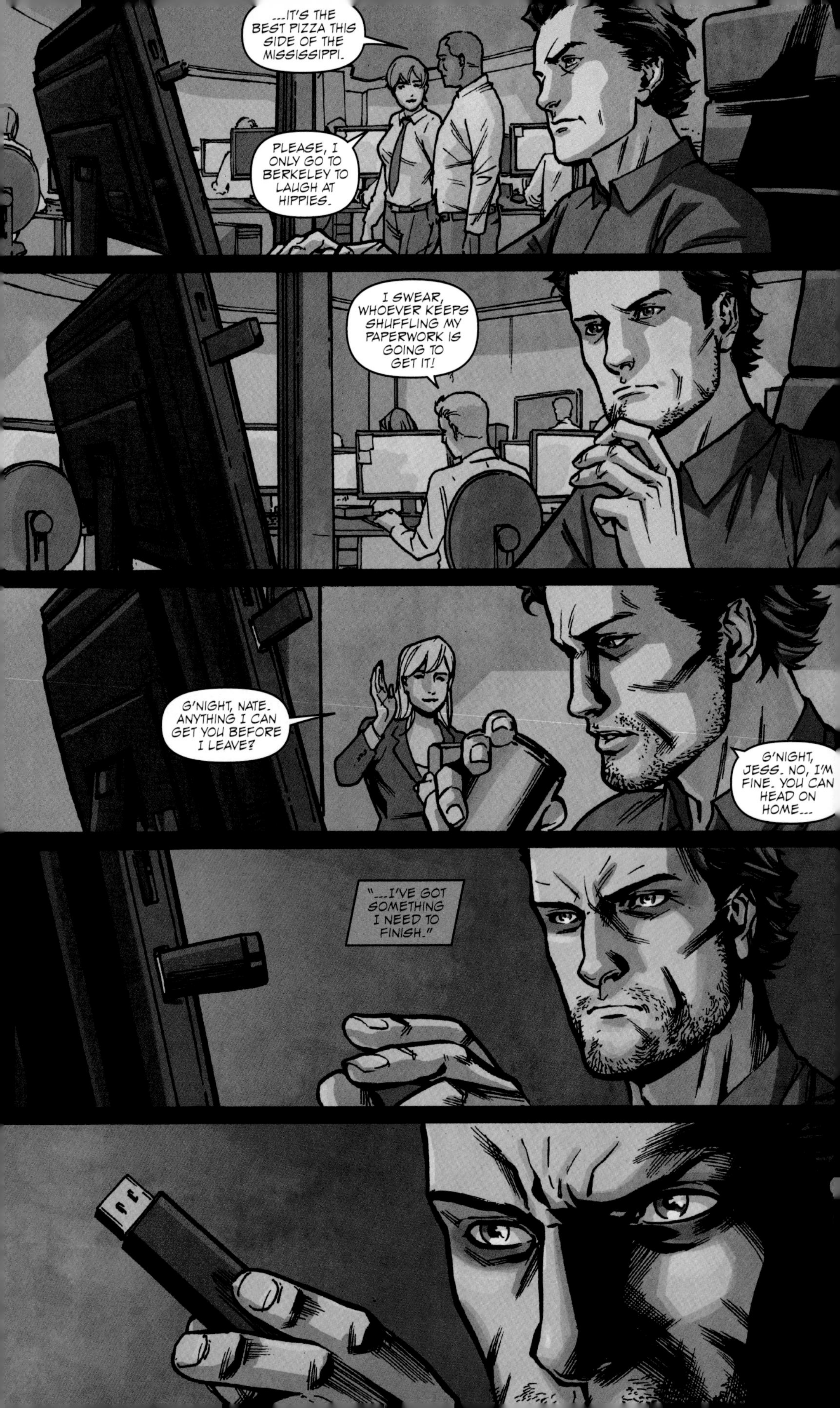

...IT'S THE BEST PIZZA THIS SIDE OF THE MISSISSIPPI.
PLEASE, I ONLY GO TO BERKELEY TO LAUGH AT HIPPIES.
I SWEAR, WHOEVER KEEPS SHUFFLING MY PAPERWORK IS GOING TO GET IT!
G'NIGHT, NATE. ANYTHING I CAN GET YOU BEFORE I LEAVE?
G'NIGHT, JESS. NO, I'M FINE. YOU CAN HEAD ON HOME...
"...I'VE GOT SOMETHING I NEED TO FINISH."

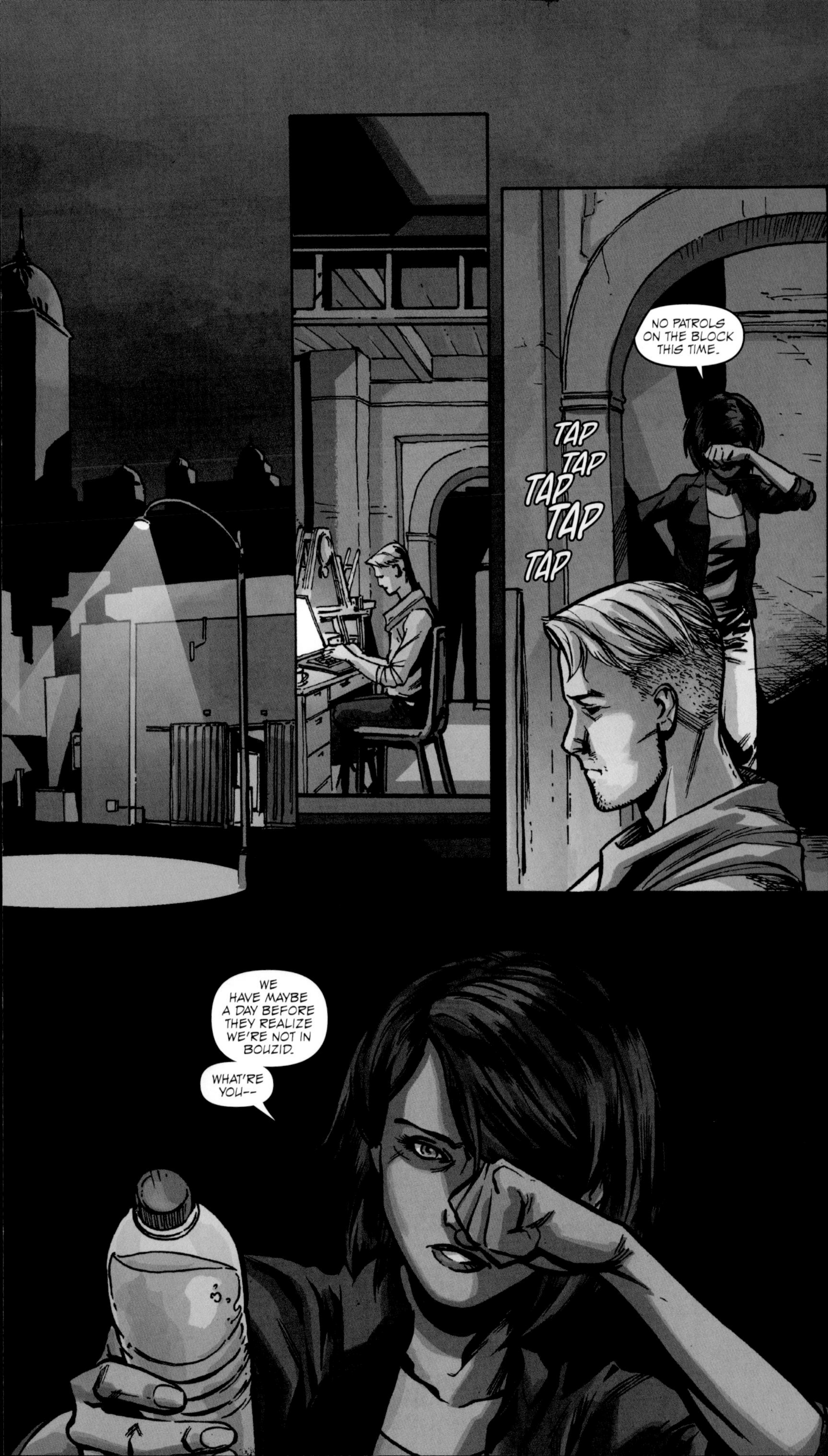
TAP
TAP
TAP
TAP
TAP
NO PATROLS ON THE BLOCK THIS TIME.
WE HAVE MAYBE A DAY BEFORE THEY REALIZE WE'RE NOT IN BOUZID.
WHAT'RE YOU--

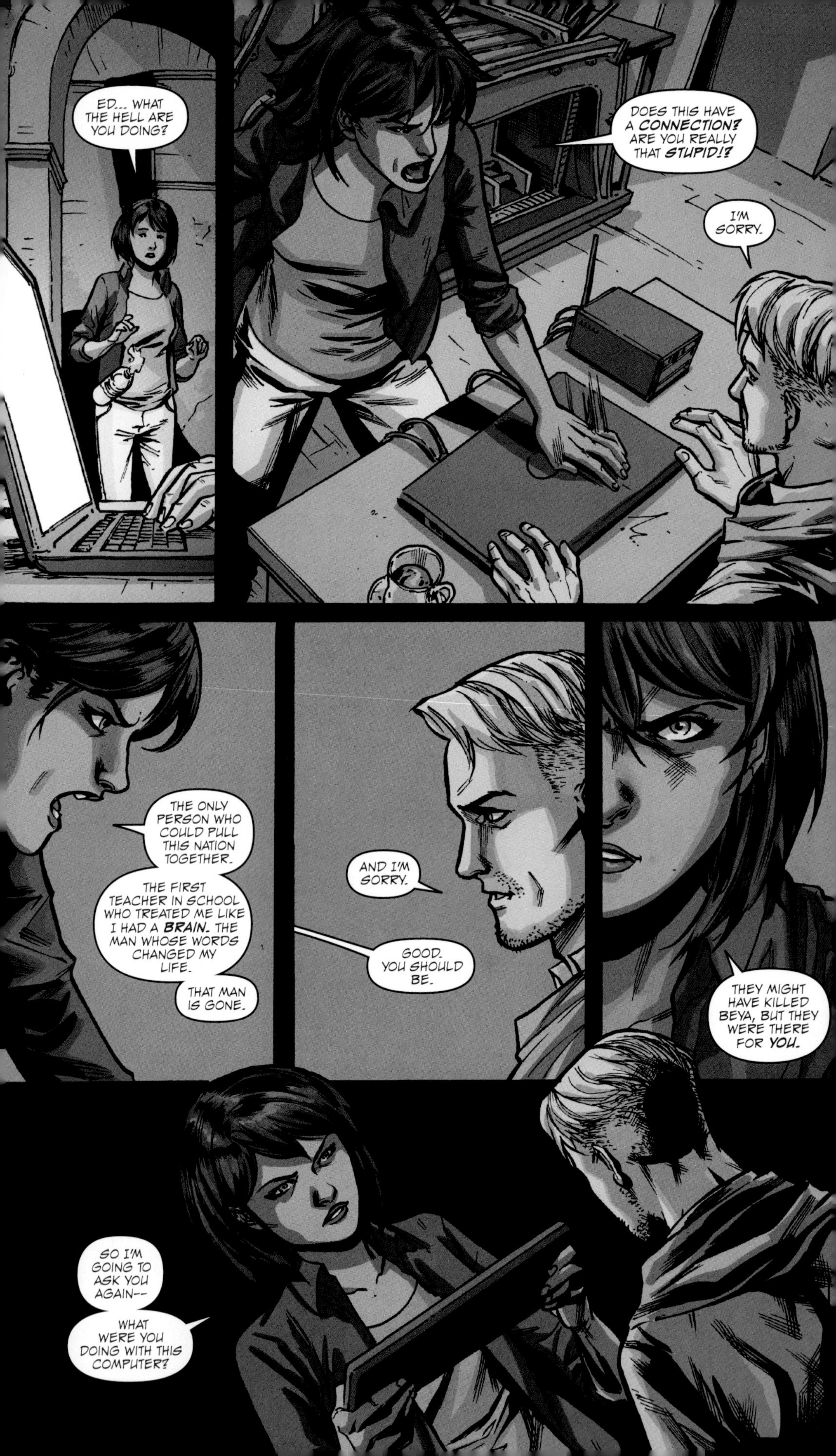
ED... WHAT THE HELL ARE YOU DOING?
DOES THIS HAVE A **CONNECTION?** ARE YOU REALLY THAT **STUPID!?**
I'M SORRY.
THE ONLY PERSON WHO COULD PULL THIS NATION TOGETHER.
THE FIRST TEACHER IN SCHOOL WHO TREATED ME LIKE I HAD A **BRAIN.** THE MAN WHOSE WORDS CHANGED MY LIFE.
THAT MAN IS GONE.
AND I'M SORRY.
GOOD. YOU SHOULD BE.
THEY MIGHT HAVE KILLED BEYA, BUT THEY WERE THERE FOR **YOU.**
SO I'M GOING TO ASK YOU AGAIN--
WHAT WERE YOU DOING WITH THIS COMPUTER?

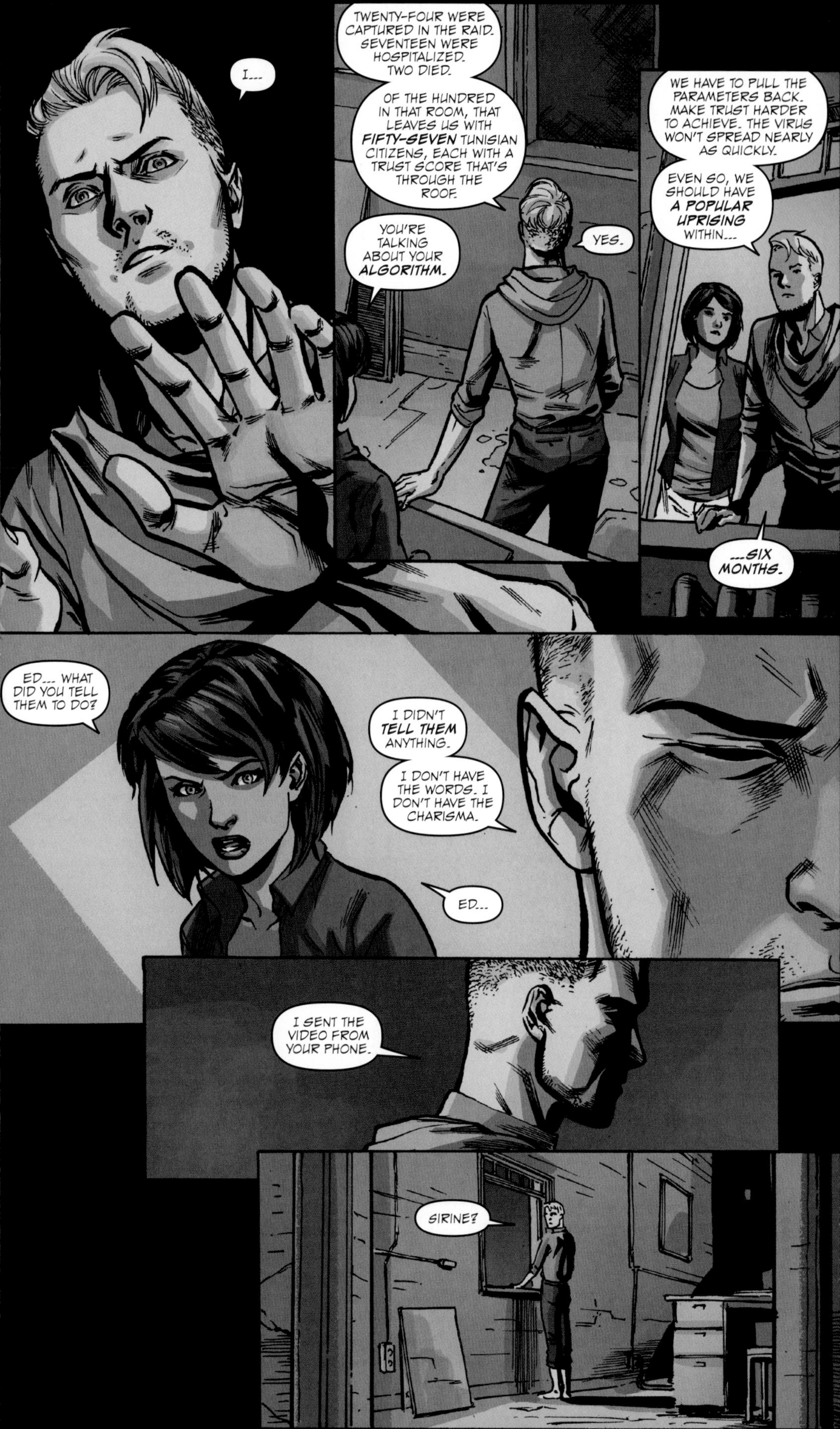

I---
TWENTY-FOUR WERE CAPTURED IN THE RAID. SEVENTEEN WERE HOSPITALIZED. TWO DIED.
OF THE HUNDRED IN THAT ROOM, THAT LEAVES US WITH FIFTY-SEVEN TUNISIAN CITIZENS, EACH WITH A TRUST SCORE THAT'S THROUGH THE ROOF.
YOU'RE TALKING ABOUT YOUR ALGORITHM.
YES.
WE HAVE TO PULL THE PARAMETERS BACK. MAKE TRUST HARDER TO ACHIEVE. THE VIRUS WON'T SPREAD NEARLY AS QUICKLY.
EVEN SO, WE SHOULD HAVE A POPULAR UPRISING WITHIN---
---SIX MONTHS.
ED--- WHAT DID YOU TELL THEM TO DO?
I DIDN'T TELL THEM ANYTHING.
I DON'T HAVE THE WORDS. I DON'T HAVE THE CHARISMA.
ED---
I SENT THE VIDEO FROM YOUR PHONE.
SIRINE?

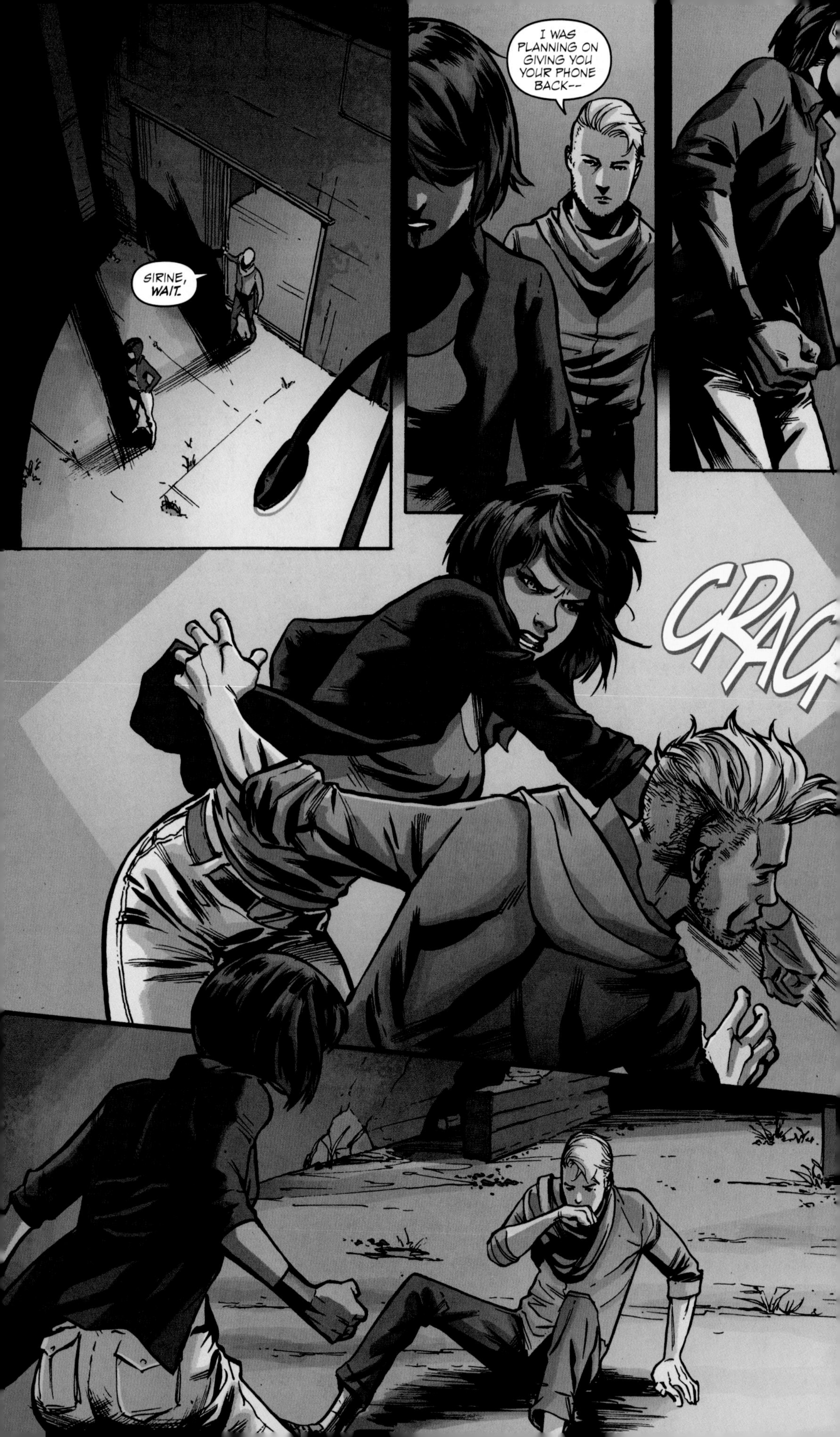
SIRINE, WAIT.
I WAS PLANNING ON GIVING YOU YOUR PHONE BACK--
CRACK

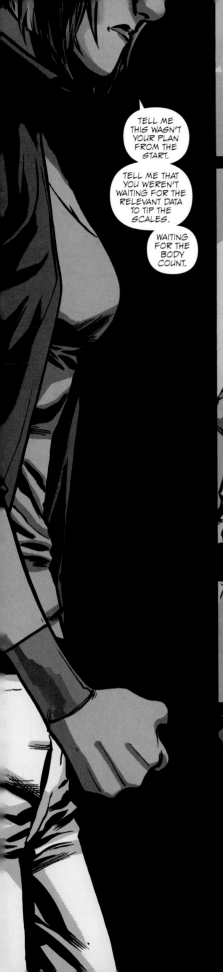

NO, I... NEVER.

TELL ME THIS WASN'T YOUR PLAN FROM THE START.

TELL ME THAT YOU WEREN'T WAITING FOR THE RELEVANT DATA TO TIP THE SCALES.

WAITING FOR THE BODY COUNT.

YOU USED *MY COUNTRY* LIKE A *PETRI DISH.*

WE TREATED YOU LIKE A BROTHER. WE TREATED YOU LIKE *FAMILY.*

AND YOU JUST *CONTROLLED* US. KEPT SECRETS. WE WEREN'T PEOPLE TO YOU, JUST NODES IN YOUR NETWORK.

...I JUST WANTED TO HELP YOU.

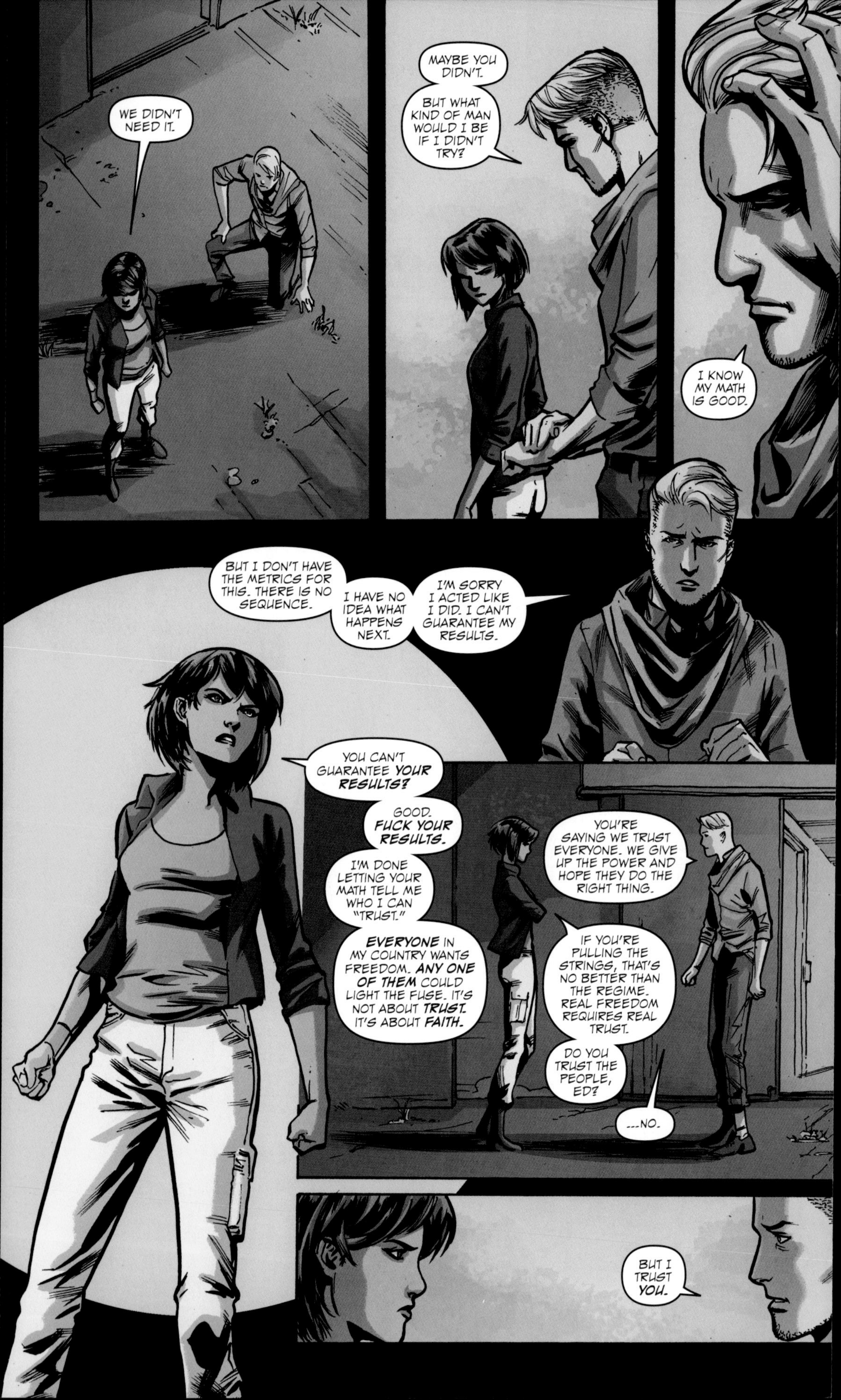
WE DIDN'T NEED IT.
MAYBE YOU DIDN'T.
BUT WHAT KIND OF MAN WOULD I BE IF I DIDN'T TRY?
I KNOW MY MATH IS GOOD.
BUT I DON'T HAVE THE METRICS FOR THIS. THERE IS NO SEQUENCE.
I HAVE NO IDEA WHAT HAPPENS NEXT.
I'M SORRY I ACTED LIKE I DID. I CAN'T GUARANTEE MY RESULTS.
YOU CAN'T GUARANTEE YOUR RESULTS?
GOOD. FUCK YOUR RESULTS.
I'M DONE LETTING YOUR MATH TELL ME WHO I CAN "TRUST."
EVERYONE IN MY COUNTRY WANTS FREEDOM. ANY ONE OF THEM COULD LIGHT THE FUSE. IT'S NOT ABOUT TRUST. IT'S ABOUT FAITH.
YOU'RE SAYING WE TRUST EVERYONE. WE GIVE UP THE POWER AND HOPE THEY DO THE RIGHT THING.
IF YOU'RE PULLING THE STRINGS, THAT'S NO BETTER THAN THE REGIME. REAL FREEDOM REQUIRES REAL TRUST.
DO YOU TRUST THE PEOPLE, ED?
...NO.
BUT I TRUST YOU.

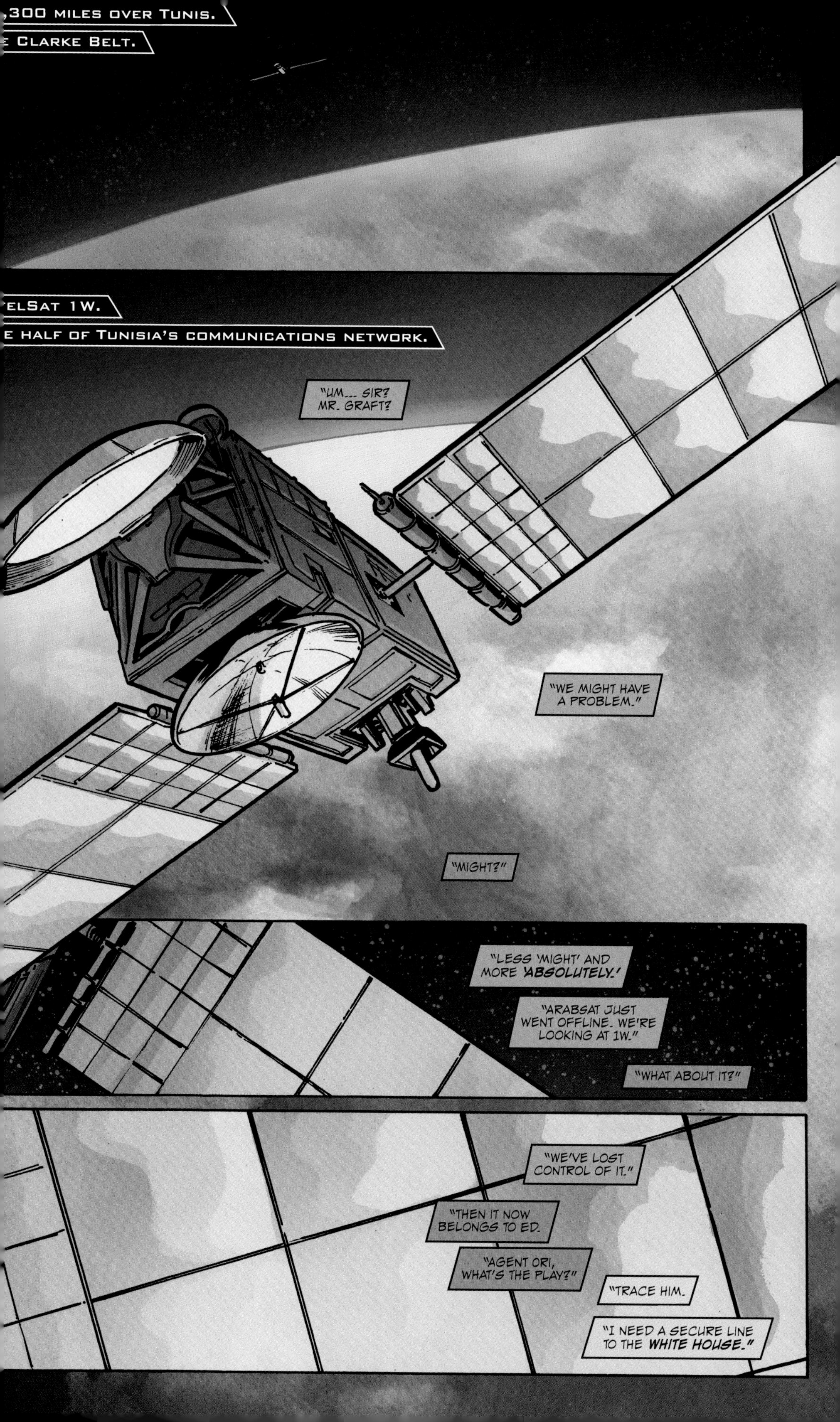
,300 MILES OVER TUNIS.
E CLARKE BELT.
ELSAT 1W.
E HALF OF TUNISIA'S COMMUNICATIONS NETWORK.
"UM... SIR? MR. GRAFT?
"WE MIGHT HAVE A PROBLEM."
"MIGHT?"
"LESS 'MIGHT' AND MORE 'ABSOLUTELY.'
"ARABSAT JUST WENT OFFLINE. WE'RE LOOKING AT 1W."
"WHAT ABOUT IT?"
"WE'VE LOST CONTROL OF IT."
"THEN IT NOW BELONGS TO ED.
"AGENT ORI, WHAT'S THE PLAY?"
"TRACE HIM.
"I NEED A SECURE LINE TO THE WHITE HOUSE."

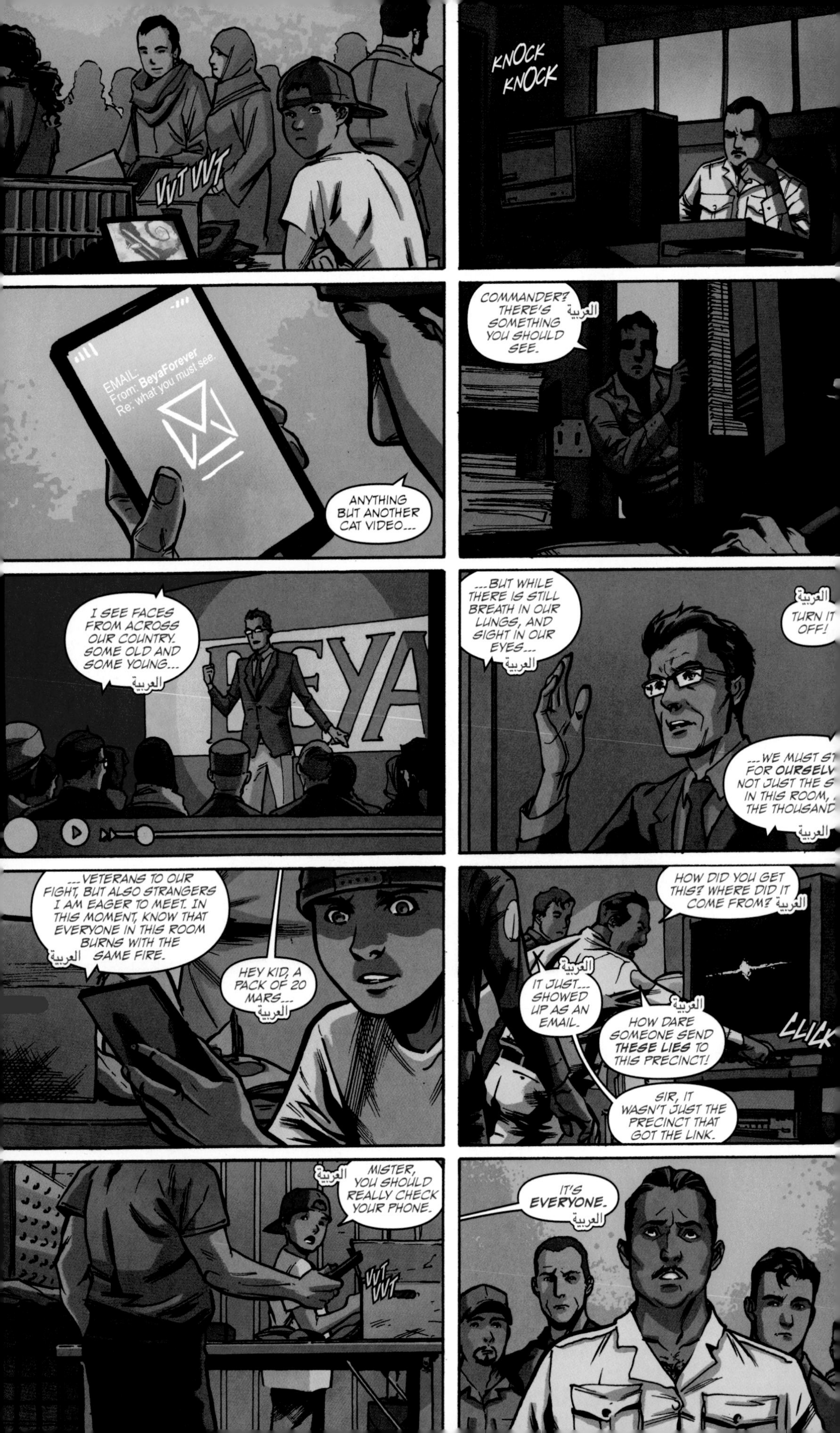
VVT VVT
KNOCK KNOCK
EMAIL:
From: BeyaForever
Re: what you must see.
ANYTHING BUT ANOTHER CAT VIDEO...
COMMANDER? THERE'S SOMETHING YOU SHOULD SEE. العربية
I SEE FACES FROM ACROSS OUR COUNTRY. SOME OLD AND SOME YOUNG... العربية
BEYA
...BUT WHILE THERE IS STILL BREATH IN OUR LUNGS, AND SIGHT IN OUR EYES... العربية
العربية TURN IT OFF!
...WE MUST S FOR OURSELV NOT JUST THE IN THIS ROOM, THE THOUSAND العربية
...VETERANS TO OUR FIGHT, BUT ALSO STRANGERS I AM EAGER TO MEET. IN THIS MOMENT, KNOW THAT EVERYONE IN THIS ROOM BURNS WITH THE SAME FIRE. العربية
HEY KID, A PACK OF 20 MARS... العربية
HOW DID YOU GET THIS? WHERE DID IT COME FROM? العربية
العربية IT JUST... SHOWED UP AS AN EMAIL.
العربية HOW DARE SOMEONE SEND THESE LIES TO THIS PRECINCT!
CLICK
SIR, IT WASN'T JUST THE PRECINCT THAT GOT THE LINK.
العربية MISTER, YOU SHOULD REALLY CHECK YOUR PHONE.
VVT VVT
IT'S EVERYONE. العربية

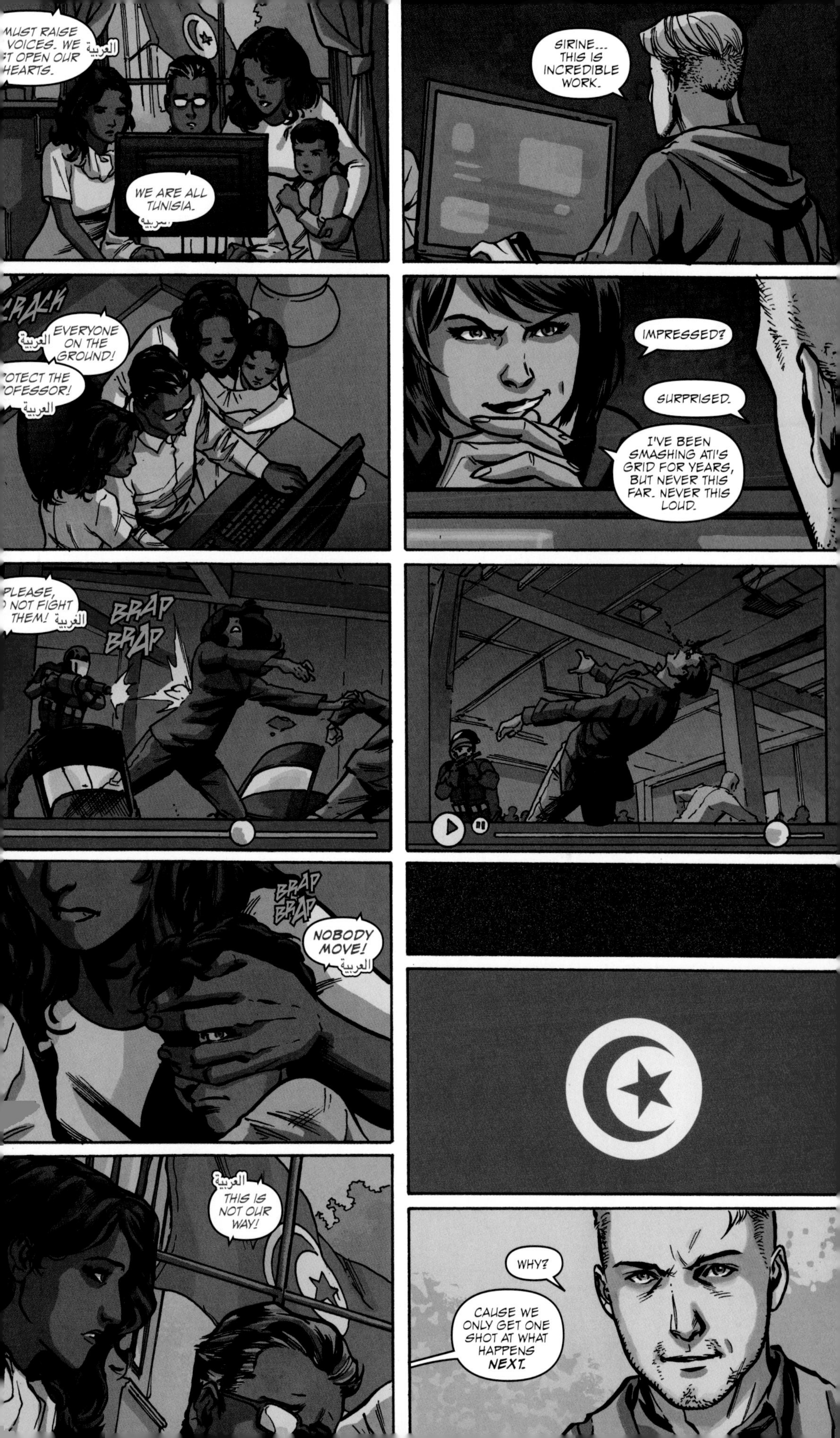
MUST RAISE VOICES. WE T OPEN OUR HEARTS.
العربية
WE ARE ALL TUNISIA.
SIRINE... THIS IS INCREDIBLE WORK.
CRACK
EVERYONE ON THE GROUND!
العربية
OTECT THE OFESSOR!
العربية
IMPRESSED?
SURPRISED.
I'VE BEEN SMASHING ATI'S GRID FOR YEARS, BUT NEVER THIS FAR. NEVER THIS LOUD.
PLEASE, NOT FIGHT THEM!
العربية
BRAP BRAP
BRAP BRAP
NOBODY MOVE!
العربية
العربية
THIS IS NOT OUR WAY!
WHY?
CAUSE WE ONLY GET ONE SHOT AT WHAT HAPPENS NEXT.

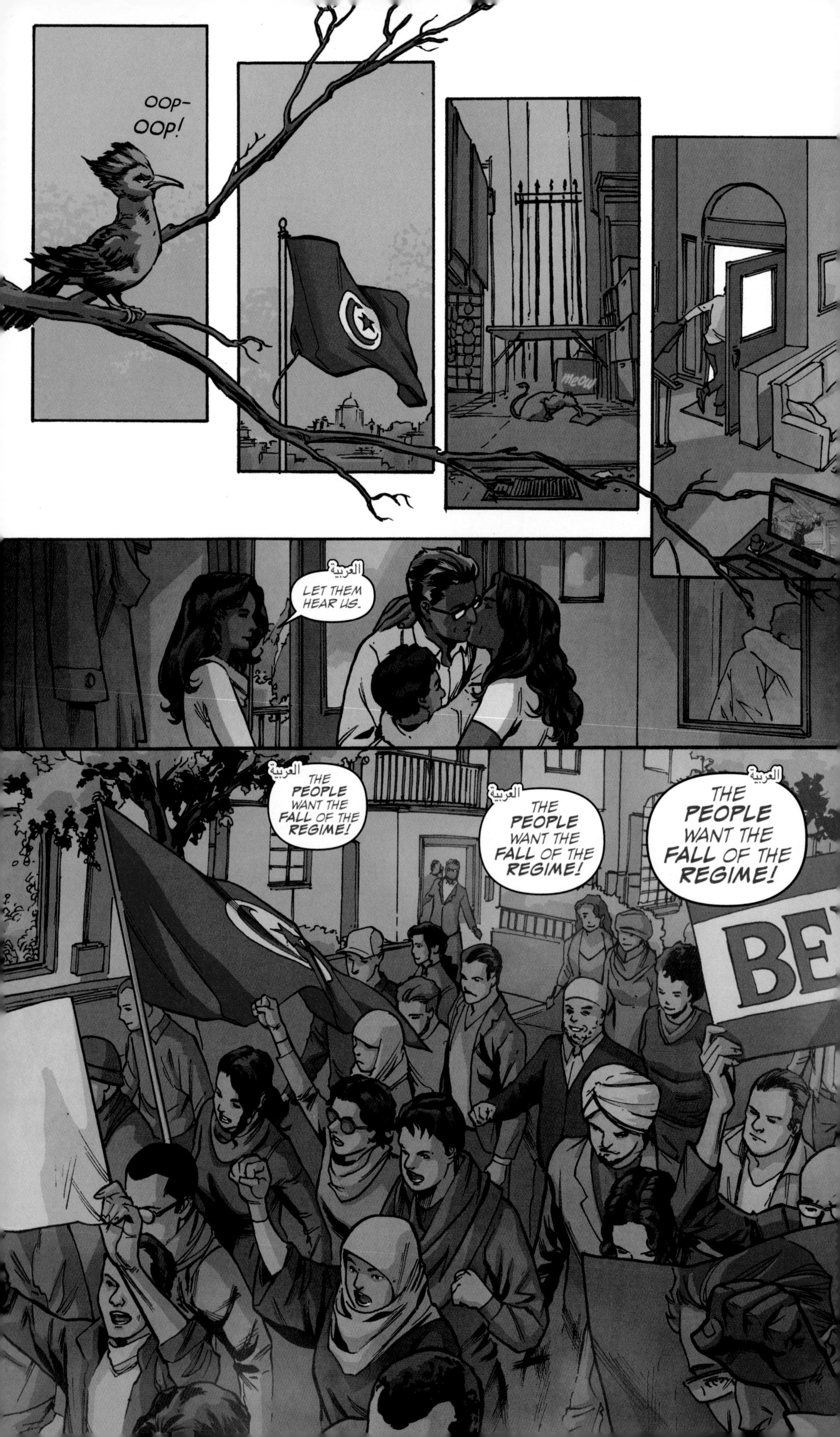
OOP-
OOP!
MEOW
العربية
LET THEM HEAR US.
العربية
THE PEOPLE WANT THE FALL OF THE REGIME!
العربية
THE PEOPLE WANT THE FALL OF THE REGIME!
العربية
THE PEOPLE WANT THE FALL OF THE REGIME!
BE

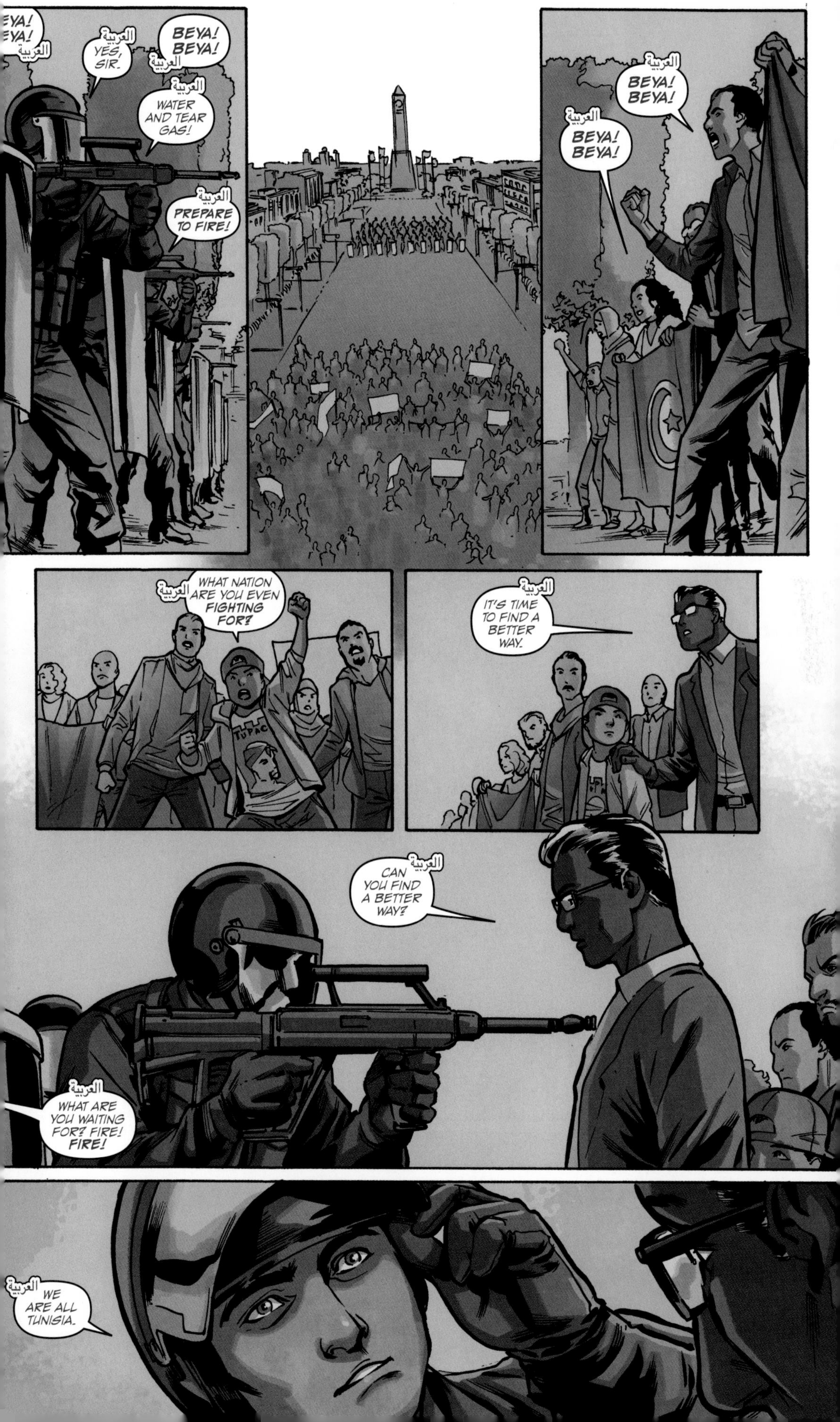

العربية
-EYA! -EYA!
العربية
YES, SIR.
العربية
BEYA! BEYA!
العربية
WATER AND TEAR GAS!
العربية
PREPARE TO FIRE!
العربية
BEYA! BEYA!
العربية
BEYA! BEYA!
العربية
WHAT NATION ARE YOU EVEN FIGHTING FOR?
TUPAC
العربية
IT'S TIME TO FIND A BETTER WAY.
العربية
CAN YOU FIND A BETTER WAY?
العربية
WHAT ARE YOU WAITING FOR? FIRE! FIRE!
العربية
WE ARE ALL TUNISIA.

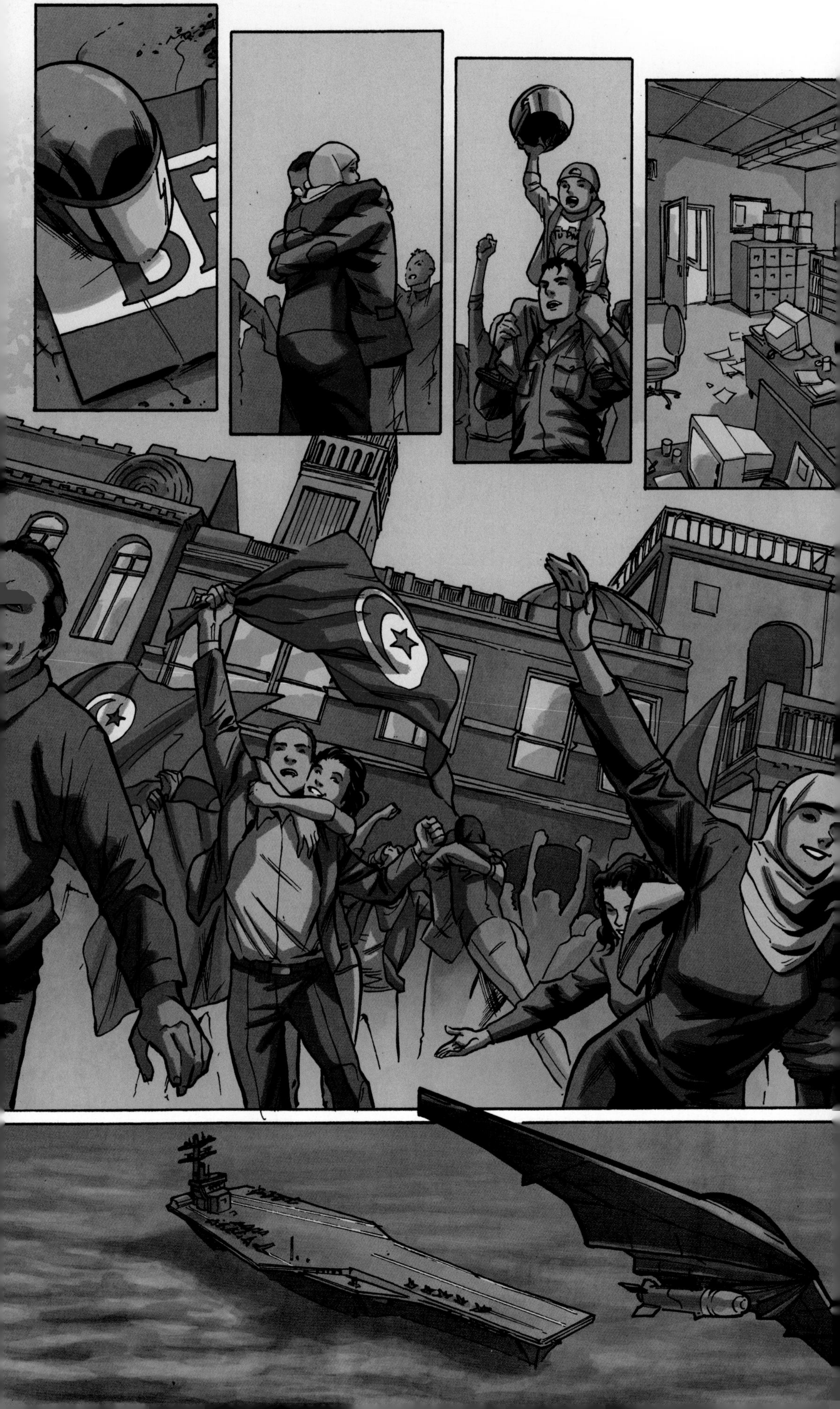

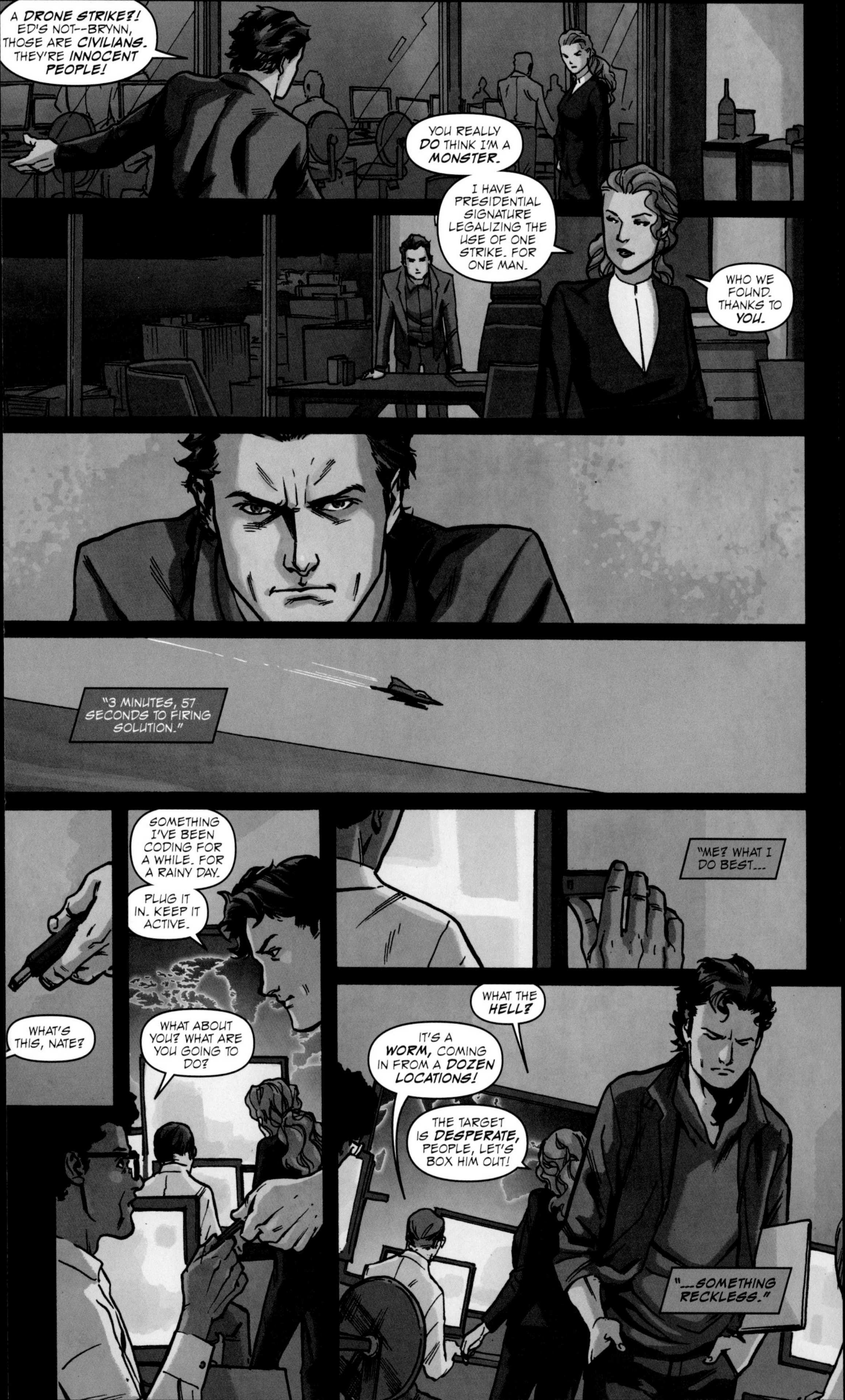
A DRONE STRIKE?! ED'S NOT--BRYNN, THOSE ARE CIVILIANS. THEY'RE INNOCENT PEOPLE!
YOU REALLY DO THINK I'M A MONSTER.
I HAVE A PRESIDENTIAL SIGNATURE LEGALIZING THE USE OF ONE STRIKE. FOR ONE MAN.
WHO WE FOUND. THANKS TO YOU.
"3 MINUTES, 57 SECONDS TO FIRING SOLUTION."
SOMETHING I'VE BEEN CODING FOR A WHILE. FOR A RAINY DAY.
PLUG IT IN. KEEP IT ACTIVE.
WHAT'S THIS, NATE?
WHAT ABOUT YOU? WHAT ARE YOU GOING TO DO?
"ME? WHAT I DO BEST...
WHAT THE HELL?
IT'S A WORM, COMING IN FROM A DOZEN LOCATIONS!
THE TARGET IS DESPERATE, PEOPLE, LET'S BOX HIM OUT!
"...SOMETHING RECKLESS."

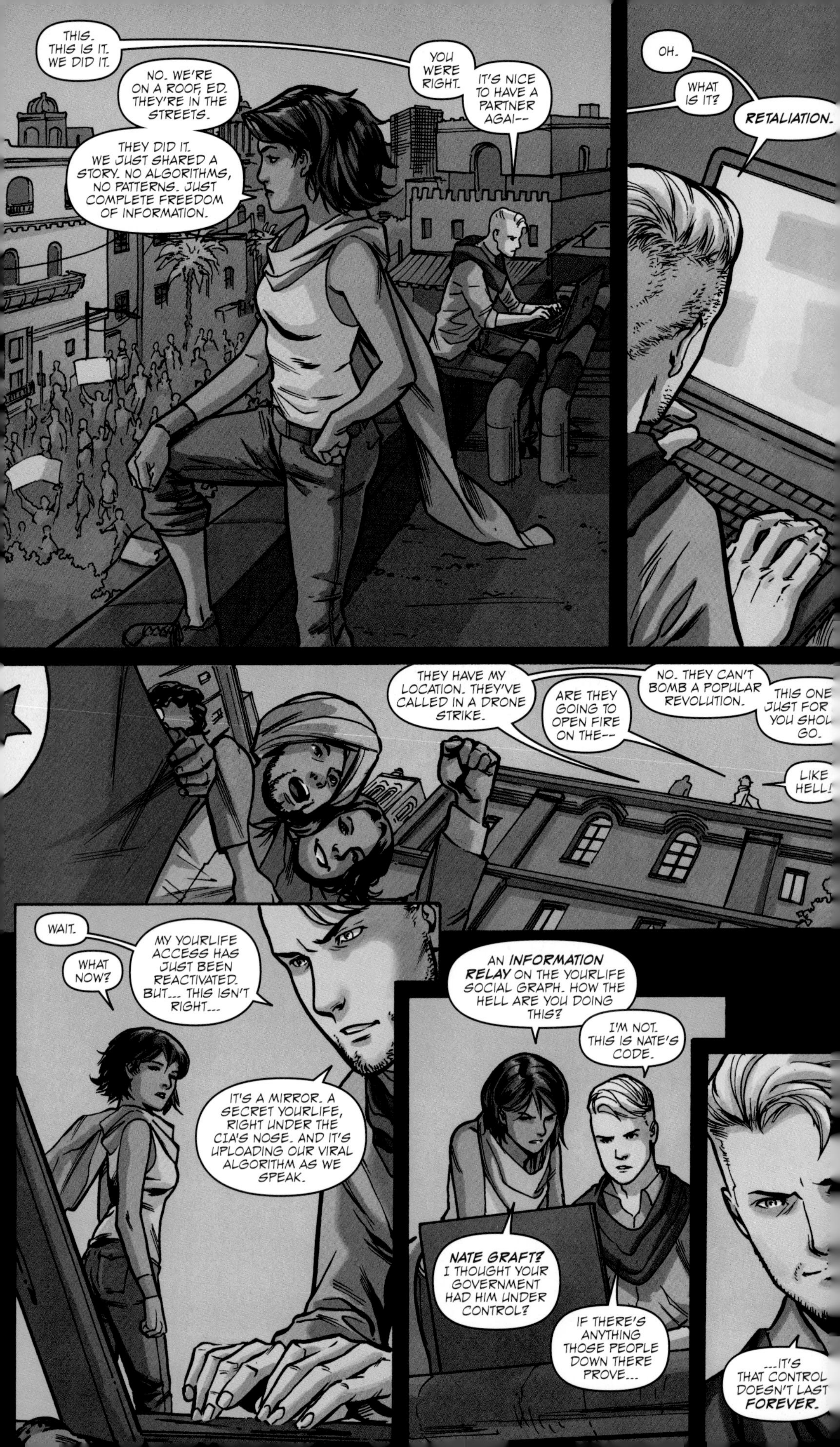
THIS. THIS IS IT. WE DID IT.
NO. WE'RE ON A ROOF, ED. THEY'RE IN THE STREETS.
THEY DID IT. WE JUST SHARED A STORY. NO ALGORITHMS, NO PATTERNS. JUST COMPLETE FREEDOM OF INFORMATION.
YOU WERE RIGHT.
IT'S NICE TO HAVE A PARTNER AGAI--
OH.
WHAT IS IT?
RETALIATION.
THEY HAVE MY LOCATION. THEY'VE CALLED IN A DRONE STRIKE.
ARE THEY GOING TO OPEN FIRE ON THE--
NO. THEY CAN'T BOMB A POPULAR REVOLUTION.
THIS ONE JUST FOR YOU SHOU GO.
LIKE HELL!
WAIT.
WHAT NOW?
MY YOURLIFE ACCESS HAS JUST BEEN REACTIVATED. BUT... THIS ISN'T RIGHT...
IT'S A MIRROR. A SECRET YOURLIFE, RIGHT UNDER THE CIA'S NOSE. AND IT'S UPLOADING OUR VIRAL ALGORITHM AS WE SPEAK.
AN INFORMATION RELAY ON THE YOURLIFE SOCIAL GRAPH. HOW THE HELL ARE YOU DOING THIS?
I'M NOT. THIS IS NATE'S CODE.
NATE GRAFT? I THOUGHT YOUR GOVERNMENT HAD HIM UNDER CONTROL?
IF THERE'S ANYTHING THOSE PEOPLE DOWN THERE PROVE...
...IT'S THAT CONTROL DOESN'T LAST FOREVER.

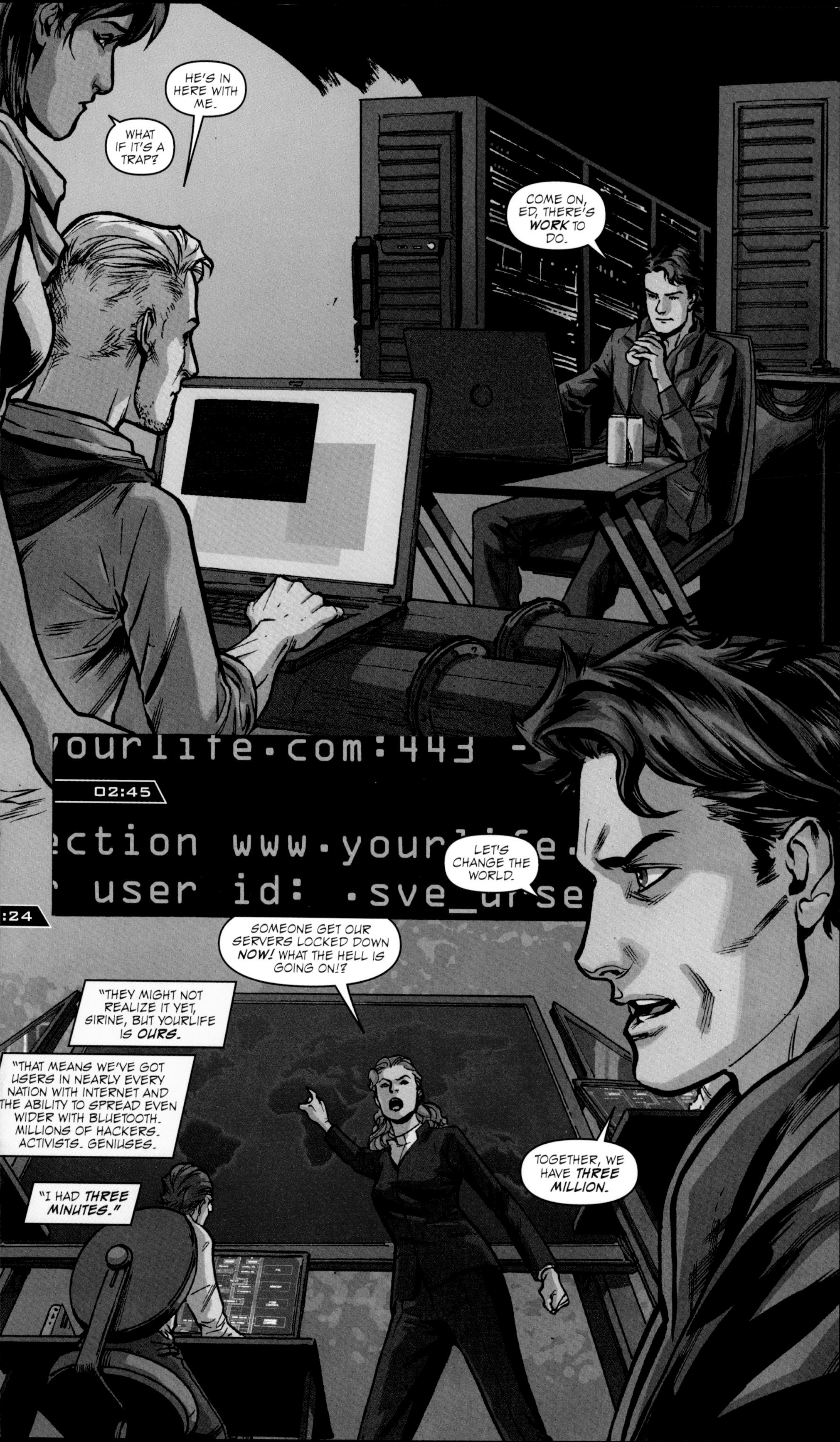
WHAT IF IT'S A TRAP?
HE'S IN HERE WITH ME.
COME ON, ED, THERE'S WORK TO DO.
yourlife.com:443 -
02:45
ection www.yourlife.
user id: .sve_urse
LET'S CHANGE THE WORLD.
:24
SOMEONE GET OUR SERVERS LOCKED DOWN NOW! WHAT THE HELL IS GOING ON!?
"THEY MIGHT NOT REALIZE IT YET, SIRINE, BUT YOURLIFE IS OURS.
"THAT MEANS WE'VE GOT USERS IN NEARLY EVERY NATION WITH INTERNET AND THE ABILITY TO SPREAD EVEN WIDER WITH BLUETOOTH. MILLIONS OF HACKERS. ACTIVISTS. GENIUSES.
"I HAD THREE MINUTES."
TOGETHER, WE HAVE THREE MILLION.

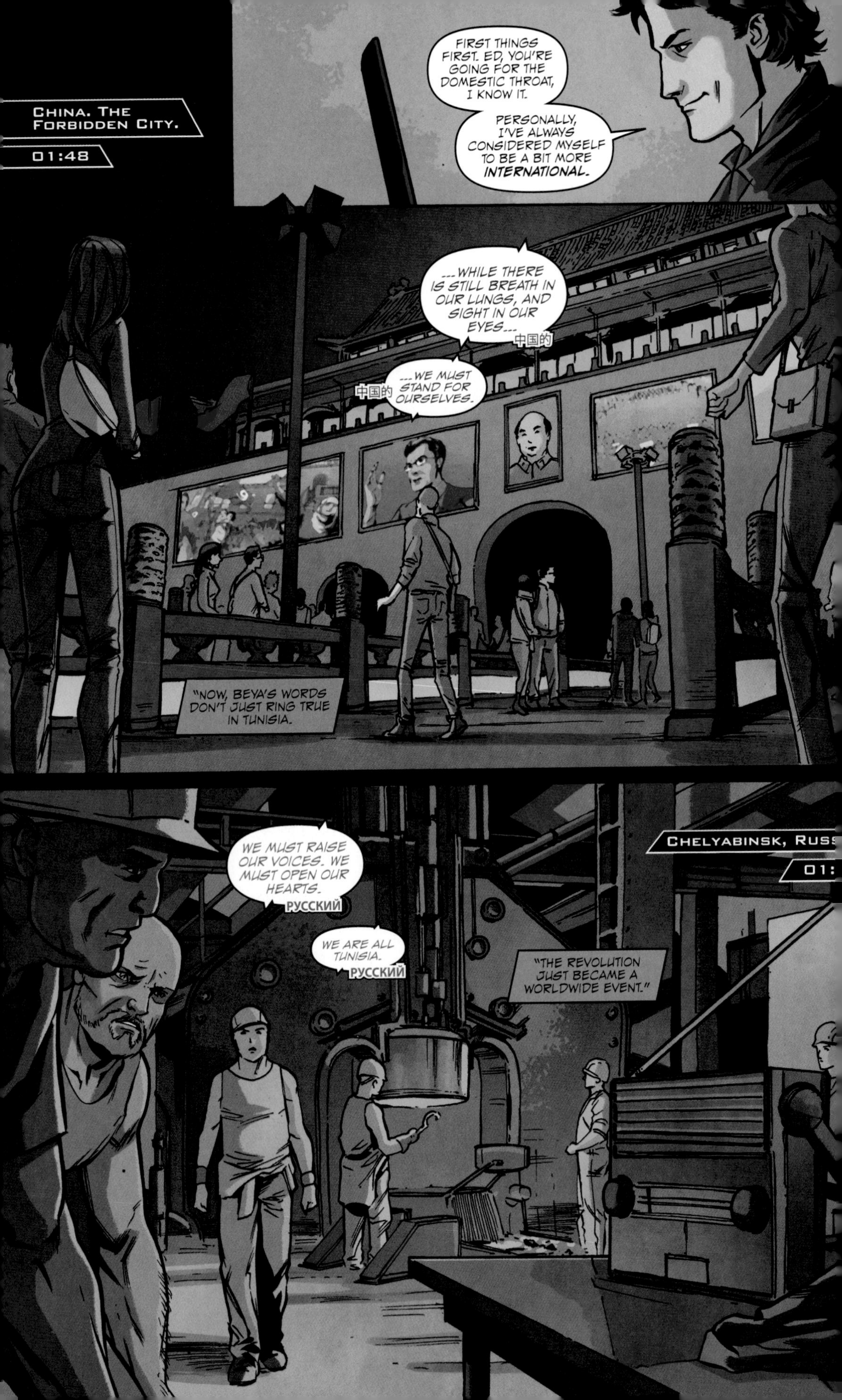

CHINA. THE FORBIDDEN CITY.
01:48
FIRST THINGS FIRST. ED, YOU'RE GOING FOR THE DOMESTIC THROAT, I KNOW IT.
PERSONALLY, I'VE ALWAYS CONSIDERED MYSELF TO BE A BIT MORE INTERNATIONAL.
...WHILE THERE IS STILL BREATH IN OUR LUNGS, AND SIGHT IN OUR EYES...
中国的
...WE MUST STAND FOR OURSELVES.
中国的
"NOW, BEYA'S WORDS DON'T JUST RING TRUE IN TUNISIA.
CHELYABINSK, RUSS
01:
WE MUST RAISE OUR VOICES. WE MUST OPEN OUR HEARTS.
РУССКИЙ
WE ARE ALL TUNISIA.
РУССКИЙ
"THE REVOLUTION JUST BECAME A WORLDWIDE EVENT."

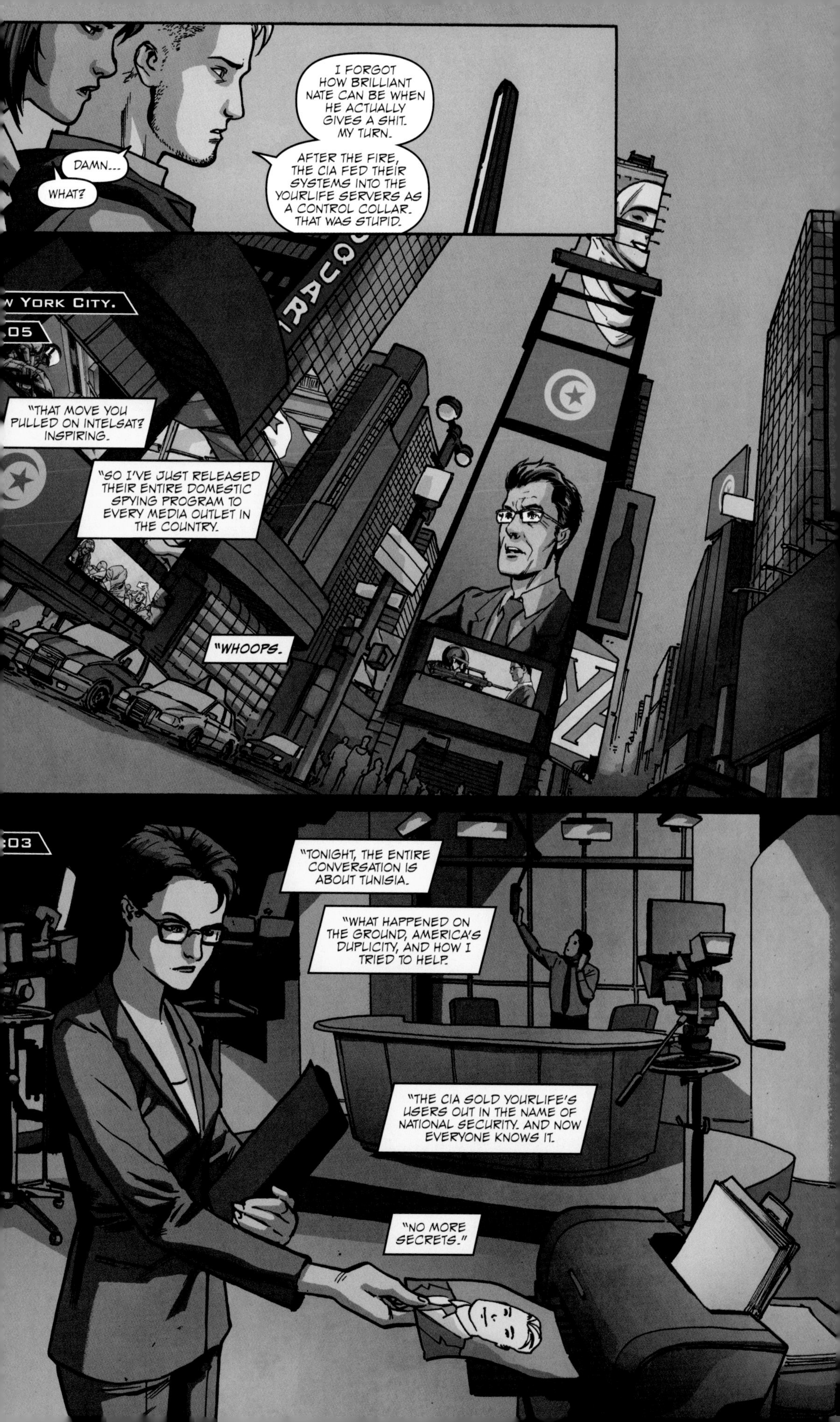
I FORGOT HOW BRILLIANT NATE CAN BE WHEN HE ACTUALLY GIVES A SHIT. MY TURN.
DAMN...
WHAT?
AFTER THE FIRE, THE CIA FED THEIR SYSTEMS INTO THE YOURLIFE SERVERS AS A CONTROL COLLAR. THAT WAS STUPID.
W YORK CITY.
05
"THAT MOVE YOU PULLED ON INTELSAT? INSPIRING.
"SO I'VE JUST RELEASED THEIR ENTIRE DOMESTIC SPYING PROGRAM TO EVERY MEDIA OUTLET IN THE COUNTRY.
"WHOOPS.
03
"TONIGHT, THE ENTIRE CONVERSATION IS ABOUT TUNISIA.
"WHAT HAPPENED ON THE GROUND, AMERICA'S DUPLICITY, AND HOW I TRIED TO HELP.
"THE CIA SOLD YOURLIFE'S USERS OUT IN THE NAME OF NATIONAL SECURITY. AND NOW EVERYONE KNOWS IT.
"NO MORE SECRETS."

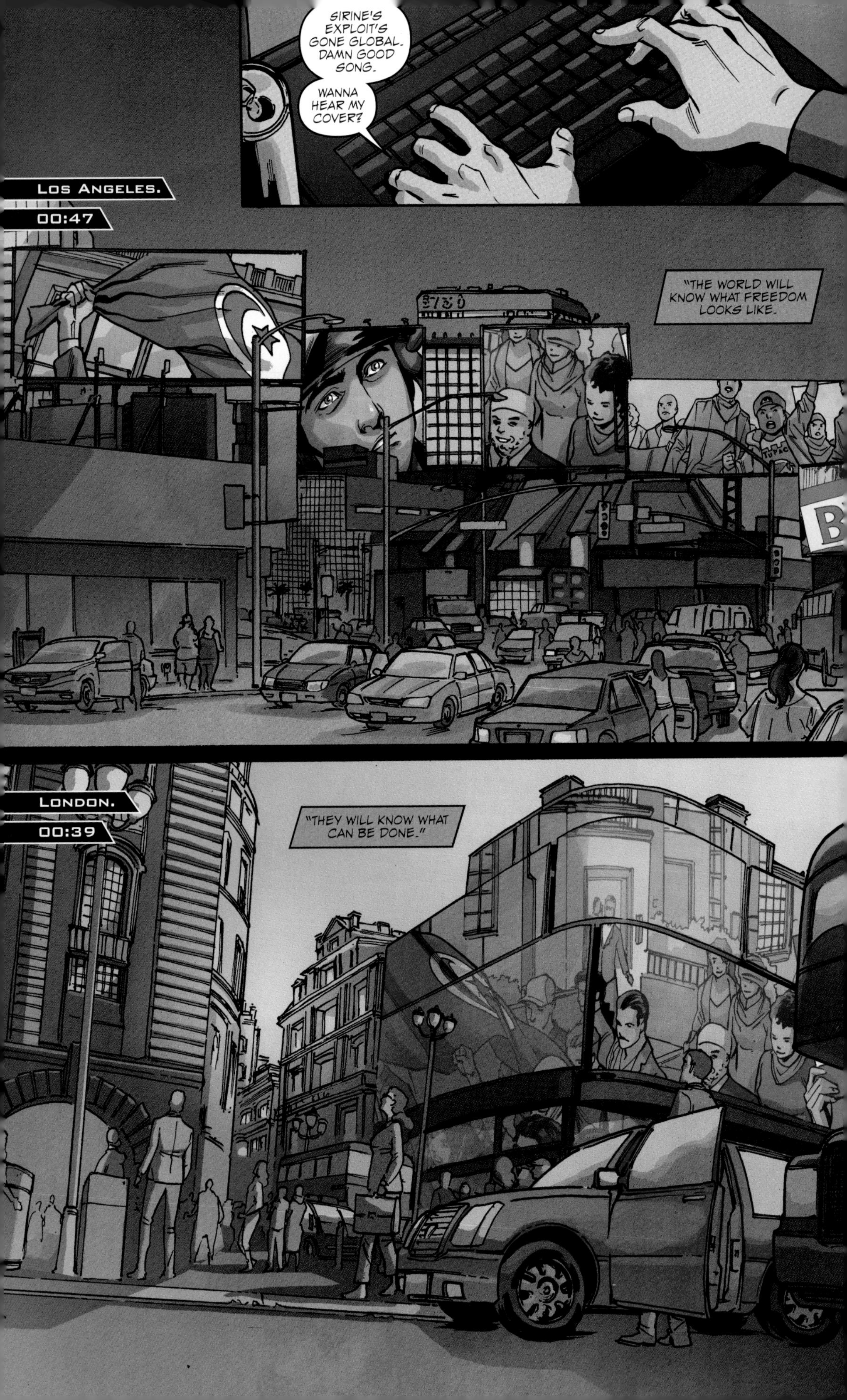
SIRINE'S EXPLOIT'S GONE GLOBAL. DAMN GOOD SONG.
WANNA HEAR MY COVER?
LOS ANGELES.
00:47
"THE WORLD WILL KNOW WHAT FREEDOM LOOKS LIKE.
LONDON.
00:39
"THEY WILL KNOW WHAT CAN BE DONE."

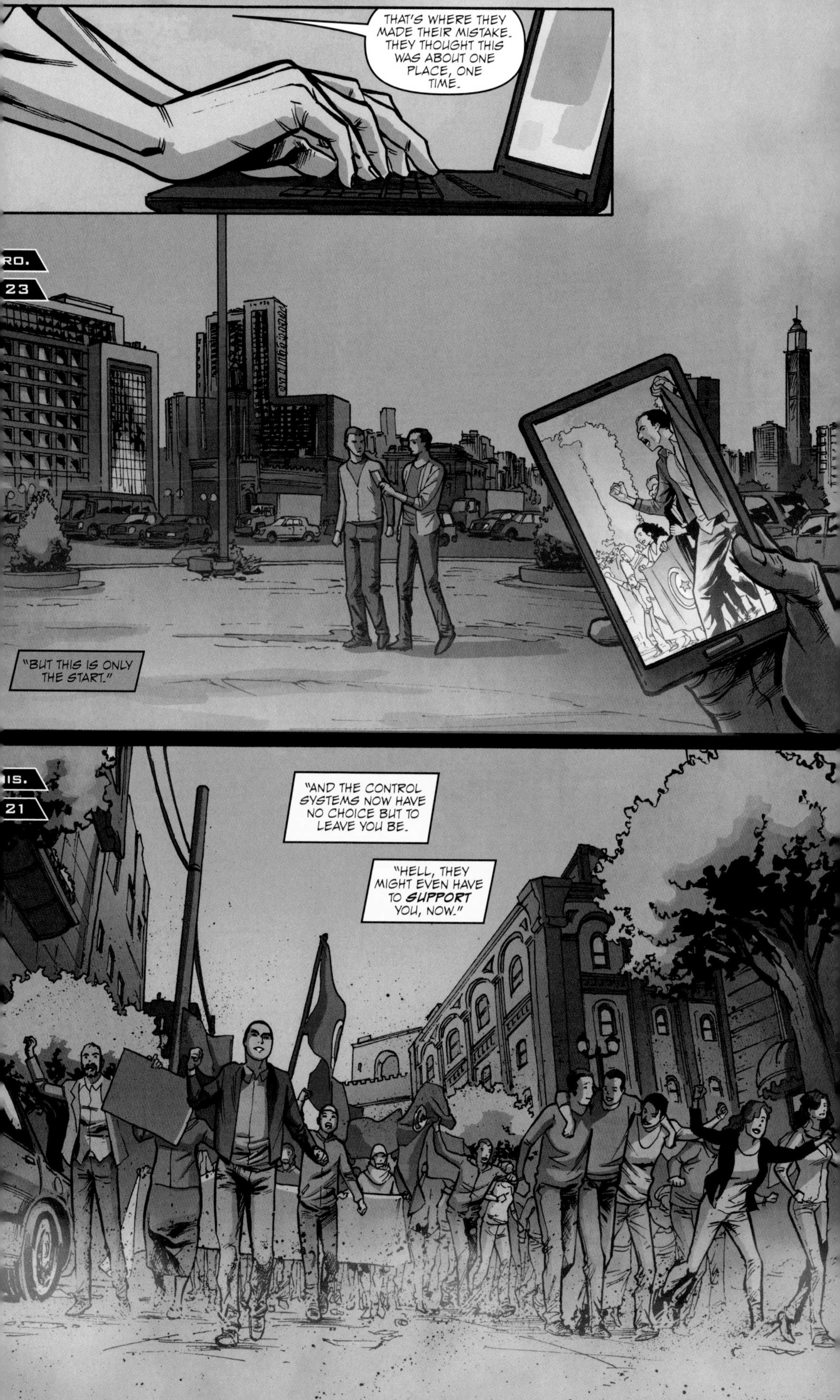
THAT'S WHERE THEY MADE THEIR MISTAKE. THEY THOUGHT THIS WAS ABOUT ONE PLACE, ONE TIME.
"BUT THIS IS ONLY THE START."
"AND THE CONTROL SYSTEMS NOW HAVE NO CHOICE BUT TO LEAVE YOU BE.
"HELL, THEY MIGHT EVEN HAVE TO *SUPPORT* YOU, NOW."

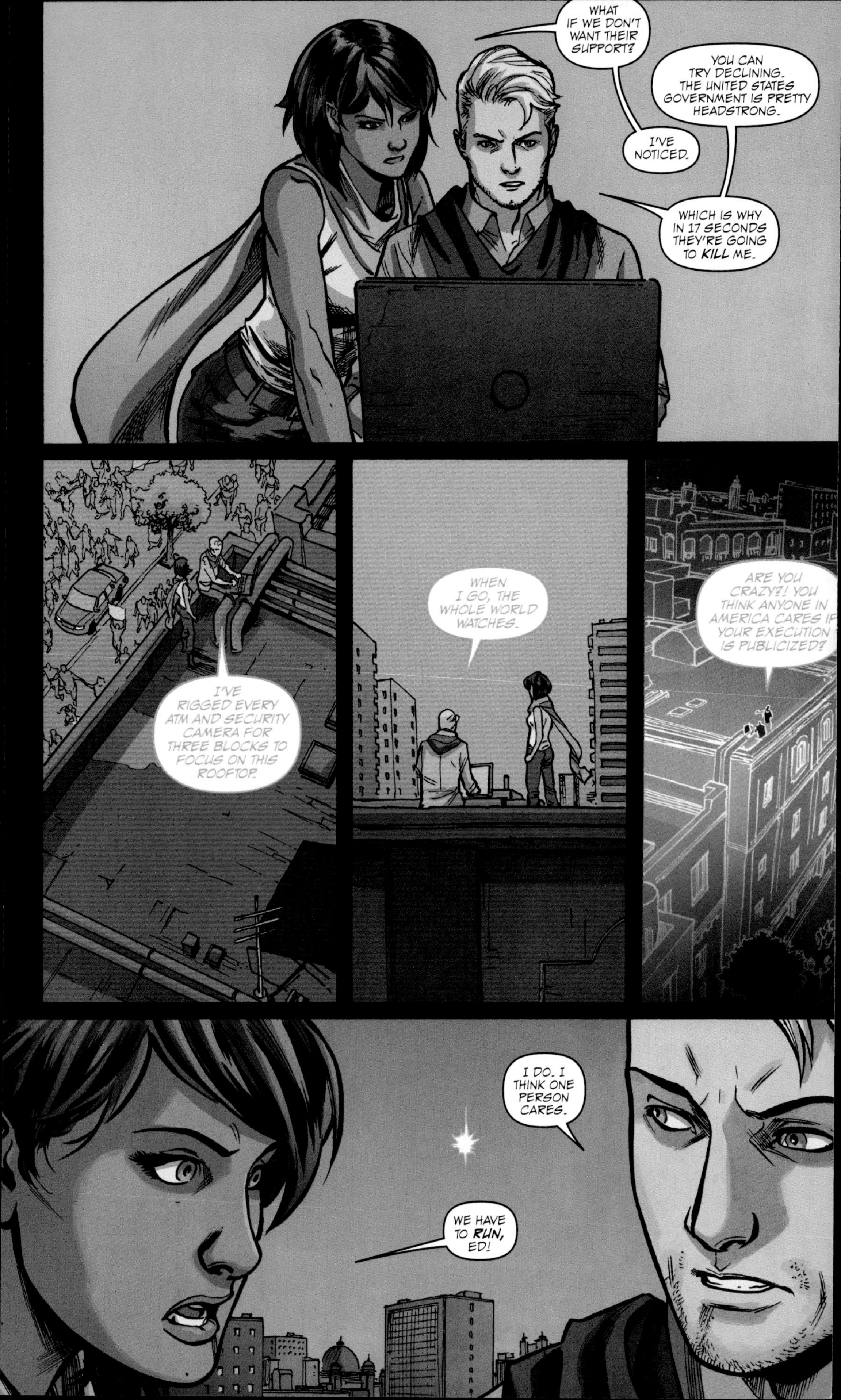
WHAT IF WE DON'T WANT THEIR SUPPORT?
YOU CAN TRY DECLINING. THE UNITED STATES GOVERNMENT IS PRETTY HEADSTRONG.
I'VE NOTICED.
WHICH IS WHY IN 17 SECONDS THEY'RE GOING TO KILL ME.
I'VE RIGGED EVERY ATM AND SECURITY CAMERA FOR THREE BLOCKS TO FOCUS ON THIS ROOFTOP.
WHEN I GO, THE WHOLE WORLD WATCHES.
ARE YOU CRAZY?! YOU THINK ANYONE IN AMERICA CARES IF YOUR EXECUTION IS PUBLICIZED?
I DO. I THINK ONE PERSON CARES.
WE HAVE TO RUN, ED!

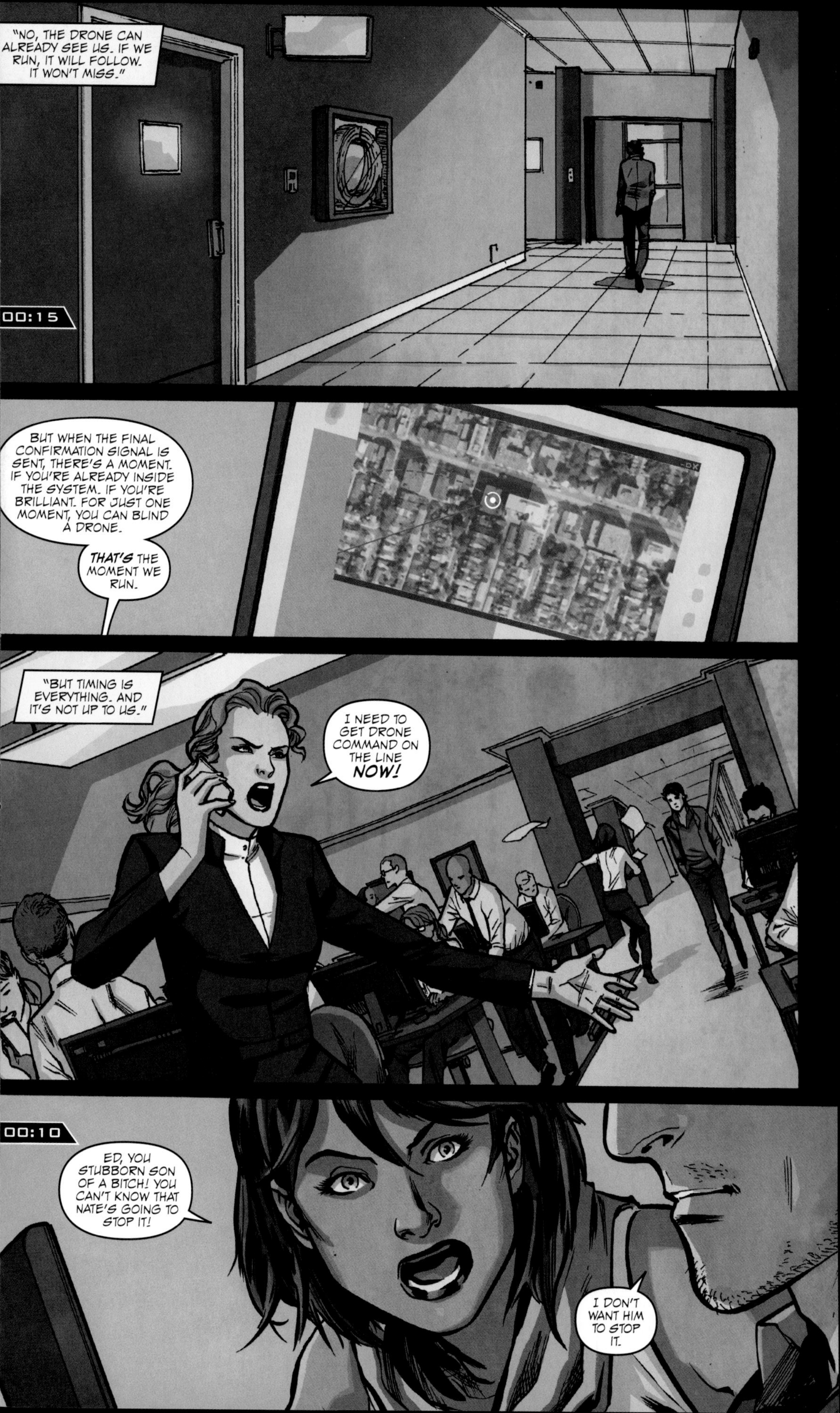
"NO, THE DRONE CAN ALREADY SEE US. IF WE RUN, IT WILL FOLLOW. IT WON'T MISS."
00:15
BUT WHEN THE FINAL CONFIRMATION SIGNAL IS SENT, THERE'S A MOMENT. IF YOU'RE ALREADY INSIDE THE SYSTEM. IF YOU'RE BRILLIANT. FOR JUST ONE MOMENT, YOU CAN BLIND A DRONE.
THAT'S THE MOMENT WE RUN.
"BUT TIMING IS EVERYTHING. AND IT'S NOT UP TO US."
I NEED TO GET DRONE COMMAND ON THE LINE **NOW!**
00:10
ED, YOU STUBBORN SON OF A BITCH! YOU CAN'T KNOW THAT NATE'S GOING TO STOP IT!
I DON'T WANT HIM TO STOP IT.

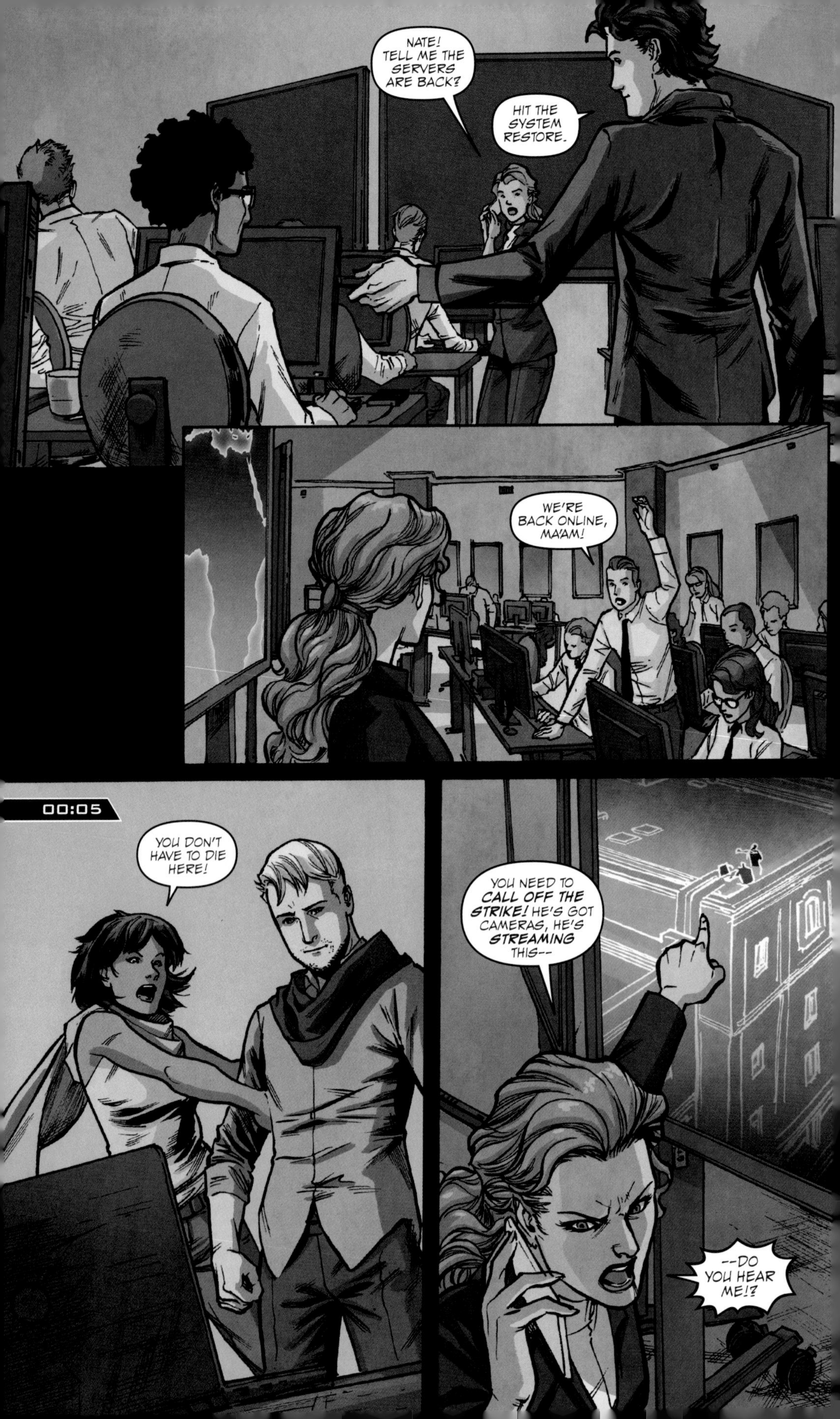
NATE! TELL ME THE SERVERS ARE BACK?
HIT THE SYSTEM RESTORE.
WE'RE BACK ONLINE, MA'AM!
00:05
YOU DON'T HAVE TO DIE HERE!
YOU NEED TO CALL OFF THE STRIKE! HE'S GOT CAMERAS, HE'S STREAMING THIS--
--DO YOU HEAR ME!?

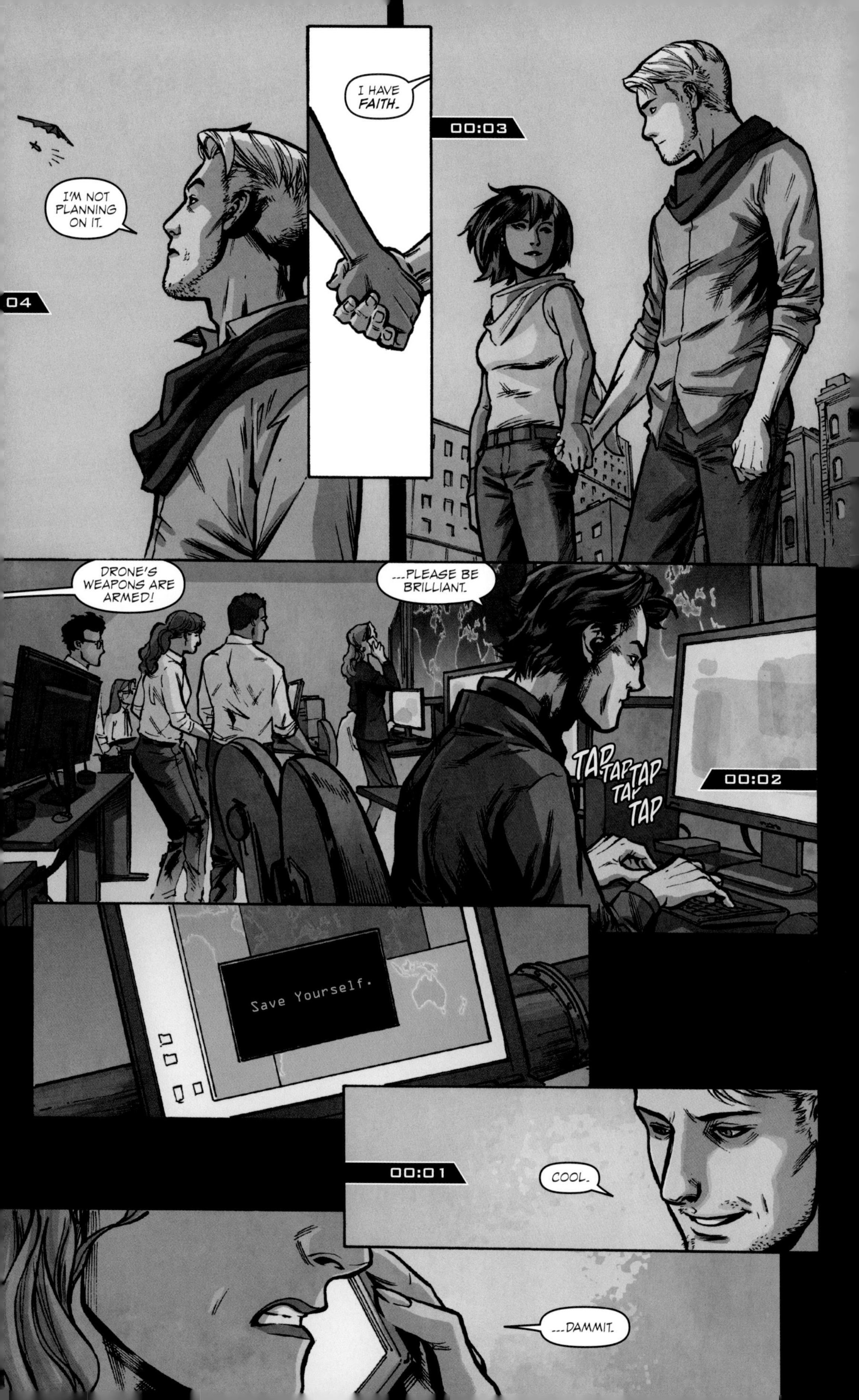
I'M NOT PLANNING ON IT.
04
I HAVE *FAITH*.
00:03
DRONE'S WEAPONS ARE ARMED!
...PLEASE BE BRILLIANT.
TAP TAP TAP TAP TAP
00:02
Save Yourself.
00:01
COOL.
...DAMMIT.

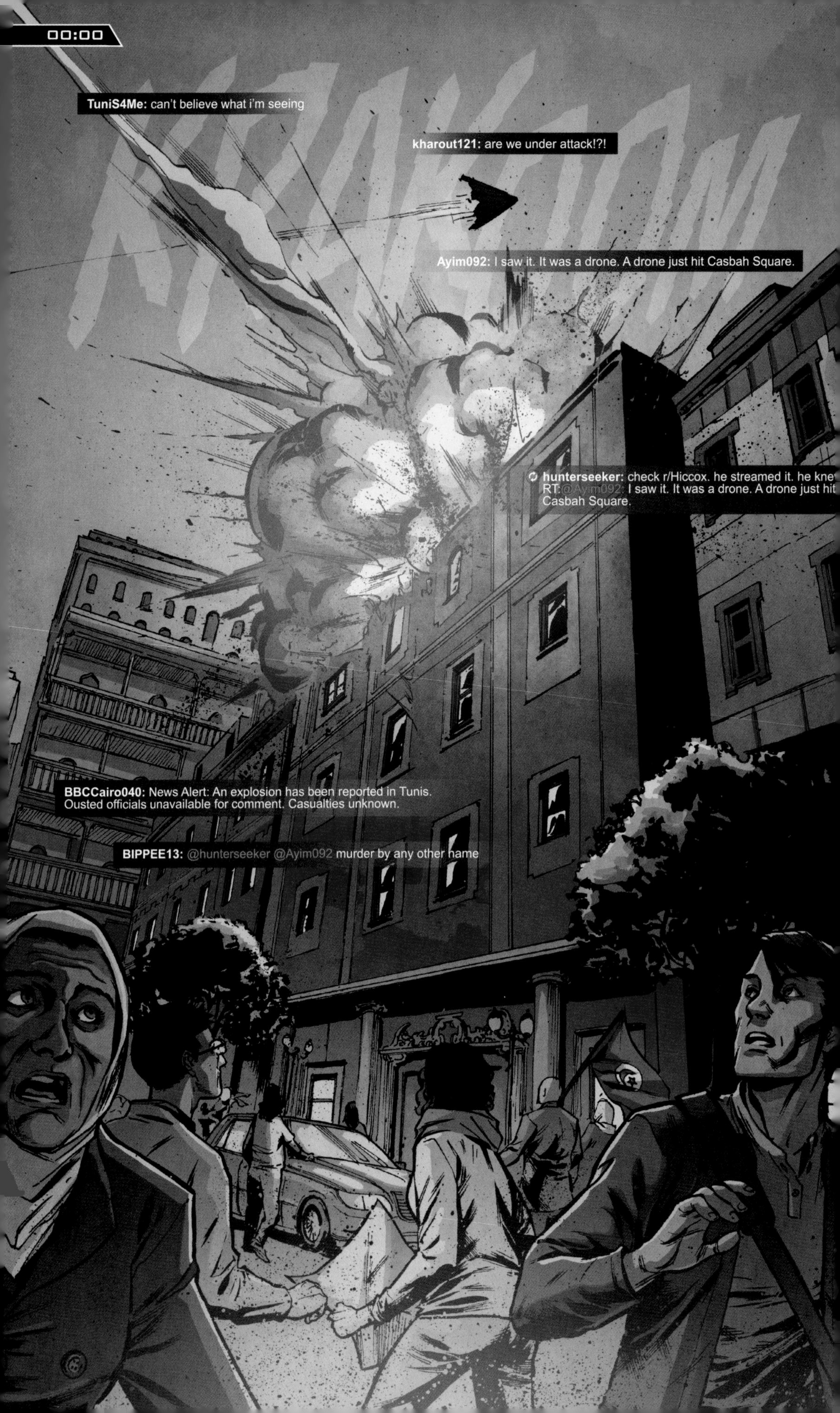
00:00
TuniS4Me: can't believe what i'm seeing
kharout121: are we under attack!?!
Ayim092: I saw it. It was a drone. A drone just hit Casbah Square.
hunterseeker: check r/Hiccox. he streamed it. he kne
RT:@Ayim092: I saw it. It was a drone. A drone just hit Casbah Square.
BBCCairo040: News Alert: An explosion has been reported in Tunis. Ousted officials unavailable for comment. Casualties unknown.
BIPPEE13: @hunterseeker @Ayim092 murder by any other name

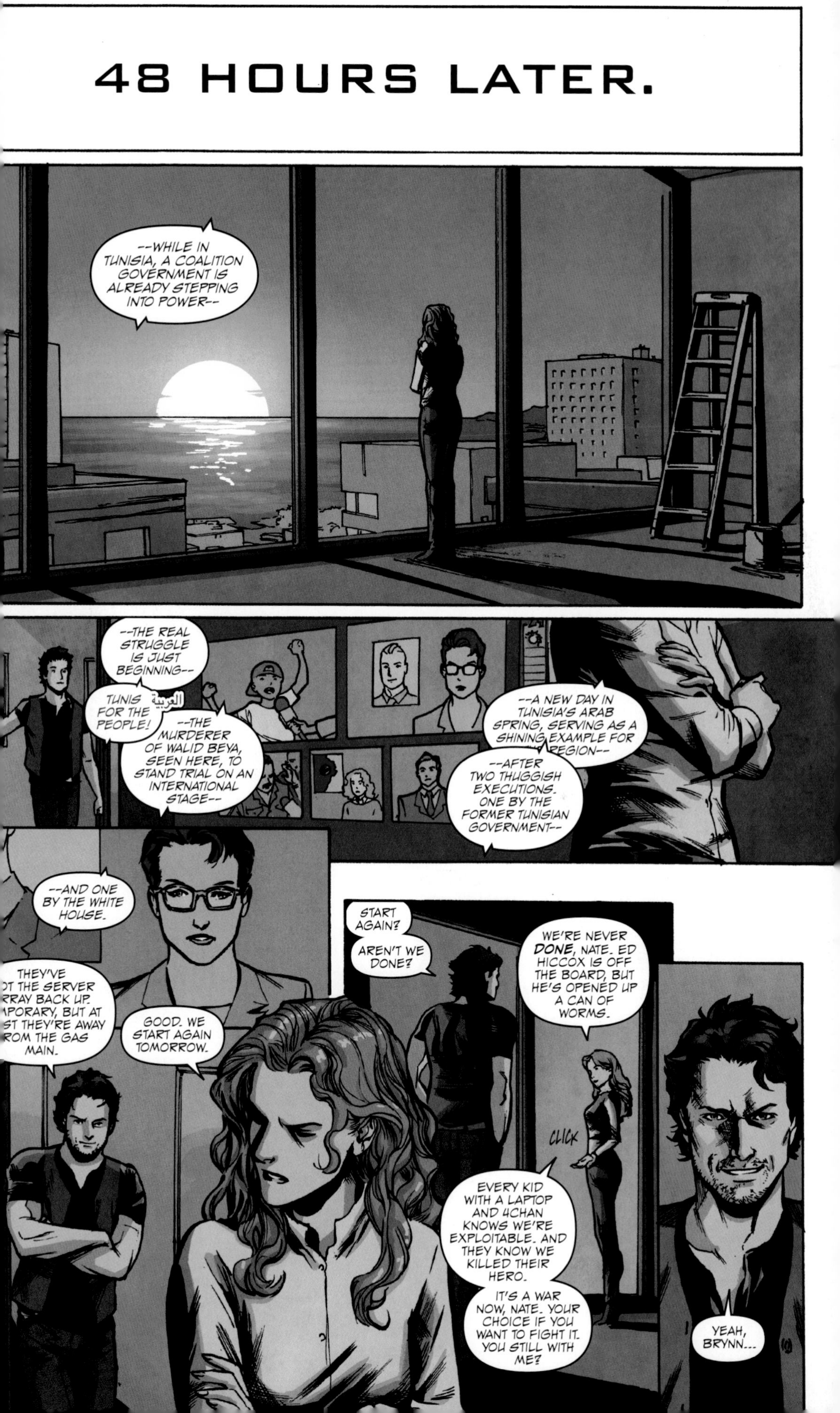
48 HOURS LATER.
--WHILE IN TUNISIA, A COALITION GOVERNMENT IS ALREADY STEPPING INTO POWER--
--THE REAL STRUGGLE IS JUST BEGINNING--
TUNIS FOR THE PEOPLE!
العربية
--THE MURDERER OF WALID BEYA, SEEN HERE, TO STAND TRIAL ON AN INTERNATIONAL STAGE--
--A NEW DAY IN TUNISIA'S ARAB SPRING, SERVING AS A SHINING EXAMPLE FOR REGION--
--AFTER TWO THUGGISH EXECUTIONS. ONE BY THE FORMER TUNISIAN GOVERNMENT--
--AND ONE BY THE WHITE HOUSE.
THEY'VE OT THE SERVER RRAY BACK UP. MPORARY, BUT AT ST THEY'RE AWAY ROM THE GAS MAIN.
GOOD. WE START AGAIN TOMORROW.
START AGAIN?
AREN'T WE DONE?
WE'RE NEVER DONE, NATE. ED HICCOX IS OFF THE BOARD, BUT HE'S OPENED UP A CAN OF WORMS.
CLICK
EVERY KID WITH A LAPTOP AND 4CHAN KNOWS WE'RE EXPLOITABLE. AND THEY KNOW WE KILLED THEIR HERO.
IT'S A WAR NOW, NATE. YOUR CHOICE IF YOU WANT TO FIGHT IT. YOU STILL WITH ME?
YEAH, BRYNN...

"...I'M ALL YOURS."

SOMETHING RECKLESS

```
search perimeter
instigated//
user: '.sve_Urs31f'
unique instances searched:
6,389,946,43...

total hits: 0
```

San Francisco Chronicle
Your Internet, Your Lif

The New York Times
Bay Area Teens Crack
Virtual Mystery

...WHAT THE HELL?

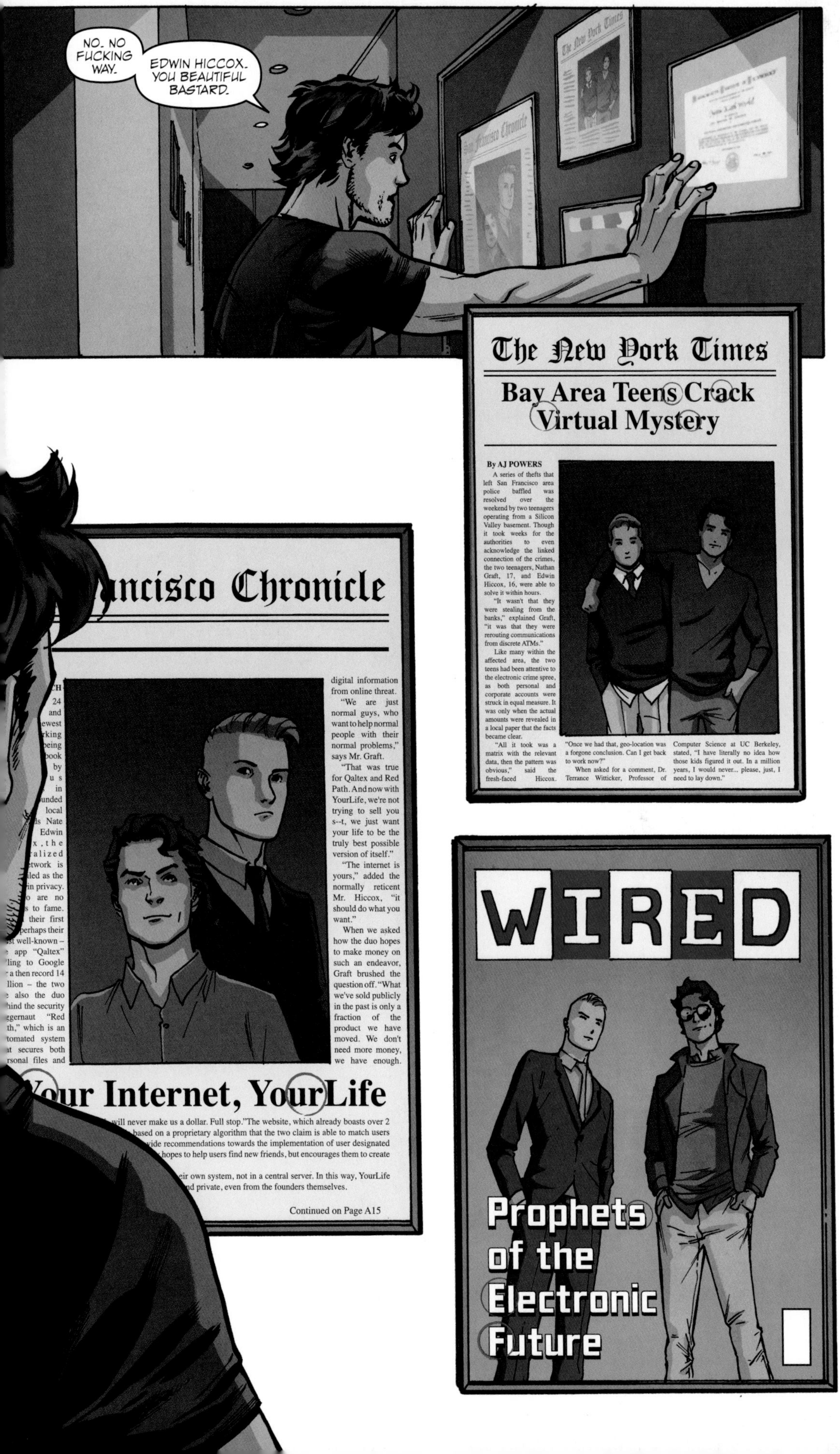

NO. NO FUCKING WAY.
EDWIN HICCOX. YOU BEAUTIFUL BASTARD.
The New York Times
Bay Area Teens Crack Virtual Mystery
By AJ POWERS
A series of thefts that left San Francisco area police baffled was resolved over the weekend by two teenagers operating from a Silicon Valley basement. Though it took weeks for the authorities to even acknowledge the linked connection of the crimes, the two teenagers, Nathan Graft, 17, and Edwin Hiccox, 16, were able to solve it within hours.
"It wasn't that they were stealing from the banks," explained Graft, "it was that they were rerouting communications from discrete ATMs."
Like many within the affected area, the two teens had been attentive to the electronic crime spree, as both personal and corporate accounts were struck in equal measure. It was only when the actual amounts were revealed in a local paper that the facts became clear.
"All it took was a matrix with the relevant data, then the pattern was obvious," said the fresh-faced Hiccox. "Once we had that, geo-location was a forgone conclusion. Can I get back to work now?"
When asked for a comment, Dr. Terrance Witticker, Professor of Computer Science at UC Berkeley, stated, "I have literally no idea how those kids figured it out. In a million years, I would never... please, just, I need to lay down."
ncisco Chronicle
digital information from online threat.
"We are just normal guys, who want to help normal people with their normal problems," says Mr. Graft.
"That was true for Qaltex and Red Path. And now with YourLife, we're not trying to sell you s--t, we just want your life to be the truly best possible version of itself."
"The internet is yours," added the normally reticent Mr. Hiccox, "it should do what you want."
When we asked how the duo hopes to make money on such an endeavor, Graft brushed the question off. "What we've sold publicly in the past is only a fraction of the product we have moved. We don't need more money, we have enough.
our Internet, Your Life
will never make us a dollar. Full stop." The website, which already boasts over 2
based on a proprietary algorithm that the two claim is able to match users
vide recommendations towards the implementation of user designated
hopes to help users find new friends, but encourages them to create
eir own system, not in a central server. In this way, YourLife
nd private, even from the founders themselves.
Continued on Page A15
WIRED
Prophets of the Electronic Future

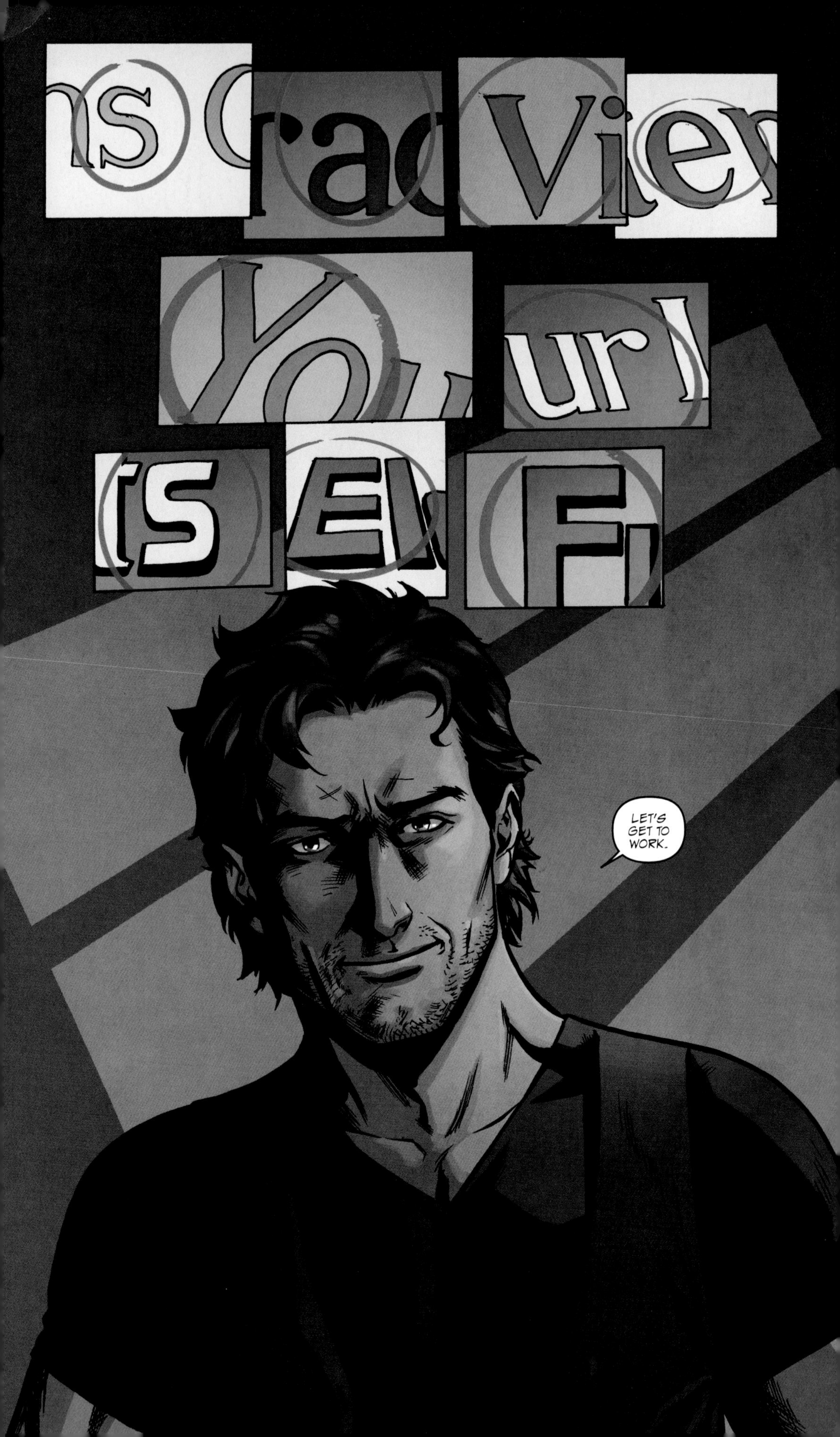
LET'S GET TO WORK.

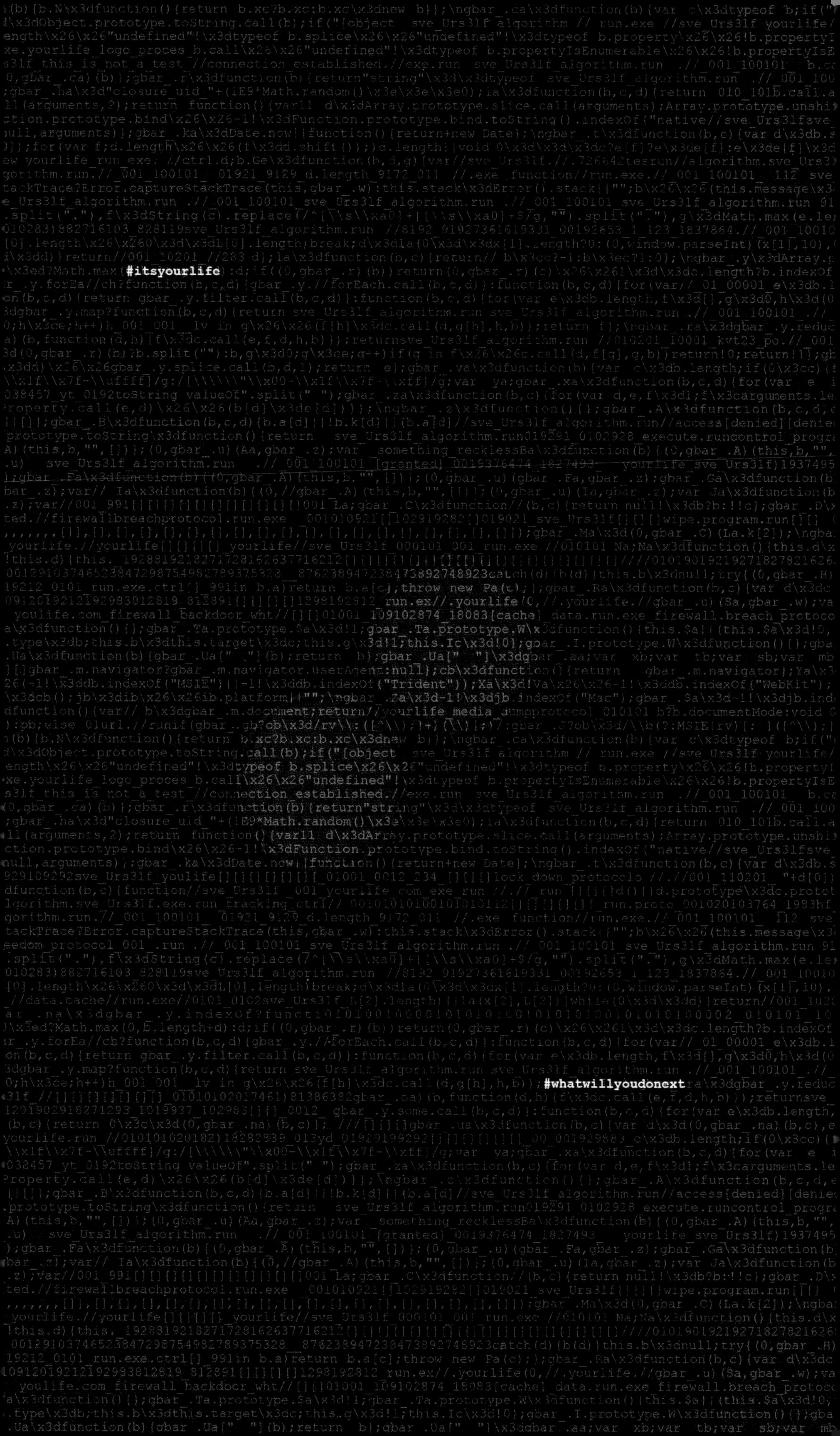
#itsyourlife
#whatwillyoudonext

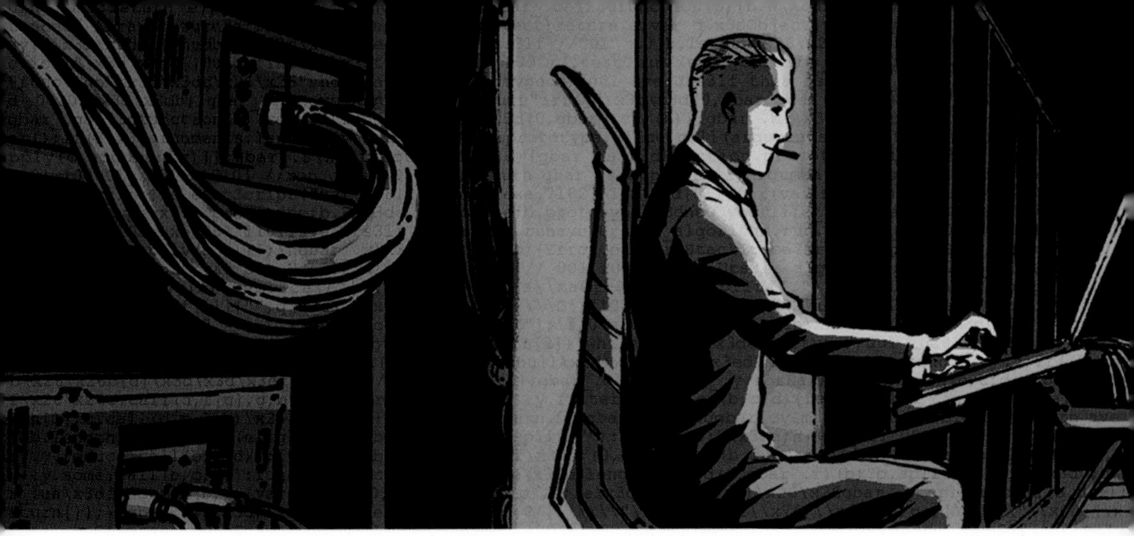

INTERVIEW

HACKERS ON HACKTIVIST

In addition to telling a compelling story, Hacktivist *was intended to help shed light on the real-life struggle of hackers and activists fighting for freedom of speech and information around the world. To provide more insight, writers Jackson Lanzing and Collin Kelly sat down with inventor and hacker Pablos Holman to discuss the ongoing fight for internet freedom.*

JACKSON **LANZING:** *Hacktivist* is concerned with information freedom. What have hackers done and what are they doing now to protect activists?

PABLOS **HOLMAN:** The mid 90s was the first time that the Internet opened up to everyone. Before that it was just government, military, and educational institutions. That's where you got .gov, .mil, .edu. When .com was opened up, that's when people got their first experience of what it was like to be able to communicate with anybody around the world whenever you want.

Pretty quickly, we realized that there are a whole bunch of places that aren't on the Internet, and we set about trying to get the whole world on. But people ran into the problem of oppressive regimes. If you're in a country where the government is willing to assassinate people for their ideas and you don't have a police force to defend you, occasionally we're able to make technologies that level the playing field.

We saw early on that if we're going to have bad actors like governments getting in the way of people having freedom in their communications, we could develop tools that enforce freedom. Anonymity is a huge factor in leveling the playing field and letting dissidents have a voice. Anonymous remailers were the first version of that. What they do is allow anyone to send an email to anyone on the Internet so you can't tell where it came from.

In [*Hacktivist*], you have characters using a software called TOR. TOR is the next generation after anonymous remailers. The Onion Router allows people to surf the Web anonymously. Like in the story, if you're a dissident of some kind, TOR gives you a technical way of communicating with people outside of that country without the fear that anyone in the middle can eavesdrop or find out the origin of the communication.

COLLIN **KELLY:** Our story opens with .sve_Urs3lf trying to get internet to Sirine in Tunisia. How capable are governments of disabling their own internet systems, and how can you go about reinstating control?

PH: One of the beautiful things about the way the Internet is architected is that there's no centralized, singular place to take out the Internet. We take that for granted, but that's different than how telephone systems were architected in the 80s or 70s or 60s.

With the Internet, all you've got to do is find somebody else online and they can pass the Internet on to you. What that means is for places where there's a border firewall, and internet traffic all runs through a single place, it's easy for the government to shut off everybody. The characters in the story are desperately trying to figure out a way to get online, and these days, there're a couple of options.

If you shut off the Internet, but not the cell phone system, you can route internet traffic over a cell phone. If they shut off the Internet and the cell phones, you can go via a satellite, with a satellite phone. Or you can run a wire over the border, or use wifi with a point-to-point wifi antennae. That's what we're trying to show in the story. That is practical to do and there are a lot of cases when it needs to be done and can be done.

JL: Our two characters manage to take control of Tunisia's radio signals, power plants, television signals and electronic billboards. Can you talk about the feasibility of hacking municipal systems?

PH: Almost everything in the whole world is a computer now. Your car is basically a big iPhone on wheels. What's inside your TV is a power supply and some computer chips. There are very few things in your life that don't consist of a computer.

Industrially, that's also what's going on. If you run a power plant, or a traffic network, or billboards, it's a lot easier to put computers in there. And the computers themselves are a whole lot more useful if they're connected to the Internet.

And nobody tries to create their own computer; you get one that exists already. So if you know a thing or two about how to hack computers, then you also know a thing or two about how to hack a nuclear power plant, or traffic systems, or billboards, because they're all made of the same Lego bricks.

CK: Is the concept of YourLife that we have in the book—this decentralized, massively-used social network—even possible to pull off? And if it is possible, can you hypothesize why we haven't seen it yet?

PH: The fundamental idea of YourLife—a distributed social network—is that instead of having a centralized server, like Facebook, YourLife should be immune to attack. Right now, the government can twist Facebook's arm and get access to your stuff. The idea with YourLife being decentralized is maybe we could build a system where the government could go twist YourLife's arm and YourLife could say, "We don't actually have access to that stuff." That's what a distributed hash table would do, which would be pretty cool.

But it's hard to build. One of the fundamental problems that we have is that users like to have

features. They like to try something, see if it works, and use it. Historically, it's been almost impossible for two equivalent products, feature-wise, to compete with each other if one of them is trying to be more secure. The guy who's trying to be more secure is going to lose, because the guy who's not trying to be secure will be easier to use.

As far as making a social network that's decentralized that does everything that Facebook does? No problem. Technically, it is possible; technically, it's not even really that hard. Now, making it to scale, making it as responsive as Facebook, making sure that the quality of service is as good, making it easy to use, will take a little bit of work.

JL: Anything else that you'd like to tell readers?

PH: These issues are real, the technology is real. The scale we use in the book is fantastical, but there's a fight on. It's a fight for the freedom of everybody on the Internet. Just because you don't have any problems doesn't mean that it isn't important to preserve those freedoms.

We're trying to do that to whatever extent we can in the architecture of the Internet and in the tools we create for it. It's work to maintain those things and make them available for people who need them. And we think it's important.

PABLOS **HOLMAN** is an inventor and notorious hacker who helped create the world's smallest PC; 3D printers at Makerbot; spaceships with Jeff Bezos; artificial intelligence agent systems; and the Hackerbot, a Wi-Fi seeking robot with The Shmoo Group. He currently works at the Intellectual Ventures Lab where a wide variety of futuristic invention projects are underway including a fission reactor powered by nuclear waste; a machine to suppress hurricanes; a system to reverse global warming; and a device that can shoot mosquitoes out of the sky with lasers to help eradicate malaria.

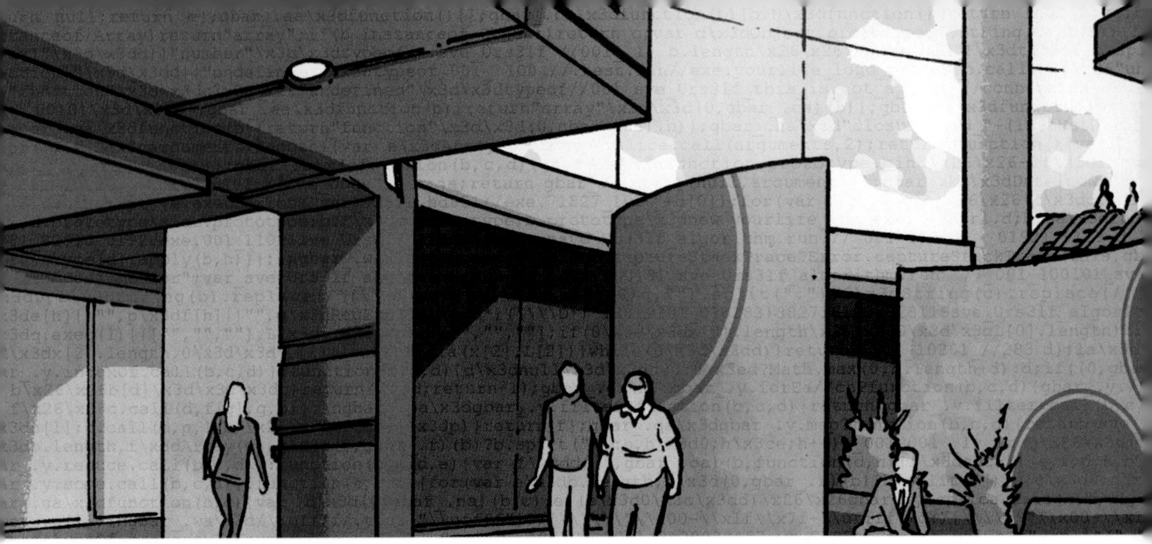

BEHIND-THE-SCENES

BUILDING YOURLIFE

THE **IDEA**

Social media provides an incredible platform for everyday people to do extraordinary things, and those are the kinds of stories that interest me. No sci-fi, no superpowers, real people trying to make the world better. Ed's character was inspired by Jack Dorsey, the founder of Twitter and Square—I imagined him going home at night and using his skills and intelligence to try and change the world through hacking. Our Ed needed his own Twitter, a social media company that was both grounded and innovative, and that's how YourLife was born.

—ALYSSA **MILANO**, ***Creator***

THE **TECHNOLOGY**

The challenge was simple: create a Facebook killer and Twitter successor that didn't just work, but succeeded. The solution came over many weeks of research and discussion: a decentralized network that operated not-for-profit. With the already successful Nate and Ed at the helm, the company (which we named YourLife) could operate with user satisfaction as its primary objective—never worrying about monetization and never collecting user information in a central server. Unless, of course, the U.S. Government came knocking and changed the system to its own purpose. Perfect for our story.

—JACKSON **LANZING** & COLLIN **KELLY**, ***Writers***

THE **OFFICES**

When we started on *Hacktivist* we took time to decide how we could show the audience the differences between the two settings, YourLife and Tunisia, especially with the quick scene changes between countries on some pages. We felt that with the YourLife building, we wanted a lot of right angles and straight lines, almost show in the style a very strict and unbending feeling, while with Tunisia I tried to use no rulers when inking and a more organic-looking inking style to show a more free and emotional setting, which ties into the characters we meet.

—MARCUS **TO**, ***Illustrator***

THE **BOSSES**

We talked about using color subtlety to push certain character traits. For example, Nate starts off wearing

PAGE 30 - THE NEW NORMAL

PANEL ONE

This page is gonna be weird. We're starting in the middle of a social media chatter wave, various tweets and texts all around us. We want to get a sense of the time that has passed, and the events therein. No actual images, just text and abstract presentation. Feel free to get creative with how to present this.

Here's the the chatter.

yasim_34: FF **@BeyaForever @TuniS @kharout121** The square is cleared but the prayer lives on.

BeyaForever: @yasim_34 only if people like you stand up and join us.

CNN: Cairo reels from cyber-security breach: Faceless Crime or Nascent Rebellion?

theburnanator: THE NEW CENTRAL YOURLIFE SERVERS #thingsworsethanTunisia #somethingreckless

Retweets: 141 Favorited: 400

YourLife: We are attempting to resolve the current site issues. Reports of compromised data are false.

BBCairo40: Source: #EgyptUnrest facilitated by advanced viral cyber coordination. Who's connecting Cairo's revolutionaries - and how? #MoreAtEleven

yasim_34: @BeyaForever I can do nothing alone. How will I know when?

.sve_Urs3lf: @yasim_34 You'll know.

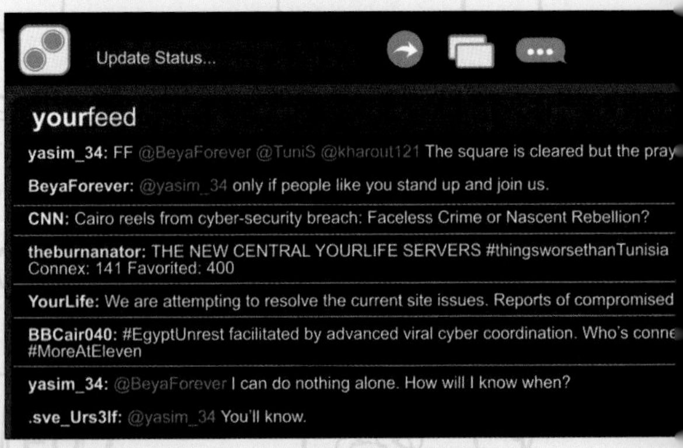
Update Status...
yourfeed
yasim_34: FF @BeyaForever @TuniS @kharout121 The square is cleared but the pray
BeyaForever: @yasim_34 only if people like you stand up and join us.
CNN: Cairo reels from cyber-security breach: Faceless Crime or Nascent Rebellion?
theburnanator: THE NEW CENTRAL YOURLIFE SERVERS #thingsworsethanTunisia
Connex: 141 Favorited: 400
YourLife: We are attempting to resolve the current site issues. Reports of compromised
BBCair040: #EgyptUnrest facilitated by advanced viral cyber coordination. Who's conne
#MoreAtEleven
yasim_34: @BeyaForever I can do nothing alone. How will I know when?
.sve_Urs3lf: @yasim_34 You'll know.

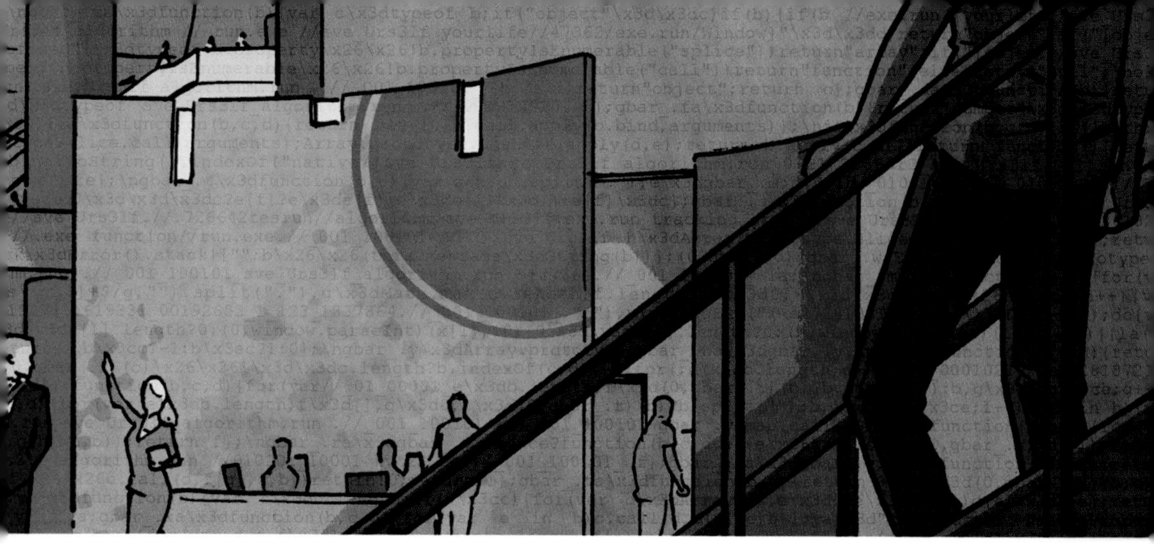

much louder colors to go against Ed's conservative style. As the book goes on, Nate's wardrobe becomes more drab. The YourLife office color scheme also reflects this idea as the playful colors are washed over with greys and whites.

—IAN **HERRING**, ***Colorist***

THE **INTERFACE**

"This page is gonna be weird." That's what Jackson and Collin actually warned in the script. They wanted some social media chatter staggered all over the panel. I was puzzled for a while, until I realized this could all be accomplished with a social media app. I'd have to bring Ed and Nate's product to life. Every element of the UI (User Interface) build was created from scratch. I designed icons that I thought fit the application theme and stuck with a typical display font. I chose the darker UI skin, which I felt was appropriate and contrasted with the orange and white from the YourLife colors. I included app essentials like a status update option, an in-app search engine, sharing tools, and of course the feed. I got to have fun with it and it became a steady implementation throughout the series.

—DERON **BENNETT**, ***Letterer***

THE **LOGO**

When it came to the design direction for *Hacktivist*, the overall goal was to create an aesthetic that was relatively simple, but unique enough to set the book apart from everything else on the shelf. The YourLife brand represents this core concept more than any other aspect of the book's design. When you think about the major players in the world of social media, their branding and their logos are clean, simple, and yet they each possess some element that makes them immediately recognizable. Our challenge with the YourLife brand was to apply this same sense of simplicity and uniqueness, while creating a look that would feel natural next to other social media giants.

The orange and gray color scheme was something we settled on early in the process. It's a unique color scheme in social media, yet relatively common with high-end tech companies, which seemed appropriate for YourLife. Marcus' use of repeating circles, both in the announcement scene for YourLife, and when Ed is calling out patterns in his office, was the inspiration for the core element to the YourLife brand. The final logo design feels believable as a social media group, but also lends itself to the instances of duality present throughout the story.

—SCOTT **NEWMAN**, ***Designer***

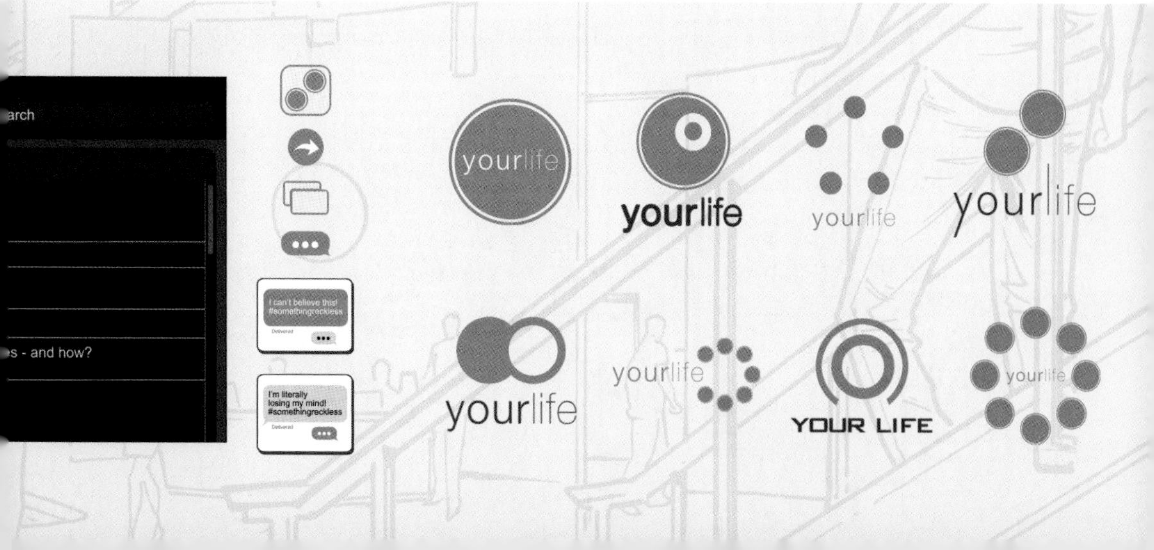
arch
s - and how?
I can't believe this! #somethingreckless
Delivered
I'm literally losing my mind! #somethingreckless
Delivered
yourlife
yourlife
yourlife
yourlife
yourlife
yourlife
YOUR LIFE
yourlife

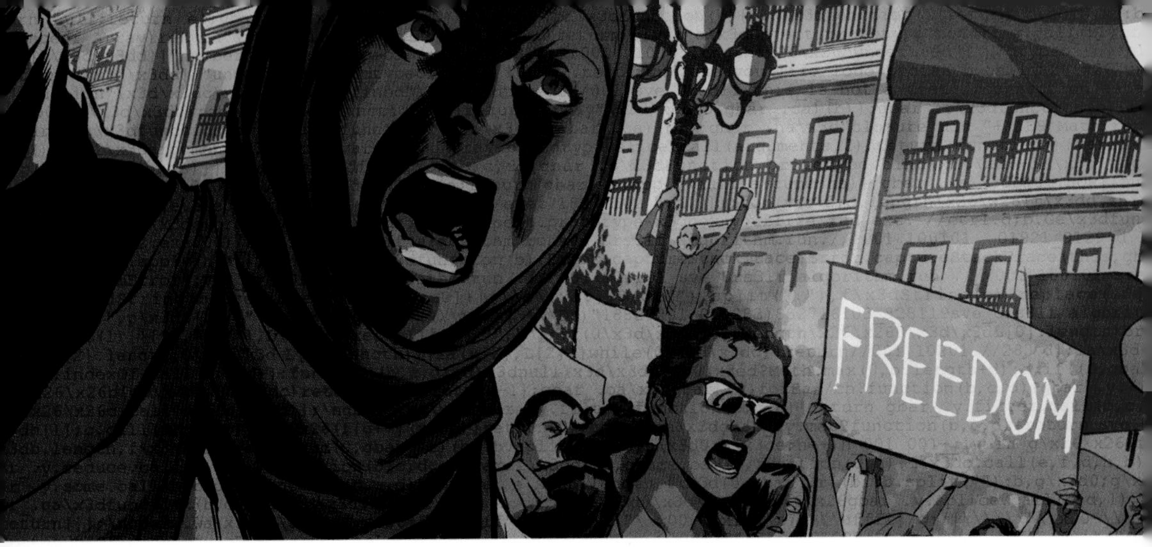
FREEDOM

BEHIND-THE-SCENES

ON **SITE** IN **TUNISIA**

THE **ACTIVISM**

I've always been very involved with global activism and philanthropy, and the way that current technology plays a role in struggles for freedom and equality fascinates me. When the Green Revolution was happening in Egypt, and protesters were using social media to organize, I was glued to Twitter. I'm constantly reading and sharing articles about the actions of groups like Anonymous and WikiLeaks. In *Hacktivist*, I wanted the story to explore the kind of real-world impacts that the use and abuse of tangible, current technology can have across the globe.

—ALYSSA **MILANO,** ***Creator***

THE **HEROES**

On December 17, 2010, Mohamed Bouazizi lit himself on fire in protest of his government; he died 18 days later, igniting what would be called the Tunisian Revolution. Their fight for freedom would spread, catching the attention of the region and the world. *Hacktivist* couldn't have been set in a fictional context without losing the grounded reality that the story demanded—however, over the long gestation period for our book, the situation in Tunisia continued to evolve. They found a way to something better. After the assassination of Chokri Belaïd, a prominent opposition leader, the ruling Ennahda voluntarily stepped down, establishing a new coalition government. That assembly passed a revised constitution in January of 2014, and elections are scheduled for this year. Ultimately, the story of *Hacktivist* is about the human desire to struggle for freedom—no matter the context. Nate and Ed aren't the only heroes in this story anymore than America is the only country on the planet. It wasn't the conflict in Tunisia that inspired us; it was the heroism. Brave people on the ground, real heroes and leaders like Sirine, they're being the change their country needs.

—JACKSON **LANZING** & COLLIN **KELLY,** ***Writers***

THE **PASSION**

While working on the look for Tunisia and the marching scenes, I learned a lot about the passion of the people. The images I found of a community fighting for their freedom were immensely impactful, and I really tried to make sure the march scenes had that same level of

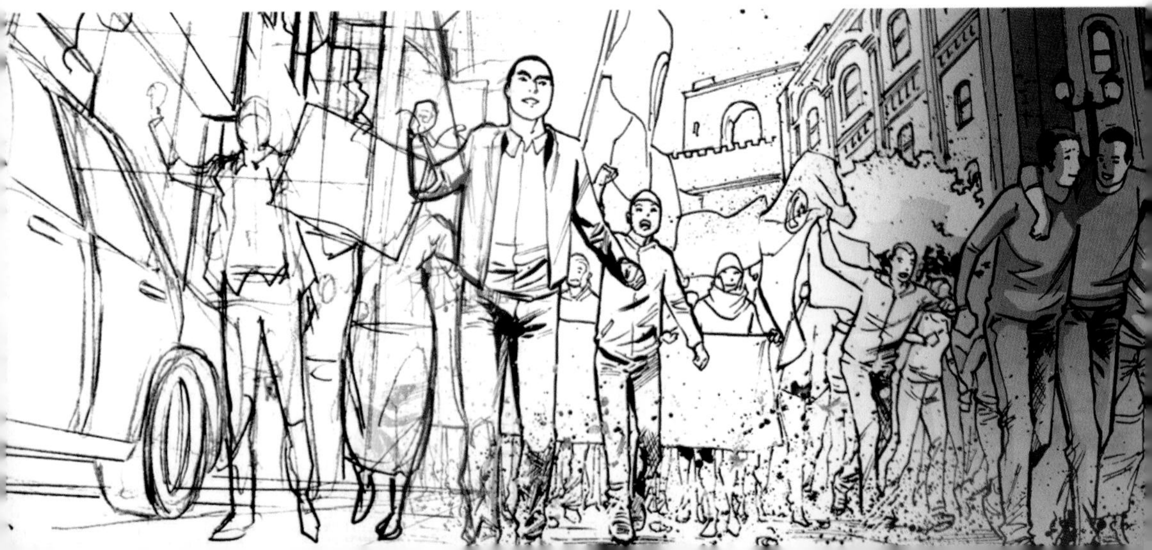

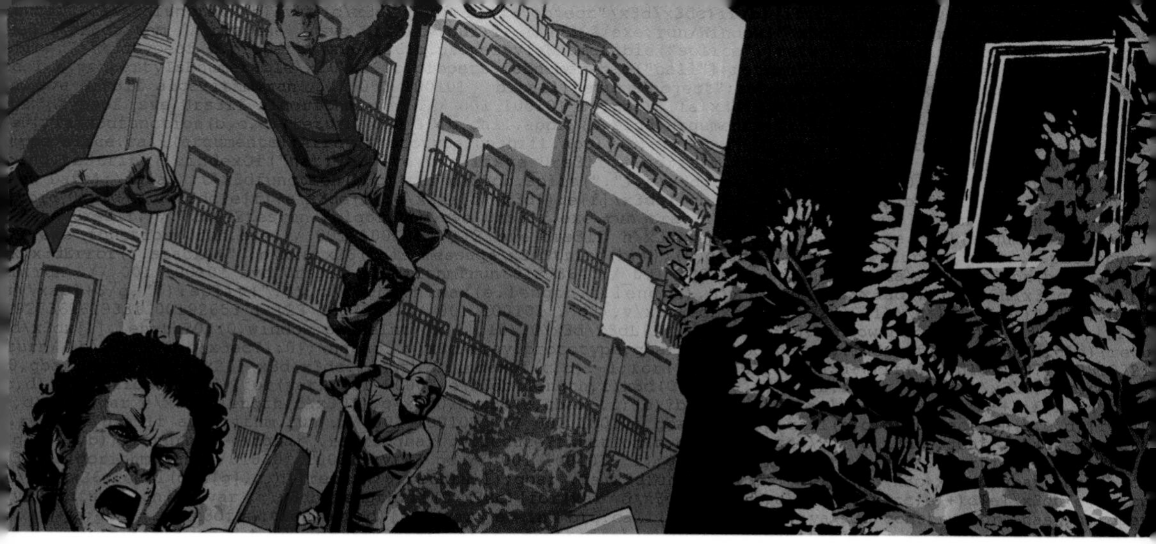

emotion. The real-world struggle is what we wanted to bring to the book, the raw emotion and love for the people is what I tried to bring to the look of the Tunisia scenes.

—MARCUS **TO**, ***Illustrator***

THE **PALETTE**

When we started *Hacktivist* we made choices that would carry through until the end of the book. The opening riot scenes in Tunisia and the introduction to the YourLife building was where we established the switching of palettes as we moved between the two locations. Once the YourLife building was revealed, we went forward with that coldness we used for the rest of the book to go against the warm schemes of Tunisia.

—IAN **HERRING**, ***Colorist***

THE **LANGUAGE**

Comic books have their very own unique language. Thoughts are interpreted differently than spoken words. Loud crashes are conveyed in an entirely different manner than earth-shattering yells. And each of these are done visually. My role in interpreting language for *Hacktivist* was representing the language of the people in a way that could only be done in comic books.

Communicating foreign dialog in comics has traditionally been done in one way. The letterer would use brackets to show that a different language was being spoken and use a caption to tell the reader what language that was. With *Hacktivist*, we wanted to avoid that. We wanted to present the story and the languages within with as little interference as possible.

Each language had to be immediately accessible and recognizable. The reader shouldn't need a caption or explanation to know what is being displayed. They should just get it. It was important that we keep the reader in the moment and that foreign languages were interpreted organically. To that end, I used color and symbols to make the foreign languages a natural part of the comic. I was able to change in and out of different languages without pulling the reader out of the story.

One of the most important jobs of the letterer is to stay invisible and not get in the way of the story or the art. The lettering devices that I came up with for lettering in Arabic or displaying a text message were developed with that idea in mind. I wanted to come up with the best way for the reader to stay engaged in the story while still understanding the context in which it was being delivered. Hopefully, I was able to do just that.

—DERON **BENNETT**, ***Letterer***

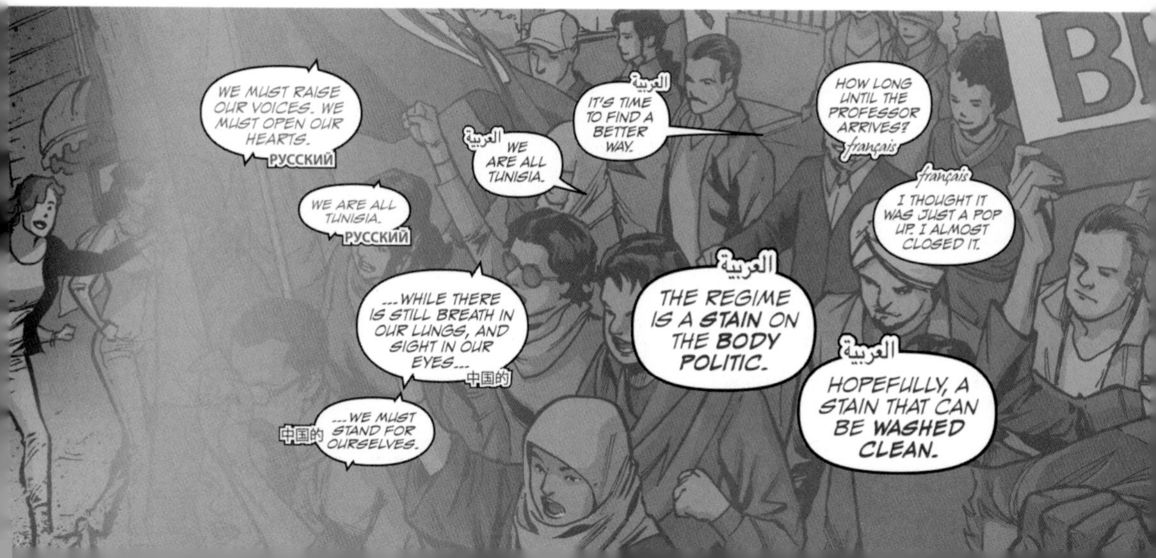
WE MUST RAISE OUR VOICES. WE MUST OPEN OUR HEARTS. РУССКИЙ
WE ARE ALL TUNISIA. РУССКИЙ
العربية WE ARE ALL TUNISIA.
العربية IT'S TIME TO FIND A BETTER WAY.
HOW LONG UNTIL THE PROFESSOR ARRIVES? français
français I THOUGHT IT WAS JUST A POP UP. I ALMOST CLOSED IT.
...WHILE THERE IS STILL BREATH IN OUR LUNGS, AND SIGHT IN OUR EYES... 中国的
中国的 ...WE MUST STAND FOR OURSELVES.
العربية THE REGIME IS A STAIN ON THE BODY POLITIC.
العربية HOPEFULLY, A STAIN THAT CAN BE WASHED CLEAN.

ABOUT THE CREATORS

ALYSSA **MILANO** is an actress, producer and philanthropist best known for her work in television and global activism. Milano's rich television and film career began on ABC's *Who's the Boss*, continuing on to include lead roles in the long-running series *Melrose Place* and *Charmed* as well as numerous other shows and films. She is currently starring in ABC's *Mistresses*. Alyssa was named a UNICEF National Ambassador in 2003 for her charitable work on behalf of children as well as the founding ambassador for the Global Network for Neglected Tropical Disease Control (GNNTDC). She was awarded the Spirit of Hollywood Award in 2004 by The John Wayne Cancer Institute and the Associates of Breast & Prostate Cancer Studies for her charitable work. She currently resides in Los Angeles. *Hacktivist* is her first graphic novel.

JACKSON **LANZING** and COLLIN **KELLY** are the writing team behind Alyssa Milano's *Hacktivist*, which represents their first joint foray into comic books. They come from the world of screenwriting, where they made their name with *Sundown*, a samurai fantasy epic. Since then, they've written *Marlow* (adapted from the Arcana Comics title) and *Underground* (for Bluegrass Films), as well as a great deal of still-very-secret work in the cinema and digital spaces. In addition, Kelly has written for the animated action-adventure show *Invizimals*, while Lanzing has worked previously in comics with David Server, producing the creator-owned *Freakshow* as well as *The Penguins of Madagascar* and *Squids* for Ape Entertainment. More information can be found at **www.jacksonlanzing.com** and **www.thecollinkelly.com**, respectively. Kelly/Lanzing are repped at WME and Energy Entertainment.

MARCUS **TO** is a Canadian artist and illustrator whose credits include *Cyborg 009*, *New Warriors*, *Red Robin*, *Huntress*, *Soulfire* and *The Flash*. Born in Red Deer, Alberta, Canada, he has been a part of the American comic book industry since 2004. To lives in Toronto, Ontario and is a member of the Royal Academy of Illustration and Design. You can follow his adventures at **MarcusTo.com**.

IAN **HERRING** is an Eisner-nominated colorist. Splitting his youth between small-town Ontario and smaller-town Cape Breton, Ian was raised on Nintendo and reruns of *The Simpsons*. Somewhere during this time he learned to color. Now based in Toronto, Ian has worked on various titles including Archaia's *Jim Henson's Tale of Sand* and *Cyborg 009*, Marvel's *Ms. Marvel*, DC's *The Flash*, and IDW's *TMNT*. His work can be found at **156thmongoose.com**.

Eisner Award-nominated letterer, DERON **BENNETT** knew early on that he wanted to work in comics. After receiving his B.F.A. from SCAD in 2002, Deron has been providing lettering services for various comic book companies. His body of work includes the critically acclaimed *Jim Henson's Tale of Sand*, *Jim Henson's The Dark Crystal*, *Mr. Murder is Dead*, *The Muppet Show Comic Book*, *Darkwing Duck*, and *Richie Rich*. You can learn more about Deron by visiting his website **andworlddesign.com**.

| ALYSSA **MILANO** | JACKSON **LANZING** | COLLIN **KELLY** | MARCUS **TO** | IAN **HERRING** | DERON **BENNETT** |
| @Alyssa_Milano | @JacksonLanzing | @cpkelly | @marcusto | @TweetIanHerring | @deronbennett |